THE
VIRTUOUS
ORGANIZATION

Insights from Some of the
World's Leading Management Thinkers

THE
VIRTUOUS
ORGANIZATION

Insights from Some of the World's Leading Management Thinkers

Editors

Charles C Manz
University of Massachusetts Amherst, USA

Kim S Cameron
University of Michigan, USA

Karen P Manz
Hartford Seminary, USA

Robert D Marx
University of Massachusetts Amherst, USA

Consulting Editor
Judi Neal
International Center for Spirit at Work, USA

 **World Scientific**

NEW JERSEY · LONDON · SINGAPORE · BEIJING · SHANGHAI · HONG KONG · TAIPEI · CHENNAI

#234380374

Published by

World Scientific Publishing Co. Pte. Ltd.

5 Toh Tuck Link, Singapore 596224

USA office: 27 Warren Street, Suite 401-402, Hackensack, NJ 07601

UK office: 57 Shelton Street, Covent Garden, London WC2H 9HE

The cover art, "Tikun Olam" © 2007 Nancy Adler, is used with her permission. "Tikun Olam" is Hebrew and means to repair or perfect the world. Adler was an artist-in-residence at The Banff Center in 2007. Her works have been exhibited in Canada and the United States and are held in private collections worldwide.

THE VIRTUOUS ORGANIZATION
Insights from Some of the World's Leading Management Thinkers

ISBN-13 978-981-281-859-1
ISBN-10 981-281-859-6

Typeset by Stallion Press
Email: enquiries@stallionpress.com

Printed by Fuisland Offset Printing (S) Pte Ltd. Singapore

DEDICATION

We dedicate this book
to
leaders
and
organization members
who have embodied *virtue*
in
crises,
ordinary
and
exemplary times
and
who have inspired others
to do the same.

ACKNOWLEDGMENTS

It has been a long journey and many sources of support and several people in particular need to be acknowledged for their contributions to this book. First, we want to give special credit to the *Journal of Management Spirituality & Religion* (JMSR) since many chapters in this volume are based on and adapted from articles that originally appeared in a special issue on "*Values and Virtues in Organizations*" (Volume 3, Issues 1 & 2, 2006) guest edited by the editors of this book. We especially thank the editors of *JMSR*, Yochanan Altman and Jerry Biberman, for their permission to include material from the special issue and enthusiastic support of our publication of *The Virtuous Organization*.

We also express our appreciation to our Universities — the University of Massachusetts, University of Michigan, and Hartford Seminary — and the respective staff and faculties of these institutions who have provided support to members of the Editor team. And we thank *World Scientific Publishing* and our editors, Teng Poh Hoon and Ms. Sandhya and acquisitions editor, David Sharp, for their encouragement and belief in this project and support in bringing it to publication.

In addition, Charles Manz expresses his appreciation to his many colleagues and co-authors who have provided encouragement and support for his work over the years. He offers a special thanks to Charles and Janet Nirenberg for their generous gift that made the Nirenberg Leadership Chaired Professorship possible that Charles now holds, and for their ongoing support and encouragement. He also expresses his appreciation to his immediate and extended family for all the inspiration and encouragement they have provided over the years.

Kim Cameron offers appreciation to colleagues in the Center for Positive Organizational Scholarship who contribute to our understanding of virtues and virtuousness in organizations — Wayne Baker, Jane Dutton, Robert Quinn, Gretchen Spreitzer and Lynn Wooten.

Karen Manz wishes to acknowledge the virtuous leadership and inspiring work of Donna Queeney, Jerry Haas, David K. Scott, Aaron Feuerstein, Michael Volkema and the members of The Solomon Group.

Robert Marx wishes to acknowledge the mentorship of Peter Frost and Andre Delbecq who have been inspiring role models of virtuousness in their work and in their lives. The Solomon Group has been a creative, supportive, and productive community to generate ideas and then nurture them along into the books and articles that can help foster virtuousness in persons and their organizations. Finally, Mitzi and Martin Marx who taught me the paths to a virtuous life and my wife, Susan, who always helps me remember the moment.

We also want to thank all the contributing authors to this volume and the many organizational members that were in anyway part of the research projects and otherwise enabled the thinking and learning that went into the writing of the various chapters of this book. Finally, we especially offer our appreciation to the many people whom in their work and lives embody virtue day by day and both directly and indirectly contribute to the "*The Virtuous Organization.*"

CONTENTS

THE VIRTUOUS ORGANIZATION: AN INTRODUCTION

Charles C. Manz

University of Massachusetts Amherst

Kim S. Cameron

University of Michigan

Karen P. Manz

Hartford Seminary

Robert D. Marx

University of Massachusetts Amherst

Even though the concept of virtues may seem more at home in philosophy, religion, and social services than in the for-profit world of business, *The Virtuous Organization* focuses on virtuous practices in work contexts. Much attention has been paid to values in organizations, of course, but the definition and roles played by virtues in organizations differ from values. We briefly discuss the concept of virtues in organizations and differentiate it from the concept of values with which it is sometimes confused. This will serve as a backdrop to the contributions made by the various chapters contained in this book.

1

What are Virtues?

Until recently the concept of virtue has been out of favor in the scientific community. Virtues have been traditionally viewed as relativistic, culture-specific, and associated with social conservatism, religious or moral dogmatism, and scientific irrelevance (Chapman and Galston, 1992; MacIntyre, 1984; Schimmel, 1997). Scholarly research has not only paid scant attention to virtues, especially in organizations, but also has remained largely undiscussable among practicing managers faced with economic pressures and stakeholder demands.

Walsh *et al.* (2003), for example, surveyed the appearance of terms depicting virtue in the business press. They found that virtues are largely ignored as topics associated with business performance. In an analysis of word usage in the *Wall Street Journal* from 1984 through 2000, Walsh *et al.* reported that the appearance of terms such as "win," "advantage," and "beat" had risen more than four-fold over that 17-year period, whereas terms such as "virtue," "caring," and "compassion" seldom appeared at all. Moreover, their appearance had remained negligible across the 17-year period. Although organizations, as well as individuals, aspire to be virtuous (e.g., honest, caring, courageous), such concepts have been replaced by more morally neutral terms in organizational studies such as corporate social responsibility, prosocial behavior, and employee morale (McNeely and Meglino, 1994; George, 1991; Piliavin and Charng, 1990). One result of this neutralizing of the language of organizational studies is that there has been little systematic investigation of the expression and effects of virtue in organizations. The attributes of organizations "that move individuals toward better citizenship, responsibility, nurturance, altruism, civility, moderation, tolerance, and work ethic" (Seligman and Csikszentmihalyi, 2000, p. 5) have been largely absent from empirical investigations in organizational studies.

The concept of virtue has been defined in a variety of ways in the literature but mainly as a link to meaningful life purpose (Becker, 1992; Overholster, 1999) or a transcendent principle that ennobles human beings (Eisenberg, 1990; Lipman-Blumen and Leavitt, 1999). For example, in early Greek culture virtue was associated with personal health and flourishing (Weiner, 1993; Nussbaum, 1994) and that which leads to health, happiness, transcendent meaning, and resilience in suffering (Ryff and Singer, 1998; Myers, 2000a,b). Virtue also has been defined as an attribute of personal character, and it possesses cognitive, affective, volitional, and behavioral characteristics (Peterson, 2003; Nodding, 1984; Doherty, 1995). Still another view of virtue is a quality of psychological strength, "moral muscle," or willpower that promotes stamina in the face of challenges (Emmons, 1999; Seligman, 1999; Baumeister and Exline, 1999, 2000).

At the aggregate level, virtue has been treated as embedded in communities, cultures, and organizations, and being virtuous has meant adhering to the highest qualities of the social system of which one is a part (Jordan and Meara, 1990; Roberts, 1988). Virtuousness, in this sense, is the internalization of moral rules that produces social harmony (Baumeister and Exline, 1999). Because the concept of virtue captures the highest aspirations of human beings (Peterson and Seligman, 2000), the study of virtue is a study of the capacity, attributes, and reserve in organizations that facilitate the expression of positive deviance among organization members (Cameron, 2003). This area of study includes not only an examination of extraordinary outcomes (e.g., the best of the human condition) but also the extraordinary behaviors within organizations that may lead to positive outcomes (Sandage and Hill, 2001; Dutton *et al.*, 2002).

Virtues in organizations appear to have at least five attributes (Cameron, 2003):

(1) Virtues foster a sense of meaning, well-being, and ennoblement in human beings.
(2) Virtues are experienced cognitively, emotionally, and behaviorally.
(3) Virtues foster harmony in relationships.
(4) Virtues are self-reinforcing and positively deviation amplifying.
(5) Virtues serve a buffering function and foster resilience.

These attributes differentiate virtues from the concept of values, which serve different functions in individuals and organizations.

A Shift to Virtues

Psychologist Martin Seligman, the primary founder of the Positive Psychology movement, reported that 99 percent of research in the last 50 years has neglected the positive virtuous aspects of people in favor of an emphasis on human dysfunction (Seligman, 2002). Luthans *et al.* (2002) have explained that the shift toward Positive Psychology is a response to the over-emphasis of the field over the years on what is wrong with the people. This has led to collaborative work centered at the University of Nebraska on both a positive approach to Organizational Behavior in general as well as to leadership specifically that recognizes more virtuous considerations such as optimism and hope.

Similarly, a research center at the University of Michigan has been formed which examines Positive Organizational Scholarship, or that which leads to the development of human strength, resiliency, and healing; cultivates extraordinary individual and organizational performance; leads to flourishing outcomes and the best of the human condition; and fosters and enables virtuous behaviors and emotions such as compassion, forgiveness, dignity, respectful encounters, optimism, integrity and positive affect (Cameron *et al.*, 2003). Results of this research have included investigations of the impact of virtues on organizational performance as well as on individual cognitions and physical well-being (Dutton and Ragins, 2006; Cameron and Lavine, 2006).

Still another group of scholars at the University of Massachusetts at Amherst has written extensively about virtues and their effects on leaders and organizations (cf. Manz *et al.* 2001, 2003, 2004; Marx *et al.*, in press). Drawing from ancient scripture as a rich source of inspiration with its emphasis on virtuous aspects of struggling with the human condition, six virtues were identified by these writers. These virtues — faith, courage, compassion, integrity, justice and wisdom — related well to exemplary cases of positive contemporary leadership and action at work (Manz *et al.* 2001, 2006).

This book focuses on this new, yet as old as recorded history, emerging set of concepts that can be referred to as virtues. The concept of virtues is also very consistent with the growing emphasis on spirituality in the workplace, a primary focus of the recently established journal — the *Journal of Management, Spirituality and Religion* — where much of the content of this book originally appeared in a special issue on "Values and Virtues in Organizations" as journal articles. Virtues have recently become topics of serious examination among organizational researchers and progressive companies who are exploring their role in creating new, more holistic, healthy and humane work environments.

Values

The concept of *value* has long been assigned an important role in the organization literature. Hofstede (1980, p. 19) has defined the term value as "a broad tendency to prefer certain states of affairs over others". Individuals as well as organizations have values. At the individual level a value can be described as "a specific mode of conduct or end-state of existence — that is personally or socially preferable to an opposite or converse mode of conduct or end-state of existence" (Rokeach, 1973, p. 5). Values help to identify appropriate goals and behaviors (Schwartz and Bilsky, 1987) as well as roles. Values emerge over time and are affected by family, work units, societies, and national cultures. And, much empirical evidence confirms that values significantly affect behavior and attitudes at work (Gamble and Gibson, 1999).

At the organizational level, values represent the beliefs and attitudes that permeate the organization. Values are a key part of defining an organization. They help shape its culture (Schein, 1985; O'Reilly and Chatman, 1996) and identity (Albert and Whetten, 1985). Values also link organization members in ways that can facilitate the achievement of goals (Meglino and Ravlin, 1998).

Shifts in dominant values have occurred in organizations over the last 50 years or so; at least four major shifts can be identified (Cameron and Quinn, 2006). The early organizational literature emphasized traditional business values such as efficiency, control, specialization, and rationality (Weber, 1947). These values were highly effective in helping organizations achieve efficient, reliable, smooth-flowing, and predictable output, especially in relatively stable environments. A turn in dominant organizational values also occurred toward market mechanisms, mainly monetary exchange. That is, the major values focused on transactions (exchanges, sales, contracts) designed to create competitive advantage. Profitability, competitiveness, bottom line results, strength in market niches, stretch targets, and secure customer bases supplemented the more traditional values (Williamson, 1975; Ouchi, 1981) and became dominant in organizations. Still later, shared values and goals, cohesion, participativeness, individuality, and a sense of we-ness began to achieve prominence. Instead of traditional rules and procedures or the competitiveness of profit centers, typical values focused on teamwork, employee involvement, and corporate commitment (Ouchi, 1981; Pascale and Athos, 1981; Lincoln *et al.*, 1980). Finally, the hyper-turbulent, complex, accelerating environments of the 21st century led to still another shift in values toward innovative and pioneering initiatives. Organizations and leaders emphasized developing new products and services and preparing for the future, and the major task of management became to foster entrepreneurship, creativity, adaptation, innovativeness and activity on the cutting edge (DeGraff and Lawrence, 2002; Tushman and O'Reilly, 1997).

These value shifts have not resulted in any set of values being predominant in organizations, and all are represented in the organizational studies literature. However, the point we are making is that whereas values have been extensively investigated, virtues have not been, even though the two terms are sometimes confused. That is, the contemporary management research literature has largely neglected the virtuous aspects of human nature.

The Virtuous Organization began with the development of a series of questions that invited response. How might the concept of virtue be best defined relative to organizational contexts, and how does it relate to the concept of value? What are the key dimensions or manifestations of virtues? Can virtues be recognized, assessed or enabled at the group or organization level of analysis, or are virtues strictly individualistic? How do we identify, characterize and select virtues for organizational purposes? How can traditional business values and virtues work together in the workplace? What is the relationship between virtues and various kinds of individual and organizational performance? How might an emphasis on organizational virtues contribute to effective teamwork and leadership? What role can organizational virtues play in establishing organizational culture that provides deeper meaning and purpose for its members? How might the presence of virtues in organizations help avoid ethical failures such as those that occurred at Enron or World Com? What organizational dynamics are associated with virtues in organizations? What contemporary examples exist of organizations and leaders emphasizing virtues and what outcomes do they experience?

The editors of this book wanted to bring together many of the leading scholars in the field for this groundbreaking effort. We think the contributions made in *The Virtuous Organization* are valuable and help to take a step forward in understanding and being able to utilize the concept of virtues in organizations. These chapters exemplify the variety of viable approaches and perspectives which are seen as important for addressing the breadth and scope of where virtues can touch, support, and shape organizational life. Thus, the contributors to this book offer their observations in several formats: research reports, more applied chapters, essays, and interviews. We organized the book into three sections connecting with the idea of virtues in organizations during crisis, ordinary, and exemplary times. More specifically this book addresses the following overall purpose:

> Historically emphasis on traditional business values such as efficiency, control, and profitability, seem to have helped organizations to achieve competitiveness and financial success. At the same time, many would say they are inadequate alone for guiding organizations into the future in a healthy and sustainable way. In addition, when pursued unchecked without being balanced by other kinds of higher level values (virtues) they can contribute to the emergence of broad scale corporate scandal. This volume provides a range of conceptual thinking, research studies, and practical applications that provide

insights about how "virtuous management"(based on transcendent values such as compassion, forgiveness and integrity) can help organizations succeed in achieving valuable and meaningful results that extend beyond financial success during:

(a)   *Crises — such as threats to the organization and its environment or scandalous leader behavior.*
(b)   *Ordinary times — absence of immediate crises or unusual prosperity and progress but with ongoing corporate and societal challenges.*
(c)   *Exemplary times — such as when significant opportunities are at hand and unusual prosperity or healthy progress is being enjoyed.*

Note that the book is designed to enable readers to select specific chapters or sections that can be read independent of the rest of the volume. While this enables the book to serve as a useful reference it may create some redundancy in points in section and chapter introductions.

The Virtuous Organization and Crises

Powley and Cameron introduce the topic of virtuousness in the chapter "Organizational Healing: Lived Virtuousness Amidst Organizational Crisis." They present a case study of the occupants of a university building who are traumatized by a gunman. Based on extensive interview data, four primary themes are identified as essential for organizational healing and how virtuousness can be enacted under such circumstances.

The next chapter by Rhee *et al.*, "Making Sense of Organizational Actions with Virtue Frames and its Links to Organizational Attachment," examines another traumatic event: the September 11, 2001 attacks in New York City. This study introduces the concept of virtue frames as a construct for understanding members' sense making experience, both cognitive and emotional, in response to the virtuousness of organizational actions.

Bright *et al.*, in "Forgiveness from the Perspectives of Three Response Modes: Begrudgement, Pragmatism and Transcendence" present an empirical analysis of the virtue "forgiveness" and how it can function not only as a healing mechanism, but also as a "life-giving, positive, uplifting" force in an organizational setting. Interview data are drawn from employees of an organization burdened with long-term union-management conflict. From this, the authors develop a five Phase Model of Forgiveness.

Finally, the essay chapter "The Spiritual Challenges of Power, Humility and Love as Offsets to Leadership Hubris" emanates from Andre Delbecq's work with executives in Silicon Valley. Many of these executives sought a more spiritual and virtuous approach to their work, but often found themselves tempted by arrogance and dominance — the two dimensions of hubris. Delbecq explores how even well-intentioned leaders can be seduced by the trappings of power and how the offsetting virtues of humility and love can negate the circumstances that lead into hubris.

The Virtuous Organization and Ordinary Times

Having identified virtuousness in organizations as a concept of increasing interest and importance to management scholars, it only follows that management educators will be attempting to examine how to "teach" these concepts to their students and/or employees. In "The Language of Virtues: Toward an Inclusive Approach for Integrating Spirituality in Management Education," Manz *et al.* address the critical issue of language when speaking about spirituality as it relates to virtuousness in the workplace. They suggest that personal sources of virtuous behavior in organizations include religious, ethical, legal, and humanistic origins. The language of virtues is suggested as a way of speaking that includes the individual sources of spirituality at work but translates these sources into actions that can be implemented by the organization as a whole.

Next, in their chapter "Leveraging Psychological Capital in Virtuous Organizations: Why and How?," Carolyn Youssef and Fred Luthans provide an engaging discussion of the important role that psychological capital plays in the manifestation of virtuousness in organizations during crises, ordinary and exemplary times. In particular, they view psychological capital as being based on psychological resources such as optimism, hope, resilience and efficacy and review research that supports its potential benefits for the firm's bottom line. They suggest that psychological capital can be effectively developed during the relative stability of ordinary times and consequently help the organization to maintain a virtuous stance during more volatile periods.

In the chapter, "Europe Versus Asia: Truth Versus Virtue" cultural scholar Geert Hofstede reflects on the values which exemplify West and East differences in social history and their effect on both short-term and long-term understandings of "a way of life." This has implications for the identification and understanding of virtue. Hofstede considers this impact on the thinking and actions of science, management and government.

Joseph Maciariello's 2005 interviews with Peter Drucker serve as the focus of the next chapter. "Peter Drucker on Mission-Driven Leadership and Management in the Social Sector: Interviews and Postscript" offers Drucker's insights "into the problems and erroneous promise of the social sector in America." This section of the chapter is followed with another interview undertaken especially to address the theme of this book. Drucker gets to the heart of the social sector and the need to create balanced organizations emphasizing virtuous purposes while still being held accountable for results.

The section concludes with Nancy Adler's chapter "Corporate Global Citizenship: Successfully Partnering with the World." Adler offers a vision and a challenge for CEOs and the largest global organizations to use their resources and influence in the spirit of positive global citizenship. She provides several examples of how virtuous organizations can work with governments, other companies and communities to help make "The Virtuous Organization" a reality. She points to significant results from such worthwhile partnerships that can yield more peace, reduced poverty and an improved environment, all while achieving profitability.

The Virtuous Organization and Exemplary Times

In all corners of the world, we periodically face difficult and destructive events. However, by no means are virtues to be understood as only important or applicable in times of crisis (during great challenge or suffering), or in the more "ordinary" times in our work and lives. Indeed, virtues can unleash significant forces for creating much good in our organizations and in the world at large during times of special opportunity and possibilities — what we describe as "exemplary times." This section includes chapters that address virtue in both theory and practice that elucidate potential ways to help establish and/or benefit from such exemplary times.

In "Virtuous Leadership: A Theoretical Model and Research Agenda," Pearce *et al.* examine the nature of virtuous leadership by defining it as "influencing and enabling others to pursue righteous and moral goals for themselves and their organization." They articulate emotional, conceptual and moral components to virtuous leadership and discuss three organizational outcomes that have been shown to result from such an approach.

The chapter by Ian Mitroff and Donna Mitroff, "Spirituality in Action: The Fred Rogers' Way of Managing Through Lifelong Mentoring" examines the philosophy and legacy of Fred Rogers of "Mister Rogers' Neighborhood." The authors, through first-hand experience with Rogers, examine his role in starting the formation of healthy values in children and then translate Fred Rogers' ideas into seven principles aimed at developing healthy adult managers and vital organizations.

In "The Positive Potential of Tempered Radicals" Rand Quinn and Debra Meyerson examine the connection between the Positive Organizational Scholarship notion of positive deviance and the complementary influences of organizational members who spearhead change processes through both an inside and outside organizational role. These so-called "Tempered Radicals" seek to make a sustainable positive difference through constructive incremental and subtle strategies that are founded on integrity and healthy influence.

In the next chapter, we are privy to a conversation with *Fortune* magazine senior journalist, Marc Gunther and Judi Neal, founder of the International Association for Spirit at Work. Neal gives background to and a follow-up interview of Gunther on the role of virtues in leadership. A case study of CEO Ricardo Levy exemplifies the application of virtuousness in the organization and provides the core focus of the follow-up interview. Neal's final questions expand Gunther's thoughts about the importance of virtue in organizations.

The section ends with Rosabeth Moss Kanter's chapter "The Corporate Conduct Continuum: From 'Do No Harm' to 'Do Lots of Good'." Kanter makes a direct connection between economic considerations and values. Beyond acknowledging increasing societal expectations for good corporate citizenship, she shares exemplary cases of companies who have succeeded both financially and in terms of service to their communities and the world at large. Ultimately, the chapter provides insights about how corporate conduct might be assessed in terms of its integrity and positive engagement with its societal context.

After the three primary sections of this book — The *Virtuous Organization and Crises, Ordinary Times, and Exemplary Times* — David Whetten provides a final comment in his chapter "Reflections on What Matters Most." After providing a new preamble, he offers his 2000 Academy of Management Presidential Address "What Matters Most" for consideration in relation to the notion of "The Virtuous Organization." This final chapter is an especially fitting way to end the book as it reminds us that organizations consist of flesh-and -blood people who create the character of their institutions one relationship and one act at a time. It brings us back to earth and poses a challenge for all of us to consider our own role in allowing virtuousness to exist in organizational life. Whether we choose positive acts of noteworthy integrity that set an example for those we encounter throughout our work days and careers or simply greet and support a newcomer with compassion and a welcoming demeanor, in the end the realization of "The Virtuous Organization" begins with each of us.

Together the chapters in this book broaden the linkages between virtuousness and organizational outcomes during crises, ordinary and exemplary times. They help to refine definitions of virtue in several aspects of organizational endeavor and offer a series of initial attempts to encourage further theory building, empirical assessment, and application of virtuousness in the organization. They also encourage deeper thinking and reflection about how virtues can affect various organizational activities and outcomes as we move further into the 21st Century.

Hopefully this volume will help move the literature, and ultimately practice, toward a clearer language and multiple perspectives for addressing organizational virtues. Such an undertaking promises to shift thinking in significant ways about living, working, leading and organizing. It may help lay the foundation for bold action based on deeply held beliefs and values regardless of the situation.

As a consequence, workplace behavior and values may eventually become more congruent with the best of what is asserted in homes and communities and present a greater good for all. Indeed, when we and our organizations embrace the concept of virtue we may be better equipped to understand and work in whole new ways with an enhanced sense of authenticity, productivity and much needed wisdom.

References

Albert, S and DA Whetten (1985). Organizational identity. *Research in Organizational Behavior*, 7, 263–302.

Baumeister, RF and JJ Exline (1999). Virtue, personality, and social relations: self-control as the moral muscle. *Journal of Personality*, 67, 1165–1194.

Baumeister, RF and JJ Exline (2000). Self-control, morality, and human strength. *Journal of Social and Clinical Psychology*, 19, 29–42.

Becker, LC (1992). Good lives: prolegomena, *Social Philosophy and Policy*, 9, 15–37.

Cameron, K (2003). Organizational virtuousness and performance. In *Positive Organizational Scholarship*. KS Cameron, JE Dutton and RE Quinn (eds.), San Francisco: Berrett-Koehler.

Cameron, KS, JE Dutton and RE Quinn (eds.) (2003). *Positive Organizational Scholarship*. San Francisco: Berrett-Koehler.

Cameron, KS and M Lavine (2006). *Making the Impossible Possible,* San Francisco: Berrett Koehler.

Cameron, KS and RE Quinn (2006). *Diagnosing and Changing Organizational Culture*. San Francisco: Jossey Bass.

Chapman, JW and WA Galston (1992). *Virtue*. New York: New York University Press.

DeGraff, J and K Lawrence (2002). *Creativity at Work.* San Francisco: Jossey Bass.

Doherty, WJ (1995). *Soul Searching: Why Psychotherapy Must Promote Moral Responsibility.* New York: Basic Books.

Dutton, JE, PJ Frost, MC Worline, JM Lilius and JM Kanov (2002). Leading in times of trauma. *Harvard Business Review,* January, 54–61.

Dutton, JE and BR Ragins (2006). *Exploring Positive Relationships at Work.* Mahwah, NJ: Lawrence Erlbaum.

Eisenberg, EM (1990). Jamming: transcendence through organizing. *Communication Research,* 17, 139–164.

Emmons, RA (1999). *The Psychology of Ultimate Concerns: Motivation and Spirituality_in Personality.* New York: Guilford Press.

Gamble, PR and DA Gibson (l999). Executive values and decision making: the relationship of culture and information flows. *Journal of Management Studies,* 36, 217–240.

George, JM (1991). State or trait: effects of positive mood on prosocial behaviors at work. *Journal of Applied Psychology,* 76, 229–307.

Hofstede, G (l980). *Culture's Consequences.* London: Sage.

Jordan, AE and N Meara (1990). Ethics and the professional practice of psychologists: The role of virtues and principles. *Professional Psychology: Research and Practice,* 21, 107–114.

Lincoln, J, M Hanada and J Olson (1980). Cultural orientations and individual reactions to organizations. *Administrative Science Quarterly,* 26, 93–115.

Lipman-Blumen, J and HJ Leavitt (1999). *Hot Groups: Seeking Them, Feeding Them, and Using Them to Ignite Your Organization.* New York: Oxford University Press.

Luthans, F, K Luthans, RM Hodgetts and BC Luthans (2002). Positive approach to leadership (PAL): Implications for today's organizations. *The Journal of Leadership Studies,* 8, 3–20.

MacIntyre, A (1984). *After Virtue: A Study in Moral Theory.* 2nd ed., Notre Dame, IN: University of Notre Dame Press.

Manz. CC, KP Manz and RD Marx (2003). The search for wisdom at work. *Ledmotiv,* (2), 42–53. Stockholm: Stockholm School of Economics.

Manz, C, K Manz, R Marx and C Neck (2001). *The Wisdom of Solomon at Work: Ancient Virtues for Living and Leading Today.* San Francisco: Berrett-Koehler.

Manz, CC, KP Manz, RD Marx and CP Neck (2004). Spiritual beliefs and scholarship: a journey with the wisdom of solomon. *Management Communications Quarterly.* 17, 611–620.

Manz. KP, RD Marx, J Neal and CC Manz (2006). The language of virtues: toward an inclusive approach for integrating spirituality in management education. *Journal of Management Spirituality and Religion,* 3, 104–122.

Marx, RD, J Neal, KP Manz and CC Manz (in press). Teaching about spirituality and work: Experiential exercises for management educators. In *Spirituality in*

Business: Theory, Practice, and Future Directions. G Biberman and L Tischler (eds.), New York: Palgrave MacMillan.

Meglino BM and EC Ravlin (1998). Individual values in organizations: concepts, controversies, and research, *Journal of Management*, 24, 351–390.

Myers, DG (2000a). The funds, friends, and faith of happy people. *American Psychologist*, 55, 56–67.

Myers, DG (2000b). *An American Paradox: Spiritual Hunger in an Age of Plenty.* New Haven, CT: Yale University Press.

McNeely, BL and BM Meglino(1994). The role of dispositional and situational antecedents in prosocial organizational behavior: an examination of the intended beneficiaries of prosocial behavior, *Journal of Applied Psychology*, 79, 836–844.

Nodding, N (1984). *Caring: A Feminine Approach to Ethics and Moral Education.* Berkeley, CA: University of California Press.

Nussbaum, MC (1994). *The Therapy of Desire: Theory and Practice in Hellenistic Ethics.* Princeton, NJ: Princeton University Press.

O'Reilly, CA and JA Chatman (1996). Culture as social control: corporations, cults, and commitment. In *Research in Organizational Behavior.* BM Staw and LL Cummings (eds.), Vol. 18, pp. 157–200, Greenwich, CT: JAI Press.

Ouchi, WG (1981). *Theory Z: How American Business Can Meet the Japanese Challenge.* Reading, MA: Addison Wesley.

Overholster, JC (1999). Elements of the socratic method: VI. Promoting virtue in everyday life. *Psychotherapy*, 36, 137–145.

Pascale, R and A Athos (1981). *The Art of Japanese Management.* New York: Simon and Schuster.

Peterson, C (2003). Classification of positive traits in youth. In *Promoting Positive Child, Adolescent, and Family Development.* RM Lerner, F Jacobs and D Wertlieb (eds.), Vol. 4, pp. 227–255. Thousand Oaks, CA: Sage.

Peterson, CM and MEP Seligman (2000). The classification of strengths and virtues: The VIA manual, working paper. University of Pennsylvania.

Piliavin, JA and H Charng (1990). Altruism: a review of recent theory and Research. *Annual Review of Sociology*, 16, 27–65.

Roberts, RC (1988). Therapies and the grammar of virtue. In *The Grammar of the Heart: New Essays in Moral Philosophy and Theology*, RH Bell (Ed.), pp. 149–170, San Francisco: Harper & Row.

Rokeach, M (1973). *The Nature of Human Values.* New York: Free Press.

Ryff, CD and B Singer (1998). The contours of positive human health, *Psychological Inquiry*, 9, 1–28.

Sandage, SJ and PC Hill (2001). The virtues of positive psychology: the rapprochement and challenges of the affirmative postmodern perspective. *Journal for the Theory of Social Behavior*, 31, 241–260.

Schein, EH (1985). *Organizational Culture and Leadership.* San Francisco: Jossey Bass.

Schimmel, S (1997). *The Seven Deadly Sins: Jewish, Christian, and Classical Reflections on Human Nature.* New York: The Free Press.

Schwartz, SH and H Bilsky (1987). Toward a universal psychological structure of human values. *Journal of Personality and Social Psychology.* 53, 550–562.

Seligman, MEP (1999). The President's address, *American Psychologist,* 54, 559–562.

Seligman, MEP (2002). *Authentic Happiness.* New York: Free Press.

Seligman, MEP and M Csikszentmihalyi (2000). Positive psychology: an introduction. *American Psychologist,* 55, 5–14.

Tushman, ML and CA O'Reilly (1997). *Winning Through Innovation,* Cambridge, MA: Harvard Business School Press.

Walsh, JP, K Weber and JD Margolis (2003). Social issues and management: Our lost cause found. *Journal of Management,* 29, 859–881.

Weiner, NO (1993). *The Harmony of the Soul: Mental Health and Moral Virtue Reconsidered.* Albany, NY: State University of New York Press.

Weber, M (1947). *The Theory of Social and Economic Organization.* TAM Henderson and T Parsons (translators). New York: Oxford.

Williamson, O (1975). *Markets and Hierarchies, Analysis and Antitrust Implications: A Study in Economics of Internal Organization.* New York: Free Press.

Section One

THE VIRTUOUS ORGANIZATION AND CRISES

Section Editor: Kim S. Cameron

In this section, the authors discuss the role of virtues and virtuousness under conditions of crisis. Brockner and James (2008) identified the five main ingredients of crisis in organizations as: (1) a highly ambiguous situation, (2) with a low probability of occurring, (3) offering little time to respond, (4) often coming as a surprise to organizational members, and (5) requiring a decision or judgment intended to improve the organization. Crises are often watershed events for organizations. They typically pose challenges in which much is at stake, for many constituencies, and in both the short- and long-term. Whereas, crises frequently give rise to a threat-rigidity response (Staw *et al.*, 1981), to organizational deterioration (Cameron *et al.*, 1988), and to the mitigation of opportunities for organizations to flourish, this section highlights the opposite consequences. In this section, the authors identify the role that virtuousness plays during crisis conditions which produces positive organizational performance.

Traditionally, virtues or virtuousness were relegated to philosophical or theological discussions, but more recently, the concepts have been associated with the best of the human condition, the most ennobling behaviors and outcomes, the excellence and essence of humankind, and the highest aspirations of human beings (Cameron *et al.*, 2004; Peterson and Seligman, 2004). The positive effects of virtuousness in human endeavor are usually explained by two key attributes: *amplifying* qualities — i.e., virtuousness can foster escalating positive consequences — and *buffering* qualities — i.e., virtuousness can protect against negative consequences (Cameron, 2003; Fredrickson and Joiner, 2002; Masten and Reed, 2002). When virtuousness is demonstrated (as when leaders or exemplars manifest virtuous behaviors), or when organizations perpetuate or legitimize virtuous behaviors (as when courageous or compassionate acts are recognized and applauded), virtuousness tends to become self-reinforcing (amplifying), and it fosters resiliency against negative and challenging obstacles (buffering).

The amplifying and buffering roles that virtues play in organizational performance, and their association with organizational outcomes, is the theme of this section of the book. Each chapter highlights a different type of crisis — a traumatic shooting and hostage crisis, the September 11th terrorist attacks, union-management conflict and downsizing and, ironically, the narcissism, arrogance, and hubris associated with leadership success — which serve as major threats to organizational flourishing. Each chapter highlights the critical role of virtues and virtuousness in these situations.

In particular, Powley and Cameron examine the role of virtuousness in fostering healing after an organization experienced the trauma of a murder and mass hostage crisis in a campus building. Organizational healing occurs during a period of liminality, and the extent to which virtuous actions occur during this liminal period determines the extent to which healing will occur in organizations.

Rhee, Dutton, and Bagozzi analyze responses to the crises associated with September 11th. They report that individuals who perceive the organization to which they belong as responding virtuously to the crisis — humanely, justly, and courageously — identify more strong with and are more ardently committed to their organization.

Bright, Fry, and Cooperrider identify three kinds of forgiving responses when organization members are faced with crises in the form of downsizing, supervisor tension, or interpersonal conflict. Forms of forgiveness fall into three categories — a begrudging response, a pragmatic response, and a transcendent response — where the third category is associated with virtuousness and interpersonal flourishing.

Delbecq examines a different form of crisis — the achievement of celebrity status as a leader and the resulting development of situational hubris. Many aspects of the role of leader sway individuals toward arrogance, narcissism, and dominance, and this chapter offers an explanation of antidotes and offsets to these tendencies.

References

Bright, DS, KS Cameron and Arran Caza (2006). The amplifying and buffering effects of virtuousness in downsized organizations. *Journal of Business Ethics*, 64, 249–269. University Press.

Brockner, J and EH James (2008). Towards an understanding on when executives see crisis as opportunity. *Journal of Applied Behavioral Sciences*, 44, 94–115.

Cameron, KS (2003). Organizational virtuousness and performance. In *Positive Organizational Scholarship* KS Cameron, J Dutton and RE Quinn (Eds.), pp. 48–65. San Francisco: Berrett-Koehler.

Cameron, KS, D Bright, and A Caza (2004). Exploring the relationships between organizational virtuousness and performance. *American Behavioral Scientist*, 47, 766–790.

Cameron, KS, RI Sutton, and DA Whetten (1988) *Organizational Decline*. Cambridge: Ballinger.

Fredrickson, BL and T Joiner (2002). Positive emotions trigger upward spirals toward emotional well-being. *Psychological Science*.

Masten, AS and MGJ Reed (2002). Resilience in development. In *Handbook of Positive Psychology*, CR Snyder and SJ Lopez (Eds.), pp. 74–88. New York: Oxford University Press.

Peterson, C and MEP Seligman (2004). *Character Strengths and Virtues*. New York: Oxford University Press.

Staw, BM, LE Sandelands, and JE Dutton (1981). Threat-rigidity effects in organizational behavior: a multi-level analysis. *Administrative Science Quarterly*, 26, 501–524.

Chapter One

ORGANIZATIONAL HEALING: LIVED VIRTUOUSNESS AMIDST ORGANIZATIONAL CRISIS

Edward H. Powley

Naval Postgraduate School

Kim S. Cameron

University of Michigan

This chapter examines how organizations heal after major trauma. The authors introduce the concept of organizational healing and differentiate it from resilience, adaptation, and hardiness. Healing refers to the actual work of repairing and mending the collective social fabric of an organization after experiencing a threat or shock to its system. Using a qualitative research method, the chapter uncovers four themes of organizational healing that reflect an organization's capacity for virtuousness: reinforcing the priority of the individual, fostering high quality connections, strengthening a family culture, and initiating ceremonies and rituals. These themes emerged from narrative accounts of the shooting incident in a Midwestern university.

The sound of shattering glass and the break-in of an army fatigue-clad gunman went undetected by all but a few of the 90 occupants of a university building on a late Friday afternoon. Hearing the crash, one student known for his gregarious personality and leadership ability, immediately approached the gunman but was shot and killed instantly. Two other individuals were

21

wounded by gunfire as the gunman roamed the building for the next seven hours, holding hostage the building occupants and keeping the police at bay.

This chapter examines how organizations heal after a major trauma, such as the one described above, in which the core values and social fabric of the organization are threatened. We return to this example after a brief review of literature on healing and organizations. According to Gordon and Wraith (1993), the main feature of trauma is "rupture," in which continuity of time, relationships and attachments, the perceptions of self and others, and expectations about the future all are torn apart. Through the examination of this incident of shooting and police standoff, we will illustrate how an organization's ability to heal rests on its capacity to facilitate and demonstrate virtuousness at the collective level. Rupture, in other words, is healed by the expression of virtuousness.

We examine the story of one organization's responses to tragedy that not only ruptured the emotional and psychological safety of the entire system but also cut into its self-identity and culture. Students, staff, and faculty had only recently moved into a new, iconic university building — constructed to symbolize the core values of the institution. This tragedy threatened to permanently tarnish the core identity of the organization by associating its magnificent new building with carnage and death. In analyzing the aftermath of this event, we introduce the concept of organizational healing. In doing so, we present four themes for how organizations deal with tragedies and crises in order to restore them to health.

While we examine themes of organizational healing based on a singular case study, the concepts are also applicable to other organizational situations in which trauma has been experienced, such as natural or technological disasters. The tragedy resulting from hurricane Katrina, for example, in which multiple organizations experienced ruptures in continuity of time, relationships and attachments, the perceptions of self and others, and expectations about the future is an apt example. The healing process that occurs in such organizations — where strength and restoration occur as a result of specific processes — is the focus of this analysis.

Organizational healing has not been examined in the organizational studies literature to date and is only anecdotally mentioned when speaking of downsizing (Ambrose, 1996). Yet, it is a relevant construct when explaining how organizations return to a state of well-being after experiencing major harm. Healing is different from resilience (bouncing back from trauma) (Sutcliffe and Vogus, 2003), adaptation (adjusting to changes or coping with aberrations) (Cyert and March, 1963; Levinthal, 1991), and hardiness (being durable or tough) (Maddi and Khoshaba, 2005). Healing refers to the actual work of repairing and mending the social fabric, continuity, expectations, and shattered self-concepts that are necessary if an organization is to return to a healthy state of functioning. Resilience, adaptation, and hardiness, all refer to the attributes of organizations which allow them to withstand major trauma or damage resulting from external or uncontrollable events (as opposed to making mistakes and human error). Because those literatures do not discuss the nature of the healing process itself in organizations, this chapter introduces themes associated with healing and the role of virtuousness in the healing process.

The concept of healing in organizational research has not been completely ignored (see Dutton *et al.* 2005). One excellent example is Frost's (2003) superb examination of healing associated with toxic emotions and toxin handlers at work. Toxin handlers help people heal from the experience of negative emotions in a variety of ways, and Frost identified ways in which organizations can play a role in that healing process. However, healing in this and all other studies we could find relates to *personal* healing rather than organizational healing. This study differentiates the healing that occurs in an individual's psyche from that which occurs in the collective identity, values, processes, and culture of an organization.

Healing and Organizations

Healing refers to the process of becoming sound, healthy, and whole after suffering illness or harm. Surprisingly, the medical and nursing sciences do not, by and large, address stages or processes of healing but rather treat the state of healing as an outcome condition. Being healed is treated as the result of other medical and pharmaceutical interventions, but the nature of the healing process itself is little examined, especially as it relates to collective entities such as organizations. The mechanisms by which this phenomenon unfolds are largely absent from the literature. One of the few examinations of the healing process relates to the responses of children to the trauma of war, violence, death, and victimization. A key finding from this work is that "the healing of trauma cannot be accomplished by an individual alone." It always requires social intervention and collective support (see Ayalon, 1998; Jareg, 1995; Lumsden, 1997; Terr, 1991).

In a collective sense, healing connotes a coordinated effort by individuals in a social context to restore harmony, security, and integrity to individuals through their social interaction. The healing of an organization means that the organizational unit itself becomes whole and returns to health. This requires specific actions and interactions on the part of individuals and groups that comprise the organization. In this chapter, we identify the relevant actions taken by individuals and groups that brought about the process of healing in this traumatized organization. We should note that organizational healing is a collective level phenomenon derived from descriptions of organizational functioning in the face of trauma, and it is detected through organization members' actions and interactions.

Healing is a relevant construct only under conditions of harm or damage. Healing is not manifest when things are going well. The extent to which the *capacity* for healing exists in an organization is difficult to determine, therefore, in as much as this capacity cannot be known until trauma or damage occurs. That is, inherent in all living systems is the capacity to heal, but just as the human body has the potential to heal more or less quickly and effectively from the effects of disease or surgery, so organizations also may possess a strong or weak capacity to heal quickly and effectively from trauma. While no one wishes for crisis, through trauma (simulated or real) organization members come to understand their organization's capacity to restore itself to health and wholeness.

Healing and Liminality

In the study of children who had experienced major trauma, Ayalon (1998), based on the work of Winnicot (1971), articulated the idea of a transition space where healing occurs, referring to it as the "intermediate zone between the personal/psychological and the social structures." Similarly, organizational healing occurs during a transition space that is both metaphorical and literal, a liminal space where social structure is suspended as individuals engage in actions that support and enable others to become whole again. The liminal space rebuilds and renews an organization's social fabric, sense of continuity, expectations, and identity.

Liminality is a key concept in the anthropological literature that refers to the interval between physical, temporal, and metaphorical spaces — as in rituals and rites of passage studied mostly by anthropologists and a few organizational scholars (Trice and Beyer, 1984; Beyer and Trice, 1987) — which are particularly applicable to organizational change processes (Powley *et al.*, 2004; Powley, 2004). Liminality in organizations also occurs during the time following a traumatic organizational incident where operational processes are interrupted and social relationships are damaged. Liminality is the time when the system reveals its capacity to heal (Powley, 2005; Turner, 1967). That is, it is in the liminal space that healing may occur for both individuals and the organization. The actions taken during this liminal period may foster healing or not, and we argue that the extent to which virtuous actions occur in the liminal space is an indication of the extent to which healing will occur. We describe this liminal space and processes — particularly the virtuous processes — that enabled healing to occur in one traumatized organization.

The Organizational Crisis

As described briefly above, the break-in and subsequent shooting spree created tremendous damage to the organization — to both the physical space and the social architecture. An examination of the actions and interactions of the participants in this event help identify the extent to which the organization demonstrated the capacity to heal. Although unique to this incident, individuals' accounts represent how virtuousness may be revealed during difficult organizational events and, consequently, may be more generally applicable to other settings. Behind the scenes of this tragedy, staff members, students, faculty, and administrators demonstrated virtues such as compassion, courage, and selfless caring. Organization members' actions to assist and support each other both during and in the aftermath of the event reflect deeply held organizational values and beliefs, and they represent the kinds of virtuous actions required for an organization to heal after crisis.

The Events

In May 2003, the business school of a mid-western private university in the United States found itself to be at the center of a school shooting. As indicated in the Introduction, one of its more popular students became a fatal victim and the school became the scene of a hostage-taking with approximately 90 building occupants. Throughout the a seven-hour stand-off, police officers, sharp shooters, and SWAT teams engaged in a cat-and-mouse-like game with the gunman before he was cornered in the building. Outside, police officers secured the area surrounding the building, evacuated and closed buildings, and redirected traffic — all while family members waited outside and the local media descended upon the campus. Sounds of gunfire echoed from inside the building, and a small number of students and staff members escaped. Helicopters circled overhead. Faculty, staff, and students inside and outside watched and waited. It was close to 11 p.m. before those in the building reunited with family and friends and SWAT officers cornered the gunman in an upstairs classroom.

Over the next week, while the school building remained closed as a crime scene and the damage from the gunfire was repaired, the school and university offered times for faculty, staff, and students to reunite and share personal experiences of the incident. Acting quickly, school administrators and staff outlined a course of action and began the process of organizational healing. They developed strategies regarding upcoming graduation events; when and how to retrieve personal effects from the building; and a process for communicating with staff, faculty, students, and alumni. One week later, the school held a memorial service, and faculty, staff and students symbolically and ceremoniously re-entered the business school building.

Methods for Uncovering Organizational Healing

The presence of virtuousness is difficult to detect by outside observers because the same behaviors may be interpreted as virtuous or as manipulative. For example, the display of kindness in order to obtain a reward or remuneration from the recipient may be interpreted as manipulation rather than virtuousness (e.g., Cameron, 2003). The trouble is, it is difficult to determine the motives of actors merely through objective observation. Consequently, in order to determine the extent to which responses during the period of liminality were virtuous or non-virtuous — and whether they led to healing or scarring — the actual actions, thoughts, and feelings of the actors had to be captured. The approach to data gathering in this investigation, therefore, consisted of open-ended, semi-structured interviews that allowed participants to share their thoughts, feelings, and experiences related to the incident. This enabled us to discover organization members' motivations and perceptions, actions and interactions, and the extent to which healing was promoted.

In this qualitative study, the first author conducted interviews over several months after the incident with nearly 60 individuals who were members of the school and university community. The procedure for conducting a narrative description of the aftermath of the shooting required inviting volunteer participants to share their experiences and reactions to the trauma. That is, in order to honor the fact that the incident produced deep psychological and emotional wounds in some individuals — and therefore some people may not wish to re-live the events associated with the break-in and its aftermath — the first author sent e-mail invitations to approximately 800 faculty, staff, and students providing them with a chance to be interviewed. Within two weeks, at least 60 members of the organization voluntarily responded to the e-mail and asked to be interviewed. No pressure was placed on any individual to participate, and in very few cases was any individual contacted directly. The respondent sample, therefore, is biased in favor of those willing to discuss the incident within a few weeks after it occurred.

In the interviews, participants were invited to first share their personal stories of the event in narrative form. They were then asked to describe events that stood out regarding the organizational responses to the incident. They also discussed other stories that were particularly remarkable and memorable. Finally, they provided information about how their background might have affected the way they experienced the incident. These in-depth interviews represented one attempt to capture the full range of emotions, motivations, and experiences as recounted by the participants. Thus, they were the means by which the first author could determine whether actions represented virtuousness as opposed to merely fearful or self-protective responses.

Having participants describe the events in this way served several purposes. First, the open-ended questions "allow[ed] respondents to construct answers, in collaboration with listeners, in ways they find meaningful" (Riessman, 1993, p. 54). That is, the interview process gave participants the opportunity to respond in ways they felt most comfortable. Having individuals share their stories aloud was also an act that had a healing effect itself, inasmuch as storytelling has the capacity to heal organization members (Fredriksson and Eriksson, 2001; Swatton and O'Callaghan, 1999). Whereas retelling traumatic events can stir up negative emotions, guilt, and sorrow again, the act of story telling in the presence of an interested and empathetic listener tends to have the opposite effect, such that sharing stories of trauma and crisis usually has a restorative effect (Herman, 1997; Pennebaker and Harber, 1993). For example, Herman noted, "Sharing the traumatic experience with others is a precondition for the restitution of a sense of a meaningful world," and "the response of the community has a powerful influence on the ultimate resolution of the trauma" (Herman, 1997, p. 70). In other words, the process of publicly sharing stories and experiences prepares individuals and organizations to experience healing, although the content and motivation of those stories may or may not lead to the fulfillment of that potential.

Key Themes Related to Organizational Healing

The healing process occurred because of the virtuous actions taken by both individuals and the organization itself during and shortly after the traumatic incident. Using a qualitative data analysis process derived from the nursing literature (Fredriksson and Eriksson, 2001), the stories and experiences were analyzed to uncover examples and themes of virtuousness and healing. To capture themes of organizational healing, we revisited narrative accounts or "realist" tales (Van Maanen, 1988) of the incident. These narrative accounts draw out individual, group level, and organizational actions and interactions effectively. The qualitative process for this study was appropriate because a narrative approach (Ludema, 1996; Nye, 1997; Swatton and O'Callaghan, 1999) and an appreciative lens with an eye toward the virtuous dynamics and processes (Cameron *et al.*, 2003; Cooperrider and Srivastva, 1987; Srivastva and Cooperrider, 1986) allowed the inquiry to be *with* rather than *on* organization members and the organizational context.

Furthermore, this narrative approach uncovers stories of relationally oriented actions and interactions and thus makes possible the analysis of underlying mechanisms and themes. Organizational healing is an explanation for the social or collective level phenomenon that occurred in this system. Our process to uncover themes of organizational healing consisted of discovering the beliefs, perceptions, actions, and interactions of individual social actors (Boje, 2001). Data collection ought to be consistent with an approach that discovers individuals' and groups' actions and perceptions; the approach, therefore, involved open-ended, semi-structured interviews that allowed participants to share their experiences of the incident freely.

The themes we identified draw from individuals' experiences of the shooting spree as well as events that occurred the week afterward. They articulate various conceptions associated with organizational healing and are not unlike Dutton *et al.* (2005) representation of workplace healing. Four key themes characterized these actions, and we describe examples and stories associated with each. Table 1 presents definitions and examples of each theme. The stories and responses illustrate how the organization became whole and sound in the aftermath of the crisis, and how its sense of continuity, relationships, and identity were restored.

Reinforcing the priority of the individual

One key theme in the stories of informants represented the extent to which the organization displayed behaviors that were consistent with its highest stated priority, the value of the individual, particularly as reflected in its care for the well-being, future, and careers of its students. The institution espoused student well-being and development as its highest priority. The school's model of education, as articulated by the university's president, intends to "inspire renaissance students…in ways that uniquely position them to serve humanity" — inspiration that promotes virtuousness and goodness. Past research on organizational downsizing (Cameron, 1998) has described organizations that make similar claims — e.g., "people are our most important asset" — yet cut jobs and eliminate headcount at the first hint of crisis. The extent to which the organization placed a high priority on individual welfare during and after crisis reflected the extent to which the organization demonstrated this fundamental value. As it turned out, several examples from the shooting spree highlight this theme.

Minutes after the shooting began, people in the building put themselves at risk by warning others and helping colleagues to safety. A group of staff in the admission's office had access to telephones and established contact with staff in the adjacent executive education building. One woman acted courageously when she crossed an office exposed to gunfire to answer a ringing telephone — it happened to be the Dean's assistant — and doing so enabled her to provide vital information about the perpetrator by sending an immediate e-mail message to the school. This message, as it turned out, was the only warning message sent to members of the school community.

Table 1. Four themes of organizational healing.

Themes	Definition	Examples
Reinforcing the priority of the individual	The extent to which the organization displays behaviors that care for individuals' well-being, future, and careers.	• University's stated intent to "inspire renaissance students… in ways that uniquely position them to serve humanity" • Virtuous and courageous acts motivated by the desire to warn and rescue colleagues in potential danger • Faculty member took time amidst crisis to assist a non-involved student
Fostering high quality connections	The extent to which organization members deliberately create deep personal connections with others throughout the system.	• Organizational leaders personally contacted affected individuals, especially students • Work groups and colleagues held events where they shared stories as a way to support, express empathy, and show caring for one another
Strengthening a family culture	The extent to which the organizational culture is a close-knit family-type organization, inclusive of individuals across boundaries.	• Reunion-like gatherings in departments brought organizational members together • Colleagues in one department treated one couple as if they were family, taking food and protecting them from the media • Faculty members visited a student's family and helped with "family duties"
Initiating ceremonies and rituals	The extent to which rituals, ceremonies, and symbolism help members regain a sense of stability, rebuild self-concept, and re-identify with the organization.	• Ceremonies, vigils, re-dedication, and memorials, for those involved, including re-claiming the building • A staff member made and offered necklaces to others who had been in the building to remember the common bond they shared during the incident

A faculty member, alarmed by the indiscernible noises outside her fifth floor office, descended five stories before she realized that the noises were gunshots echoing the in the building's atrium. She climbed the stairs again, warned her colleagues to get into safe places, and then, exposing herself to possible gunfire again, went back down the stairs to the Ph.D. study areas so that she could direct students to secure offices. Despite possible lethal danger to herself, she acted to preserve the security and well-being of the students for whom she felt some responsibility. The virtuousness of her actions was not interpreted by her as especially noteworthy or unusual, and certainly not heroic. She interpreted them as merely a reflection of the core values that she and the organization held dear — supporting and recognizing the value of the colleagues with whom she works.

A second incident also illustrates the virtuousness of the organization's members. At the time of the shooting, a faculty member received a telephone call from an MBA student asking about the material for an upcoming class. The student remembered hearing screams in the background and, assuming that it was a department party, she proceeded to relate her request to the faculty member. During the telephone call, the faculty member put the telephone down briefly to learn from the secretaries in the office about the shooting. After taking a message from the student, he hung up and quickly moved staff members to safety as well as calling building security. It was not until much later the student realized the motivation for the screaming. To her, the faculty member demonstrated an unflinching motivation to help students regardless of the circumstances.

A third example involves a staff member who, after the incident was at home reading the newspaper accounts of the incident. She experienced an epiphany: "the building and the school belong to the students." Prior to the shooting incident, students were depleting her department's coffee supply. It had become a problem for the department, especially since the school was trying to cut unnecessary costs. But as she read the newspaper that morning and recognized that the students have nowhere to get coffee in the middle of the night, she decided to leave out the coffee pot and extra packets of coffee for the students. The deeply held values espoused by the institution were brought to the surface by the trauma. A compassionate, benevolent response was the immediate aftermath of the incident.

These examples suggest that crises have the potential to reorient organization members to the core purposes of the organization by re-centering organization members' thoughts and actions on those purposes. Whereas the fight–flight response could have predominated, self-protection was replaced by virtuousness aimed at reflecting the priority of the individual.

Fostering high quality connections

A second theme associated with the stories of organizational healing focuses on the extent to which organization members deliberately created deep personal connections with others throughout the system. Connections characterized by virtuousness enable individuals to help one another through difficulty by maintaining and forming cohesive groups and teams. The mechanism for building and reinforcing these connections during crisis is derived from the liminal state where social structure becomes less pronounced and organization members have an opportunity to strengthen and develop personal bonds with others. Connections made during this time are characterized as high quality connections (Dutton and Heaphy, 2003) which refer to momentary interactions or encounters of mutual influence and concern.

One administrator heard about a student who came face-to-face with the gunman but escaped when the gun misfired several times. The student ran from the building, and then left the scene before the police arrived. The administrator learned of this student's encounter with the gunman after the incident, and went out of his way to contact the young man personally. The administrator sought out the traumatized student, listened to his story, and apologized that he felt that no one was available to comfort him immediately after running from the building. The student reported being moved by this gesture because he had not felt supported in the aftermath. This reaction triggered an important question for the school administrator: How many more individuals had similar experiences? The administrator subsequently sought out the individual students and staff members who may have experienced similar trauma but received little help. Other individuals reported doing the same for their colleagues and friends. Instead of cloistering themselves away at home, they sought opportunities to reach out, create new connections, and listen to others' stories, thus witnessing and empathizing with their colleagues' trauma. In another instance, faculty in one department came face-to-face with the gunman. They heard the noises, looked out office windows to see police cars surrounding the building, and then, while trying to figure out how to help a faculty member in a wheelchair into an office, found that the gunman had entered the department office area. Without knowing what was behind him, but sensing danger, the wheelchair-bound faculty member sped off, just as his colleague looked up to see the gunman. She quickly closed her office door, just as he pulled the trigger. The hollow-head bullets exploded and slowed down as they hit the door. This resulted in the bullets hitting her and knocking her to the floor, but her life was preserved. The wheel-chaired faculty member was also fired upon, but the gun misfired and he "played dead" as the gunman left the area.

The department chair of these two faculty members was sitting on the tarmac waiting for his plane to depart when he received a call about the shooting. Understandably, he was distraught during his flight, and once his plane touched down, he initiated continuous contact with his wife and other colleagues as to what was happening at the school. While away for less than 48 hours, he connected, nevertheless, with each department member (faculty and staff) while his wife arranged for the entire department to come to their home upon his arrival on Sunday evening. To him, his job was to listen and to encourage people to share their stories, to offer comfort and understanding, and to promote and foster supportive relationships.

This kind of reaching out to create connections with others in the organization reflects a key element of healing — receiving social support from others, experiencing empathy and caring, and simply being heard. The administrator, the department chair and the chair's wife demonstrated that virtuousness in crisis and traumatic situations requires finding spaces for people to connect by listening and being heard, by sharing stories and recounting events, and by receiving the support necessary to deal with difficult emotions caused by the struggle. Healing can begin to take place as organization members share this liminal space through high quality interpersonal connections.

Strengthening a family culture

All organizations are characterized by identifiable cultures, but most cultural attributes in systems are hidden and rarely brought to the surface. Just as most people did not make a conscious decision this morning about which language to speak or whether or not to get dressed before going outside, most organizations also operate on a taken-for-granted set of assumptions, rituals, and values. Crises and traumas surface some deeply embedded cultural attributes. The capacity to heal, for example, is seldom noticed unless it is called forth by injury or damage.

In this organization, certain cultural traits enabled the school to heal quickly after the shooting. One interview respondent described one key attribute of this culture: "I've always thought of the school as a family. It's a very unique environment... And families don't always get along. It is in a sense a *real* family. I understand a lot of people in [other departments] would like to work here, because the atmosphere is different."

Just as families tend to gather regularly, so the aftermath of the tragedy fostered multiple gatherings and family-type get-togethers. And, notably, instead of attending these events alone, people came to meetings and gatherings in pairs and groups. They made telephone calls to colleagues inviting them to attend gatherings together, encouraged others to attend meetings, offered to provide rides, and provided meals for individuals affected by the trauma at their homes. Family members and the employees themselves were contacted, and expressions of concern were extended to loved ones affected and the employee directly involved.

As an illustration of the school's familial culture, one staff member and her husband, who had had previous interactions with the gunman, received support from co-workers while they remained out of the public eye and stayed at home the entire next week. The evening of the shooting, the wife's co-workers stayed with her until her husband came out of the building. Later a co-worker noted, "It is interesting and a very positive experience to see how caring people really are, not just the people they love in their family, but people they are working with." Colleagues sent food to their home, and many people made a point to put aside personal agendas to focus instead on *this* family who had been deeply affected by the incident.

Other examples also highlight the family-centered culture that characterized this organization. A faculty member in one department went with his wife to stay with a student's wife and children during the shooting. They helped the student's wife prepare her children for bed, clean up the house, and order pizza so she could watch the news and communicate periodically with her husband trapped in the building. Faculty members in another department independently contacted a staff member's family to make sure she was effectively adapting and adjusting after the incident. Several academic and administrative units gathered all their departments together for opportunities to share stories and food together. These gatherings reflect the important family culture that had been latent within the organization.

Many attribute the family-orientated culture to several former organizational leaders who made efforts to create unity among departments and to incorporate employees' family members in organizational functions. The response to the shooting incident brought this culture to the surface. As one individual noted, "the school is known for conversation, dialogue, and deliberations, more than you see in other [places]." Its emphasis on the values of collaboration, humanistic philosophy, and emotional competence as clearly demonstrated as individuals reached out to others, including families, in the aftermath of this event. This culture of human concern and the inherent virtuousness of the school helped aid healing after the shooting.

The incident reinforced the "family feeling" in the organization's culture, so that individuals in and around the scene were able to share an experience that reinforced organization members' common bonds with one another. These bonds were not created in the moment, but they uplifted people because of the moment. Many people spoke of the virtuous inclinations of their colleagues, and as one person said, "I think the event demonstrated a lot more caring than ever before. The incident brought something to the surface that I think was there but not apparent." The incident gave rise, in other words, to something that was already inherent — some called it "unspoken unity" — which was reinforced and solidified. The events surrounding the incident did not create the culture, but they revealed the already established virtuous patterns of interaction, caring, and concern.

Initiating ceremonies and rituals

Ritual and ceremonial acts characterize the fourth theme related to organizational healing. Ritual practices function to celebrate moments in human life and death, often carrying with them sensitivity for others' positive and negative emotions (Turner, 1967). In addition, organization members experience rituals together to celebrate their relationships or to mourn the loss of family or friends thus helping to re-establish a sense of peace, stability, and order for organization members. When organization members come together in this way, they acknowledge the pain and suffering, or joy and happiness of life.

This theme is connected to the previous three themes in the sense that ceremonies and rituals allow individuals to share stories of purpose and rebuild self-concept, re-connect with others and re-identify with the organization, and demonstrate and reinforce inherent cultural attributes. Not only do rituals help the organization members heal from the trauma, but also the interactions and conversations during ritual gatherings surface the virtuousness of organization members, establish common bonds, and enable the organization to re-establish wholeness. In essence, rituals and ceremonies following traumatic events serve as a holding space for organization members to grieve, to regroup, and to re-orient themselves to the organization.

The rituals and ceremonies in the aftermath of the shooting incident illustrate these functions of rituals. At the beginning of the week following the shooting, departments held gatherings where employees told their personal stories — whether they were on-campus at the time or not — physically held each other, and listened carefully and respectfully to one other. People reported that it felt good to be together and to connect physically and psychologically with others. These planned support group gatherings were coupled with formal departmental meetings, each of which served as a kind of healing ceremony. The large number of opportunities provided by these gatherings also enabled the organization to return to a sense of order and wholeness in the aftermath of the incident.

Formal ritual gatherings served not only to bring people together to connect with each other but to re-orient organization members to fundamental organizational purposes. For example, one week after the incident, members of the school community met and ceremoniously reclaimed the building. At this gathering, school leaders reminded organization members of the school's strategic mission, core values, and identity saying that the event should not prevent the organization from moving forward in positive ways. The new building still symbolized a positive future, and it could now be seen even more as an icon of healing and a healthy system. The university leadership presided at these meetings encouraging people to focus on the organization's virtues and strengths.

The building had been closed for the week as a crime scene, and it required extensive clean up and repairs. For some, this event was the first time they had met since the shooting. Prior to a ceremonial procession into the building was an ecumenical service where several schools leaders made short speeches about the school. This speech was oriented toward bringing people together psychologically and emotionally and reminding them of the organization's values, mission and purpose. The message was one of comfort but also of moving forward together. After the brief ceremony, organization members walked across the street together and re-entered their building.

A retired professor, unable to attend the ceremony, had purchased and sent 200 roses which individuals handed to construction workers — lined up on the sidewalk — who had worked throughout the week painting, plastering, and replacing glass.

Another poignant example of ritual and ceremony relates to the staff member who, because of her deep connection with others in the building during the incident, decided to have medallion necklaces made for those who had endured the hostage crisis in the building. She secured a small external grant from a non-profit organization and had enough medallions made for each person who witnessed the event; when they were ready, she hand-delivered them to each person who had been in the building during the shooting. One recipient said, "We got a necklace with the word 'Unity' and the date [of the shooting]. Actually my first reaction was, 'I want to forget that day, why must we remember that day.' But [now] I like that idea." A professor who received a medallion remarked how the necklace strengthened his relationships with those he was with in the building. "It was just a tight connection; we have a bond very strong... And she wanted to give each person that — and it's like you became brothers and sisters with each other." The presentation of the medallion necklace was another ceremonial act meant to solidify connections among organization members.

This theme reinforces the importance of planned ceremonies and rituals that foster organizational healing. In each case, the intent of the initiated activities was to foster healing at the organizational level, and many events represented voluntary acts of virtuousness. That is, compassionate responses, extra-mile efforts in behalf of others, and connections to spiritual and emotional themes represent spontaneous and premeditated virtuous acts. The fact that these rituals and ceremonies were tied to virtuousness made them especially effective enablers of healing.

Conclusion

This paper has outlined four primary themes associated with organizational healing. These themes illustrate the key enablers of the healing process in an organization that experienced major trauma. The four themes include *reinforcing the priority of the individual, fostering high quality connections, strengthening a family culture, and initiating ceremonies and rituals.* These themes emerged from the stories and recollections of individuals actually involved in the traumatic events of a break-in, murder, and seven-hour gun battle in a new business school building. In this description we have illustrated that healing can be a collective level phenomenon as well as an individual phenomenon. The organization itself can re-establish a sense of identify, strengthen values, and restore relationships that were ruptured by a harmful event.

The actions taken at the collective level, the messages delivered by organizational representatives, and the planned communal activities all supplemented individual actions that facilitated organization healing. Most importantly, deeply embedded in organizational healing are lived virtues and values such as caring, concern, compassion, and social support for organization members. It is clear that the virtuousness of these individual and collective efforts was most effective in producing the desired healing. That is, each theme was exemplified by examples of virtuous actions — courage, kindness, love, and faith — and healing was made possible by such expressions.

During liminal periods, which often occur during and after crisis and trauma, typical interactions, practices, and relationships are nearly canceled out by the occurrence of a trauma. New connections and opportunities for relating emerge, and alternative approaches to seeing and experiencing relationships within the organization shift. During this temporary suspension of the organization's social structure detecting demonstrations of virtuousness comes easily (Powley, 2005).

The four themes we have discussed in this paper suggest that organizational healing occurs through virtuousness. Organization members enacted the stated importance of the individual as the highest and most important priority for the organization when they focused their attention and concern on those who were in harm's way or in need of additional social and material support. The degree to which individuals developed high quality connections with colleagues, known and unknown to them, also fostered organizational healing. These momentary encounters or connections enabled organization members to reinforce and rebuild social connections. Reinforcing and building on the family culture also contributed to organizational healing. Cultural traits similar to those found in close-knit families made it common for groups and departments to support each other by providing rides, meals, or times to listen to one another. Finally, rituals and ceremonies brought organization members together to re-orient them to organizational purposes and goals, re-establish continuity of time, encourage relationships and attachments, and helping them stay focused on the future and what was important personally and for the organization.

Organizations faced with trauma have two choices: threat-rigidity (Staw *et al.*, 1981) — in which people display self-protective responses, blame others, become critical and cynical, refuse to share information, and lose confidence in leaders — or they can respond virtuously (Cameron, 2003) — with compassion, caring, mutual support, courage, and faith. The four themes addressed here indicate that within the culture and capacity of this organization resided the competence and inclination to heal by adopting the latter strategy. That is, compassion and service towards colleagues, coupled with continuous references to spiritual and emotional images, demonstrated virtuousness embedded within the organization. In all of the themes, virtuous responses were the key mechanisms that led to organizational healing as opposed to deterioration during and in the immediate aftermath of crisis.

In addition to their core operational concerns, organizations are centers of human relating and social relationships. Within those relationships reside the potential for virtuousness. When organizations face crisis — whether natural, technological, or human-induced — the virtue in those social relations and connections is what holds organizations together. As tragedies continue to increase throughout the world — portrayed as images of anger, disorganization, social distrust, chaos, or community breakdown — they are often portrayed as a society seemingly devoid of virtue. Yet, hidden beneath those images are stories of human strengths and virtues that represent narratives of hope for the world. The stories of the shooting incident in this paper are one witness to the lived virtuousness amidst organizational crisis.

References

Ambrose, D (1996). *Healing the Downsized Organization: What Every Employee Needs to Know about Today's New Workplace.* New York, NY: Harmony Books.

Ayalon, O (1998). Community healing for children traumatized by war. *International Review of Psychiatry,* 10, 224–233.

Beyer, JM and HM Trice (1987). How an organization's rites reveal its culture. *Organizational Dynamics,* 15(4), 5–24.

Boje, DM (2001). *Narrative Methods for Organizational and Communication Research,* London, UK: Sage.

Cameron, KS (1998). Strategic organizational downsizing: an extreme case. *Research in Organizational Behavior,* 20, 185–229.

Cameron, KS (2003). Virtuousness and performance. In *Positive Organizational Scholarship: Foundations of a New Discipline,* KS Cameron, JE Dutton, and RE Quinn (eds.), pp. 48–65, Berrett-Koehler, San Francisco, CA.

Cameron, KS, JE Dutton and RE Quinn (eds.) (2003). *Positive Organizational Scholarship: Foundations of a New Discipline.* San Francisco, CA: Berrett-Koehler.

Cooperrider, DL and S Srivastva (1987). Appreciative inquiry in organizational life. In *Research in Organizational Change and Development,* WA Pasmore and RW Woodman (eds.), Vol. 1, pp. 129–169, Greenwich, CT: JAI Press.

Cyert, RM and JG March (1963). *A Behavioral Theory of the Firm.* Englewood Cliffs, NJ: Prentice-Hall.

Dutton, JE and ED Heaphy (2003). The power of high-quality connections. In *Positive Organizational Scholarship: Foundations of a New Discipline,* KS Cameron, JE Dutton and RE Quinn (eds.), pp. 263–278, San Francisco, CA: Berrett-Koehler.

Dutton, JE, PJ Frost, J Kanov, J Lilius, SM Maitlis, and MC Worline (2005). *Helping Your Workplace Heal.* Leading in Trying Times website, Ann Arbor, MI: University of Michigan http://www.bus.umich.edu/FacultyResearch/Research/TryingTimes/Heal.htm [Accessed September 7, 2005].

Fredriksson, L and K Eriksson (2001). The patient's narrative of suffering: a path to health? An interpretative research synthesis on narrative understanding. *Scandinavian Journal of Caring Sciences,* 15(1), 3–11.

Frost, PJ (2003). *Toxic Emotions at Work: How Compassionate Managers Handle Pain and Conflict.* Boston, MA: Harvard Business School Press.

Gordon, R and R Wraith (1993). Responses of children and adolescents to disaster. In *International Handbook of Traumatic Stress Syndromes,* Wilson, P, and B Raphael (eds.), pp. 561–575, New York, NY: Plenum.

Herman, J (1997). *Trauma and Recovery: The Aftermath of Violence — From Domestic Abuse to Political Terror.* New York, NY: Basic Books.

Jareg, E (1995). *Main Guiding Principles for the Development of Psychosocial Interventions for Children Affected by War.* Stockholm, Sweden: ISCA Workshop.

Levinthal, DA (1991). Organizational adaptation and environmental selection — interrelated processes of change. *Organization Science,* 2(1), 140–145.

Ludema, JD (1996). *Narrative Inquiry: Collective Storytelling as a Source of Hope, Knowledge, and Action in Organizational Life,* Unpublished doctoral dissertation, Cleveland, OH: Case Western Reserve University.

Lumsden, M (1997). Breaking the cycle of violence: Are 'communal therapies' a means of healing shattered selves. *Journal of Peace Research,* 34(4), 377–383.

Maddi, SR and DM Khoshaba (2005). *Resilience at Work.* New York, NY: American Management Association.

Nye, EF (1997). Writing as healing. *Qualitative Inquiry,* 3(4), 439.

Pennebaker, JW and KD Harber (1993). A social stage model of collective coping: The Loma Prieta earthquake and the Persian Gulf War. *Journal of Social Issues,* 49(4), 125–145.

Powley, EH (2004). Underlying ritual practices of the appreciative inquiry summit: toward a theory of sustained appreciative change. In *Constructive Discourse and Human Organization: Advances in Appreciative Inquiry* DL Cooperrider and M Avital (eds.), Vol. 1, pp. 241–261, Amsterdam, The Netherlands: JAI Press.

Powley, EH (2005). *Connective Capacity in Organizational Crisis: Mechanisms of Organizational Resilience.* Unpublished doctoral dissertation, Cleveland, OH: Case Western Reserve University.

Powley, EH, RE Fry FJ Barrett, and DS Bright (2004). Dialogic democracy meets command and control: Transformation through the appreciative inquiry summit. *Academy of Management Executive,* 18(3), 67–80.

Riessman, CK (1993). *Narrative Analysis.* Vol. 30, Newbury Park, CA: Sage.

Srivastva, S and DL Cooperrider (1986). The emergence of the egalitarian organization. *Human Relations,* 39(8), 683–724.

Staw, BM, LE Sandelands, and JE Dutton (1981). Threat-rigidity effects in organizational behavior: a multilevel analysis. *Administrative Science Quarterly,* 26(4), 501–524.

Sutcliffe, KM and TJ Vogus (2003). Organizing for resilience. In *Positive Organizational Scholarship: Foundations of a New Discipline,* KS Cameron, JE Dutton and RE Quinn (eds.), pp. 94–110, San Francisco, CA: Berrett-Koehler.

Swatton, S and J O'Callaghan (1999). The experience of 'healing stories' in the life narrative: a grounded theory. *Counseling Psychology Quarterly,* 12(4), 413–429.

Terr, L (1991). Childhood traumas. *American Journal of Psychiatry,* 148, 10–20.

Trice, HM and JM Beyer (1984). Studying organizational cultures through rites and ceremonials. *Academy of Management,* 9(4), 633–669.

Turner, VW (1967). *The Forest of Symbols: Aspects of Ndembu Ritual.* Ithaca, NY: Cornell University Press.

Van Maanen, J (1988). *Tales of the Field: On Writing Ethnography.* Chicago, IL: University of Chicago Press.

Winnicot, DW (1971). *Playing and Reality.* London, UK: Tavistock.

Chapter Two

MAKING SENSE OF ORGANIZATIONAL ACTIONS WITH VIRTUE FRAMES AND ITS LINKS TO ORGANIZATIONAL ATTACHMENT

Seung-Yoon Rhee

Korea Advanced Institute of Science and Technology

Jane E. Dutton

Richard P. Bagozzi

University of Michigan

This chapter analyzes how members make sense of organizational actions after a crisis. All individuals have developed "virtue frames," or categories of interpretation that determine the extent to which actions are judged to be morally good and right. This chapter examines the effects of these virtue frames on members' identification with and attachment to their own organization as a result of that organization's responses to the events of September 11th. The authors explore the use of three virtue frames — humanity, justice, and courage — to identify the effects of interpreted virtuousness on identification and attachment. These effects are mediated through members' emotions, self-construals, and overall images of the organization.

Making sense of what an organization represents or cares about is never an easy task. Organizations are complex with rich histories and diverse activities that challenge members' capacity to make meaning out of what the organization does and why it matters. One way members infer what an organization stands for is by parsing and interpreting organizational actions in response to specific events (Weick, 1995). Despite an interest in sensemaking, researchers know little about *how* the interpretation of organizational actions shapes members' cognitive and emotional connection to the organization. This is our research focus.

September 11th, 2001, is a day etched in human history. A cluster of world events took place on that day, involving the crashes of U.S. commercial airplanes hijacked by a group of terrorists and flown into the World Trade Center, U.S. Pentagon, and a rural field in Pennsylvania. The scale and scope of this day's events called for actions of humanity, justice and courage on the part of members as well as organizations as means for healing physical and psychological wounds. What organizations did in this situation may have transformed the meaning of an organization for its members, affecting their affective and cognitive connection. This chapter empirically explores this possibility.

Our research focused on sensemaking in a U.S. university context. More specifically, we investigated how members' interpretations of organizational actions in terms of virtuousness contributed to members' identification with and attachment to the organization. Our research assumes that social actors are actively involved in the sensemaking process by constructing and using frames to parse and interpret extracted cues (Weick, 1995). In particular we explored the relative impact of the virtuousness of organizational action on members' emotions, self-conceptions and images of the organization. Thus, our study is designed to explore the mechanisms through which applications of virtue frames as sensemaking lenses affect members' relationships to their organization.

Virtue Frames

We assume that members interpret organizational actions based partly on their interpretation of the kind and degree of virtuousness of actions. We call the interpretive lens a virtue frame. A frame is "a generalized point of view that directs interpretations" (Cantril, 1941, p. 20 as cited in Weick, 1995, p. 4), which renders "what would otherwise be a meaningless aspect of the scene into something that is meaningful" (Goffman, 1974, p. 21). A virtue frame captures people's attributed meanings of virtuousness applied to a particular cluster of acts or dispositional features of members or collectivities like organizations.

Virtue frames are meaningful sensemaking devices because people are socialized to detect and understand different forms of virtuous behavior (e.g., Stilwell *et al.*, 1998). Young children learn to make sense of other people's behavior in interaction with parents, peers and teachers and they acquire a sense of whether a behavior is good or bad. As people grow, they internalize virtue principles through direct experience (e.g., Kochanska, 1995). A virtue frame is a shorthand way of capturing and communicating the level and type of virtuousness ascribed to a particular action or behavior. Virtue frames are particularly important in organizations as they are means that people use to convey their understanding that some thing (a person, an action, a unit) has a quality of moral goodness. Different virtue frames convey different forms of moral goodness — i.e., that action is courageous; that organization is wise; that person is compassionate. It is likely that virtue frames are particularly impactful when they are used to refer to actions that are ambiguous and the meaning of the actions is subject to differing interpretations.

We define "virtuous organizational action" as the perceived exercise of collective behavior that indicates the organization is following principles that lead to some form of moral or ethical betterment. At the level of individuals, virtues involve admirable qualities of one's character and conformity of one's conduct to moral and ethical principles of right (Park and Peterson, 2003), which makes oneself and society morally better and promotes well-being and the good life (Sandage and Hill, 2001). Cameron and colleagues (Cameron, 2003; Cameron *et al.*, 2004) note the rarity of consideration of organizational virtuousness, and argue that organizations vary in the virtuousness of their actions, and that these organizational qualities make a difference for financial performance. We complement their perspective by focusing on the micro-process of how members discern action virtuousness, and how this affects their relationship with the organization.

Virtue Frames and Organizational Identification and Attachment

We assume that members interpret organizational actions using virtue frames, and that the meaning members apply to organizational actions has implications for cognitive and emotional connections to the organization, through both identification and attachment. There is evidence to suggest that members' identification with and attachment to their organization partly result from perceived virtuousness of organizational actions. First, Solomon (1993) suggests that acts of caring and compassion provide a sense of belongingness for members. For example, members increased affective commitment when they perceived organizational practices to be motivated by management's genuine concern for their safety (Barling and Hutchinson, 2000). Similarly, when an organization implemented an employee support program that allowed employees to donate money to colleagues in need, employees saw the organization and themselves as more caring, resulting in higher levels of affective commitment (Grant *et al.*, 2008). Second, members who perceived organizational practices (e.g., performance evaluation) as manifesting the virtue of justice were more likely to show organizational commitment (e.g., Cropanzano *et al.*, 2001). Third, witnessing a courageous incident transformed members' involvement in the organization's mission and goals (Worline *et al.*, 2002).

The Research Context

The events of 9-11 produced an opportunity to study how members make sense of organizational actions, and how members' use of virtue frames as sensemaking lenses affects their relationship with the organization. First, organizational members exert more sensemaking efforts to understand organizational actions when uncertainty and change are present (Weick, 1995). The events of 9-11 were uncertain due to a lack of information, and disrupted "normal" life patterns, putting people into a more active, mindful state of trying to make sense of the organization, what it was doing, and what it meant.

Second, we employed three virtue frames that had particular applicability to making sense of the events of 9-11: humanity, justice, and courage (e.g., Peterson and Seligman, 2004). An organizational action is humane when it involves helping and caring oriented toward organizational members or a larger society, through which they feel the worth of their existence (e.g., Post and McCullough, 2004). A justice frame implies just treatment of members with dignity and respect, based on moral and ethical reasoning (e.g., Berkowitz and Sherblom, 2004). Our definition concerns prosocial conceptions of justice such as "justice as respect for persons" (Roberts-Cady, 2003, p. 299) rather than retributive justice conceptions that entail an eye-for-an-eye approach (e.g. Karremans and Van Lange, 2005). Finally, a courageous organizational action is one voluntarily taken by the organization in pursuit of "what is right" regardless of risks it faces (e.g., Worline et al., 2002). We selected these three virtue frames because they are salient in philosophical and psychological research and everyday experience (Peterson and Seligman, 2004), and are particularly appropriate to sensemaking of the events of 9-11. In the media and in everyday encounters, people expressed concern about hate crimes (justice), heralded kindness of volunteer workers, need for support and compassion for each other (humanity), the acts of public servants, and the actions taken by institutions such as canceling of classes by universities that might have been under criticism when occurred in ordinary situations (courage). These three virtue frames were part of the currency through which society seemed to make sense of the events and actions of 9-11.

Hypotheses

We predict that the perceived virtuousness of organizational actions as humane, just, and courageous will lead to three member responses (i.e., greater positive emotions, virtuous self-construals, and virtuous images of the organization) that, in turn, increase organizational identification and attachment. We turn now to a development of specific hypotheses.

Member responses to virtuous organizational actions

Positive emotions: positive emotions arise when an event is appraised to have positive meaning or to be related to realization of one's or others' goals and well-being (Ortony *et al.*, 1988). Organizational actions perceived as virtuous may have communicated messages that the organization was concerned about members' well-being and was committed to comforting and supporting members. It is likely that members' interpretations of organizational actions as virtuous triggered appraisals filled with positive meaning that elicited positive emotions. Hence, we hypothesize that interpreted virtuousness of organizational actions will increase members' positive emotions.

Hypothesis 1. Perceived virtuousness of organizational actions in response to tragedy increases members' positive emotions.

Virtuous self-construals: interpretations of organizational actions as virtuous influence members' self-construals. Self-construals are qualities that members apply to themselves (Baumeister, 1999), which are malleable and fluid rather than stable (Zurcher, 1977). Cialdini *et al.* (1976) found that individuals tended to publicize their affiliation with a group especially when the group was successful, thus enhancing their personal image. Attractive organizational characteristics are more easily incorporated into members' self-construals. Thus, we expect virtuous characteristics of an organization will be adopted by members, contributing to the virtuousness of their self-construals.

Hypothesis 2. Perceived virtuousness of organizational actions in response to tragedy increases the virtuousness of members' self-construals.

Virtuous images of the organization: when members see their organization as acting virtuously, they are likely to infer that the organization is virtuous as well. In Dutton and Dukerich's (1991) study of the Port

Authority, organizational members relied on the organization's treatment of homeless people to infer features of the enduring organizational identity. Organizations that act ethically in the wake of scandals or product recalls are often seen as being ethical at their core (e.g., Johnson & Johnson in Arguilar and Bhambri, 1983). Thus, we hypothesize that interpreted virtuousness of organizational actions will enhance virtuous images of the organization.

Hypothesis 3. Perceived virtuousness of organizational actions in response to tragedy increases the level of virtuousness of organizational images.

Members' cognitive and emotional connection to the organization: Organizational identification and attachment

We define organizational identification as members' cognitive self-awareness of organizational membership (Bergami and Bagozzi, 2000), that is what they think of themselves in terms of their organizational membership. By organizational attachment we refer to members' emotional involvement in or affective commitment to the organization (e.g., Allen and Meyer, 1990). We propose that members' connection to the organization involves both cognitive and emotional aspects, captured by organizational identification and attachment.

Positive emotions: past research shows that individuals are drawn to sources of positive emotions. Individuals tend to associate themselves with successful persons or groups that generate positive emotions (e.g., Cialdini *et al.*, 1976). Research suggests that members who feel positive emotions induced by virtuous organizational actions are drawn to see themselves as connected to the organizational source of these positive emotions, strengthening levels of identification.

Hypothesis 4. Positive emotions of organizational members derived from the perceptions of virtuousness of organizational actions increase members' level of identification with the organization.

Virtuous self-construals: research on organizational identification suggests that members who perceive similarity between their self and organizational attributes identify with the organization (Dutton *et al.*, 1994). Moreover, members can establish an even stronger positive self-image by identifying with an organization that possesses attractive and valuable attributes (i.e., virtuousness) (Tajfel, 1982). Thus, if members see themselves as virtuous they will more strongly identify with an organization that takes actions perceived as virtuous.

Hypothesis 5. Virtuous self-construals of organizational members derived from the perceptions of virtuousness of organizational actions increase members' level of identification with the organization.

Virtuous images of the organization: past research shows that individuals like to be members of organizations with positive identities. Research on job search processes indicates that applicants are more likely to continue the application process with organizations with positive images (e.g., Richey *et al.*, 2001). Members' interpretations of an organizational image as caring and respectful increased their commitment to the organization (e.g., Barling and Hutchinson, 2000; Grant *et al.*, 2008). Thus, virtuous images of organizations are likely to strengthen members' identification with the organization.

Hypothesis 6. Virtuous images of the organization derived from the perceptions of virtuousness of organizational actions increase members' level of identification with the organization.

Organizational identification and attachment: we propose that organizational identification precedes attachment to the organization. Bergami and Bagozzi (2000) found that affective commitment was a motivational force that directly affected members' positive behaviors on behalf of the organization, whereas organizational identification indirectly affected those behaviors through affective commitment. Their finding suggests that early organizational membership is cognitive.

Hypothesis 7. Members' identification with the organization increases their attachment to the organization.

These general hypotheses test the effects of interpreted virtuousness of organizational actions on organizational identification and attachment, and how member responses (i.e., positive emotions, virtuous self-construals, and virtuous images of the organization) mediate these effects. Our empirical investigation tests specific instances of these general hypotheses.

Methods

Participants and procedure

We administered a survey in early December, 2001. We recruited 196 students enrolled in a Midwestern University through newspaper advertisements and fliers. The sample was 59% female with a mean age of 20 years. Participants' enrollment time with the university ranged from 3 months to 6 years and 4 months with an average time of two years.

The questionnaire asked participants to think of three meaningful actions taken by the university (as a whole) in response to the events of 9-11. The data are based on the participants' retrospective thoughts of the events and their emotions, self-construals, and organizational images formed when they thought of a specific meaningful action they mentioned earlier in the questionnaire. Finally, the questionnaire measured organizational identification and attachment. More than half the participants mentioned two specific meaningful actions: Candlelight vigil the university held (63% of the sample) and the university's canceling of classes on 9-11 (58% of the sample). Because the participants' responses were action-specific, we tested the hypotheses for each action separately.

Measures

Virtuousness of organizational actions: we used three items to measure the degree of virtuousness for each action: 'Is this action humane (just, courageous)?' A 7-point scale was used: 1 = 'not at all', 7 = 'completely'.

Positive emotions: we used eight items, six from positive emotion categories (joyous, happy, excited, content, proud, hopeful) by Shaver *et al.* (1987), one from Izard (1977) (interested), and one from Haidt (2000) (elevated). These emotions are highly likely to occur when people observe or experience virtuous actions. We employed 5-point response alternatives: 1 = 'very slightly or not at all', 5 = 'extremely'.

Virtuous self-construals: from Anderson's (1968) 555 personality-trait words we selected nine words based on their relevance to individual virtuousness. Participants rated themselves on a 5-point scale anchored by two words that have opposite meaning to each other: selfish–unselfish, cold-hearted–warm-hearted, dishonest–honest, immoral–moral, unforgiving–forgiving, unethical–ethical, cowardly–courageous, tightfisted–generous, unfeeling–sympathetic.

Virtuous images of the organization: we used a count of virtue words mentioned in response to an open-ended question: 'When you think of the meaningful action taken by the university, what characteristics do you associate with the university?' Because most responses were four or fewer words, we used a 4-point scale: 0 = 'no virtue related words', 3 = 'more than three virtue related words'. Samples of virtue related words are: humanity (caring, concerned, nurturing), justice (fair, justness, equal), and courage (courageous, perseverance).

Organizational identification: we used a scale developed by Bergami and Bagozzi (2000). It includes two items, a visual measure that assesses the felt degree of overlap between one's own identity and the organization's identity, and a verbal report of organizational identification stating: 'Please indicate to what degree your self-image overlaps with the university's image.' The responses were anchored by 8 graduations of overlap and by 1 (not at all) and 7 (completely), respectively.

Organizational attachment: we used the 7-item scale developed by Allen and Meyer (1990). We used five response alternatives in a dis-agree–agree format with 1 indicating 'strongly disagree' and 5 'strongly agree'. Alphas were 0.85 for the candlelight vigil case and 0.90 for the canceling of classes case.

Analysis

We used structural equations modeling (SEM) with AMOS 4.0 and confirmatory factor analysis with SPSS 10.0 to analyze the structural model. Factor loadings and correlation coefficients of positive emotions and virtuous self-construals measurement items indicated that they were composed of two constructs. Positive emotions items included two constructs: (1) present happiness positive emotions (i.e., joyous, excited, content, happy) capturing good feelings about something current and (2) forward-looking positive emotions (i.e., proud, hopeful) capturing emotions that involve expecting a future good to happen (e.g., Shaver *et al.*, 1987). Virtuous self-construals contained two constructs: (1) moral self-construals (i.e., ethical, moral, honest) and (2) sympathetic self-construals (i.e., warm-hearted, sympathetic, generous).

Results

University's action of holding a candlelight vigil

The hypotheses received mixed support (see Fig. 1a).[1] Members who interpreted the university's action as humane and courageous experienced both (1) present happiness ($\beta = 0.21$, $p \leq 0.05$; $\beta = 0.31$, $p \leq 0.01$) and (2) forward-looking positive emotions ($\beta = 0.22$, $p \leq 0.05$; $\beta = 0.26$, $p \leq 0.05$). However, when members interpreted the university's action as just, they experienced less present happiness ($\beta = -0.21$, $p \leq 0.05$). Thus, Hypothesis 1 was partially supported.

---

[1] The model for the university's action of holding a candlelight vigil showed a good fit (RMSEA = 0.04, RMR = 0.06, NNFI = 0.97, CFI = 0.99, $\chi^2(49) = 56.77$, $p \leq 0.21$).

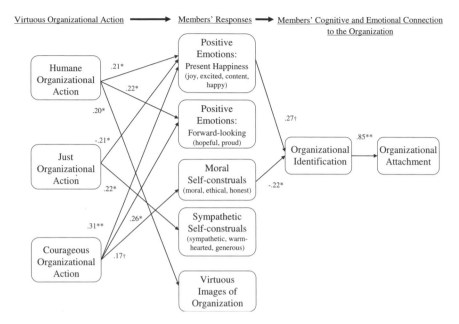

Fig. 1a: Structural equations modeling results: candlelight vigil.
Only statistically significant paths are shown:
† $p < 0.10$; * $p < 0.05$; ** $p < 0.01$

Hypothesis 2 was also partially supported. When members interpreted the university's action as courageous, they evaluated themselves as moral persons, with marginal significance ($\beta = 0.17$, $p \leq$
0.10), and sympathetic persons when they interpreted the university's
action as just ($\beta = 0.22$, $p \leq 0.05$). Members' interpretations of the
university's action as humane contributed to virtuous images of the
university ($\beta = 0.20$, $p \leq 0.05$). Thus, Hypothesis 3 was partially supported. Overall, the proposed general relationship was modestly supported that interpretations of the university's action as virtuous led to
members' positive emotions, virtuous self-construals, and virtuous
images of the university.

Hypothesis 4 was also partially supported. Members' positive
emotions of present happiness but not forward-looking positive emotions (i.e., $\beta = 0.01$, n.s.), were positively related to their identification
with the university with marginal significance ($\beta = 0.27$, $p \leq 0.10$).

Contrary to our hypothesis, members with a moral self were associated with reduced identification with the university ($\beta = -0.22$, $p \le 0.05$), thus rejecting Hypothesis 5. Virtuous images of the university were not significantly related to members' organizational identification (i.e., $\beta = -0.02$, n.s.), rejecting Hypothesis 6. Thus, only the relation between members' positive emotions and their cognitive and emotional connection to the organization was positive and marginally significant. Finally, Hypothesis 7 was supported in that members' identification with the university was associated with greater attachment to the university ($\beta = 0.85$, $p \le 0.01$).

University's action of canceling of classes

The hypotheses received mixed support (see Fig. 1b).[2] Interpretation of the university's action as humane was related to forward-looking positive emotions with marginal significance ($\beta = 0.19$, $p \le 0.10$). Members who interpreted the university's action as courageous felt positive emotions of both present happiness ($\beta = 0.21$, $p \le 0.10$) and forward-looking ($\beta = 0.35$, $p \le 0.01$). Thus, Hypothesis 1 was partially supported. Hypotheses 2 and 3 were also partially supported. Members' interpretations of the university's action as humane were related to thinking of themselves as sympathetic ($\beta = 0.30$, $p \le 0.01$) and to virtuous images of the university with marginal significance ($\beta = 0.18$, $p \le 0.10$). Overall, the results are not strong, but provide some support to the general proposition that members' interpretations of university actions as virtuous influence members' responses.

Hypothesis 4 was also partially supported. Members' forward-looking positive emotions were positively related to their organizational identification ($\beta = 0.24$, $p \le 0.10$). Hypothesis 5 was not supported. Contrary to our hypothesis, moral self-construals of members reduced their level of identification with the university but

---

[2] Although the chi-square for the structural model was significant ($\chi^2(49) = 76.56$, $p \le 0.01$), the other fit indexes in general indicated that the model fits the data well (RMSEA = 0.07, RMR = 0.06, NNFI = 0.91, CFI = 0.95). In addition, tests of non-hypothesized paths were found to be non-significant.

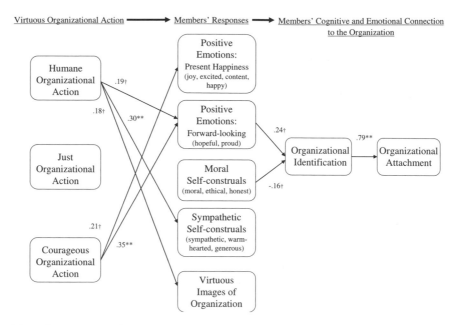

Fig. 1b: Structural equations modeling results: canceling of classes. Only statistically significant paths are shown:

$^†\, p < 0.10$; $^*\, p < 0.05$; $^{**}\, p < 0.01$

with marginal significance ($\beta = -0.16$, $p \leq 0.10$). The path coefficient from virtuous images of the university to organizational identification was not significantly different from zero (i.e., $\beta = -0.04$, n.s.). Thus, Hypothesis 6 was not supported. Overall, members' positive emotions were the only aspect of members' responses that was positively related to their cognitive and emotional connection to the organization with marginal significance. Hypothesis 7 was supported. When members cognitively identified with the university, their level of attachment to the university increased ($\beta = 0.79$, $p \leq 0.01$).

Discussion

Our research provides initial support for the general proposition that virtuousness of organizational actions influences members' responses, which lead to organizational identification and attachment. We found that members can use virtue frames in interpreting organizational actions, and that these interpretations affected members' emotions, the way they interpreted themselves and their images of the organization. In both holding a candlelight vigil and canceling of classes cases, members' positive emotions and virtuous self-construals mediated the effects of interpreted virtuousness of organizational actions on members' organizational identification.

There were two paths in the structural model that showed signs opposite to our hypotheses. First, the more members thought of themselves to be moral, ethical and honest, the less they defined themselves in terms of their membership in the organization. Three reasons may explain this finding. First, to define oneself as moral assumes independence, involving a sense of duty to follow moral law (Statman, 1997). People who see themselves this way may be relatively independent from social organizations. Second, individuals tend to view themselves as more ethical than others, including the organizations they belong to (Reynolds, 2003). Thus, members with strong moral self-construals may perceive less overlap between their self-images and the images of the organization. Finally, seeing oneself as moral might be associated with a more conservative political ideology and values. Given a large public university research site with a reputation of liberalism, this may have diminished the desire of members who see themselves as moral so as to identify with the organization. Future research will need to explore this possible explanation.

Second, the more members interpreted the university's holding a candlelight vigil to be just, the less they felt joyous, excited, content or happy. Judgments on justice usually accompany a comparison with injustice (Solomon, 1993). When members used a virtue frame of justness to interpret the organization's action, they may have been tuned into both justice and injustice. In our case, the candlelight vigil was a gathering of the whole university community with different religions and value perspectives all represented, and a few speakers even made remarks about anti-hate crime issues. At that moment, positive emotions of happiness may have diminished, replaced by a more complex set of emotional reactions to these implications of the action, including negative feelings. Alternatively, because justice is a virtue that is supposed to hold on the basis of reason and not be subject to emotional concerns, it may be that the more people hold to or judge something to be just, the less they wish to associate emotion with it.

Virtuous images of the organization did not mediate the effects of interpreted virtuousness of organizational actions on members' organizational identification. We surmise that many people could not easily or spontaneously generate instances of virtuousness when asked to give "organizational characteristics" in an open-ended format.

General Discussion

The results suggest that members engage in parsing and interpreting organizational actions in terms of how virtuous they are, which in turn relates to members' connection to the organization through their feelings and thoughts of themselves and of the organization. Our research has implications for understanding sensemaking in organizations, especially the promise of virtue as a sensemaking frame, and for research on organizational identification and attachment.

First, our study improves understanding of how organizational members make sense of organizational actions in times of trauma or stress. Members may be most attentive to organizational actions when there have been major interruptions in "normal" life patterns (Weick, 1995) such as when unexpected events of tragic proportions impact a wide universe of institutions and individuals. Our findings affirm that organizations publicly convey actions in times of trauma and these actions acquire different meanings for members in the light of how virtuous they are.

Second, our research builds on the literature on organizational virtue by introducing virtue frames as sensemaking lenses. Understanding an organization in terms of its general virtuousness has not been given much attention in organizational research. This gap exists despite the recent debate about the moral and ethical foundation of business practices. While public awareness and attention seem to be on the absence of virtuous conduct by certain organizations, we believe that people inside and outside also attend to the positive end of the virtue spectrum. People learn and internalize virtue principles from early childhood and use virtue frames throughout their lifetime in detecting and understanding virtuous behaviors in daily encounters. Virtue frames may become more salient in times of tragedy as the situation calls for virtuous actions that reveal the goodness of the society and humankind.

Third, our research contributes to work on the meanings of organizational membership. Our research addresses how positive meanings about organizational actions contribute to members' cognitive and emotional connection to the organization. While there is growing interest in how the positive meaning of work affects organizational members (e.g., Wrzesniewski, 2003) we see real promise in extending this interest to the consequences of positive meaning-making about organizational actions. By unpacking the black box between meanings of virtuous actions and organizational identification and attachment, we understand how virtuous behaviors create vital assets of positive connection to the organization.

Managerial Implications

Organizations act and members make meaning of these actions as a normal part of trying to discern what the organization is, what it stands for, and what it is likely to do in the future. In particular, this chapter draws the attention of management to the importance of virtuous organizational actions especially under crisis or tragic situations. Following the events of 9-11, there have been numerous accounts of the significance of small moves that organizations have made to provide comfort and care to members (Dutton *et al.*, 2002a). For example, Reuters America displayed concern and care for employees through its attempt to locate them worldwide and confirm their safety, and to comfort and help families of missing employees. Many of Reuters America employees, in response, reported feeling cared for, and feeling part of a family (Dutton *et al.*, 2002b). This example shows that, to the degree that certain small actions are seen as the "true heart and soul" of a workplace, the actions may transform the bases and strength of organizational membership.

Similarly, in a negative way, small actions seen as explicitly unvirtuous (e.g., inhumane, unjust, cowardly) may do lasting damage to the foundation needed for bonding members to the organization as a whole. Several news articles reported that some firms had their employees return to work right after the terrorist attack occurred, and that some firms did not consider safety issues for employees on business trips. Employees in those firms, in turn, were shocked at the management's attitude and response, and they thought of leaving their firm after the incidents.

Although members' attachment to their organization seems less important these days than before due to increased turnover rate and frequent downsizing of firms, it is nevertheless critical in determining the extent to which members exert and sustain efforts (Ellemers *et al.*, 2004) and exhibit pro-social behaviors (O'Reilly and Chatman, 1986) on behalf of the organization. In crisis or tragic situations, even small actions by an organization can substantially change the level of members' identification with and attachment to the organization. Such disruptive circumstances may provide organizations with important opportunities to shape their relationships and connection with employees. Furthermore, as members demonstrate increasing interest in organizations' socially responsible behaviors, virtuous organizational actions exhibited not only in crisis situations but also in normal daily circumstances may shape the strength of organizational membership in the long run.

Conclusion

Overall our research invites deeper exploration into the theoretical and empirical links between organizational actions and members' cognitive and emotional connections to the organization. The trauma and scale of the events of September 11th, 2001 are hopefully rare and unique. However, the process of members' sensemaking of organizational actions is common and relatively routine. Our hope is that by applying the frame of virtuousness to how members make sense, we uncover a significant and useful path for understanding members' meaning-making and its consequences. Further, by unpacking the mechanisms that explain how virtue frames shape members' positive connection to the organization, we see the potentially important role played by positive emotions and self-construals in the process of identification in organizations.

References

Allen, NJ and JP Meyer (1990). The measurement and antecedents of affective, continuance and normative commitment to the organization. *Journal of Occupational Psychology*, 63(1), 1–18.

Anderson, NH (1968). Likableness ratings of 555 personality-trait words. *Journal of Personality and Social Psychology*, 9(3), 272–285.

Arguilar, FJ and A Bhambri (1983). *Johnson & Johnson (A)*. Harvard Business School Case No. 9-384-053.

Barling, J and I Hutchinson (2000). Commitment vs. control-based safety practices, safety reputation, and perceived safety climate. *Canadian Journal of Administrative Science*, 17(1), 76–84.

Baumeister, RE (1999). The self" In *Handbook of Social Psychology*, D Gilbert, S Fiske and G Lindzey (eds.), (4th ed.), pp. 680–740. Boston, MA: McGraw-Hill.

Bergami, M and RP Bagozzi (2000). Self-categorization, affective commitment and group self-esteem as distinct aspects of social identity in the organization. *British Journal of Social Psychology*, 39(4), 555–577.

Berkowitz, MW and SA Sherblom (2004). Equity, fairness. In *Character Strengths and Virtues: A Handbook and Classification*, C Peterson and MEP Seligman (eds.), pp. 391–412. Washington, D.C.: American Psychological Association.

Cameron, KS (2003). Organizational virtuousness and performance. In *Positive Organizational Scholarship: Foundations of a New Discipline*, KS Cameron, JE Dutton and RE Quinn (eds.), pp. 48–65. San Francisco, CA: Berrett-Koehler.

Cameron, KS, D Bright and A Caza (2004). Exploring the relationships between organizational virtuousness and performance. *American Behavioral Scientist*, 47(6), 1–24.

Cialdini, RB, RJ Borden A, Thorne MR, Walker, S Freeman and LR Sloan (1976). Basking in reflected glory: Three (football) field studies. *Journal of Personality and Social Psychology*, 34(3), 366–375.

Cropanzano, R, ZS Byrne, DR Bobocel and DE Rupp (2001). Moral virtues, fairness heuristics, social entities, and other denizens of organizational justice. *Journal of Vocational Behavior*, 58(2), 164–209.

Dutton, JE and JM Dukerich (1991). Keeping an eye on the mirror: image and identity in organizational adaptation. *Academy of Management Journal*, 34(3), 517–554.

Dutton, JE, JM Dukerich and CV Harquail (1994). Organizational images and member identification. *Administrative Science Quarterly*, 39(2), 239–263.

Dutton, JE, PJ Frost, MC Worline, JM Lilius and JM Kanov (2002a). Leading in times of trauma. *Harvard Business Review*, 80(1), 54–61.

Dutton, JE, RE, Quinn and R Pasick (2002b). *The Heart of Reuters (A)*. University of Michigan Ross School of Business Case No. 002A.

Ellemers, N, D De Gilder and SA Haslam (2004). Motivating individuals and groups at work: A social identity perspective on leadership and group performance. *Academy of Management Review*, 29(3), 459–478.

Goffman, E (1974). *Frame Analysis: An Essay on the Organization of Experience.* Cambridge, MA: Harvard University Press.

Grant, AM, JE Dutton and B Rosso (2008). Giving commitment: Employee support programs and the prosocial sensemaking process. *Academy of Management Journal.*

Haidt, J (2000). The positive emotion of elevation. *Prevention and Treatment*, 3, Article 3.

Izard, CE (1977). *Human Emotions.* New York, NY: Plenum Press.

Karremans, JC and PAM Van Lange (2005). Does activating justice help or hurt in promoting forgiveness? *Journal of Experimental Social Psychology*, 41(3), 290–297.

Kochanska, G (1995). Children's temperament, mothers' discipline, and security of attachment: Multiple pathways to emerging internalization. *Child Development*, 66(3), 597–615.

O'Reilly, C and J Chatman (1986). Organizational commitment and psychological attachment: The effects of compliance, identification, and internalization on prosocial behavior. *Journal of Applied Psychology*, 71(1), 492–499.

Ortony, A, GL Clore and A Collins (1988). *The Cognitive Structure of Emotions.* Cambridge, NY: Cambridge University Press.

Park, N and C Peterson (2003). Virtues and organizations. In *Positive Organizational Scholarship: Foundations of a New Discipline,* KS Cameron, JE Dutton and RE Quinn (eds.), pp. 33–47. San Francisco, CA: Berrett-Koehler.

Peterson, C and MEP Seligman (2004). *Character Strengths and Virtues: A Handbook and Classification.* Washington, D.C.: American Psychological Association.

Post, SG and ME McCullough (2004). Kindness, generosity, nurturance. In *Character Strengths and Virtues: A Handbook and Classification,* C Peterson and MEP Seligman (eds.), pp. 325–336. Washington, D.C.: American Psychological Association.

Reynolds, SJ (2003). Perceptions of organizational ethicality: do inflated perceptions of self lead to inflated perceptions of the organization? *Journal of Business Ethics*, 42(3), 253–266.

Richey, B, HJ Bernardin, CL Tyler and N McKinney (2001). The effects of arbitration program characteristics on applicants' intentions toward potential employers. *Journal of Applied Psychology*, 86(5), 1006–1013.

Roberts-Cady, S (2003). Justice and forgiveness. *Philosophy Today*, 47(3), 293–304.

Sandage, SJ and PC Hill (2001). The virtues of positive psychology: the rapprochement and challenges of an affirmative postmodern perspective. *Journal for the Theory of Social Behaviour*, 31(3), 241–260.

Shaver, P, J Schwartz, D Kirson and C O'Connor (1987). Emotion knowledge: further exploration of a prototype approach. *Journal of Personality and Social Psychology*, 52(6), 1061–1086.

Solomon, RC (1993). *Ethics and Excellence*. New York NY: Oxford University Press.

Statman, D (1997). Introduction to virtue ethics. In *Virtue Ethics*, D Statman (ed.), pp. 1–41. Cambridge: Edinburgh University Press.

Stilwell, BM, MR Galvin, M Kopta and RJ Padgett (1998). Moral volition: the fifth and final domain leading to an integrated theory of conscience understanding. *Journal of the American Academy of Child and Adolescent Psychiatry*, 37(2), 202–210.

Tajfel, H (1982). Social psychology of intergroup relations. *Annual Review of Psychology*, 33, 1–39.

Weick, KE (1995). *Sensemaking in Organizations*. Thousand Oaks, CA: Sage Publications.

Worline, MC, A Wrzesniewski and A Rafaeli (2002). Courage and work: breaking routines to improve performance. In *Emotions in the Workplace: Understanding the Structure and Role of Emotions in Organizational Behavior*, R Lord, R Klimoski and R Kanfer (eds.), pp. 295–330. San Francisco, CA: Jossey-Bass.

Wrzesniewski, A (2003). Finding positive meaning in work. In *Positive Organizational Scholarship: Foundations of a New Discipline*, KS Cameron, JE Dutton and RE Quinn (eds.), pp. 296–308. San Francisco, CA: Berrett-Kochler.

Zurcher, LA (1977). *The Mutable Self: A Self-Concept for Social Change*. Beverly Hills, CA: Sage Publications.

Chapter Three

FORGIVENESS FROM THE PERSPECTIVES OF THREE RESPONSE MODES: BEGRUDGEMENT, PRAGMATISM, AND TRANSCENDENCE[1]

David S. Bright

Wright State University

Ronald E. Fry
David L. Cooperrider

Case Western Reserve University

This chapter explores different ways of how forgiveness is manifest in people who experience perceived offense or harm. Forgiveness is rarely considered in management research, yet it has particular relevance to the health and functioning of interpersonal connections which allow organizations to thrive. Interviews conducted in a unionized trucking company — faced with tensions, conflicts, harmful relationships, and perceived injustices — uncovered three primary responses to perceived injury and offense. One is a begrudging response, where forgiveness is an illusion. The second is a pragmatic response, where forgiveness is viewed as a necessity. The third is a transcendent response, where forgiveness is viewed as a way to help another flourish.

A t some time in life's journey, every person endures experiences in which he or she feels hurt, misunderstood, pain, suffering, or

[1] We gratefully acknowledge the assistance of Martha Shaw, Amy Bright and Linda Ghazal. The CASE Weatherhead School of Management provided funding for this research.

67

sorrow because of others' actions. During these moments of inter-personal discomfiture, forgiveness functions as a lubricant to the inherent frictions of relational engagement.

Forgiveness is an intentional response to perceived negative expe-riences in which the propensity toward harbored negativity is dis-placed or dissolved, allowing the forgiver to "refrain from causing the offender harm even though he or she believes it is morally justifiable to do so" (Aquino *et al.*, 2003, p. 212). It is an important self-man-agement and relationship preservation strategy, and has particular rel-evance in work organizations, which are centers of human connectedness (Cooperrider and Avital, 2004; Dutton and Heaphy, 2003). Forgiveness allows for the continuation of connections, even in the midst of conflict, turmoil, or change. For this reason, it is cen-tral to the establishment, preservation and maintenance of human relationships that make up and sustain organizations (Aquino *et al.*, 2003), or as Arendt (1958) argues, forgiveness is an idea that has substantial secular importance.

Forgiveness occurs when the negativity associated with workplace discomfiture is confronted. Different ideas have emerged regarding the degree of negativity transformation that must occur. The prevail-ing, "neutral" perspective suggests that the emotions, thoughts, and behaviors associated with offense are at least transformed "from neg-ative to neutral" (Yamhure Thompson and Shahen, 2003). In other words, the forgiver ceases to see offenders in an entirely negative light. In contrast, the "positive" view is that forgiveness includes a transformation from negativity to positivity. For instance, Enright *et al.* (1998) maintain that true forgiveness requires a complete shift to positive emotion, cognition, motivation, and behavior toward former offenders.

This paper seeks to explore these positions by considering how forgiveness may function as an especially positive influence. We begin by briefly reviewing the literature on forgiveness, laying a foundation for the importance of forgiveness in the workplace. We next articulate what we see as an irony in the forgiveness literature: namely that the study of forgiveness has surged as an element of Positive Psychology (Peterson and Seligman, 2004), yet because the neutrality position has prevailed, forgiveness has essentially been considered as yet another mechanism for coping with or healing from the most dour of human experiences. Thus, our study focuses on discovering how forgiveness functions in particularly life-giving, positive, or uplifting ways. Data gathered in a unionized freight company, which we refer to as LTL Trucking, reveals that the notion of forgiveness can be considered from the perspective of three response modes: *begrudgement*, *pragmatic*, and *transcendent*. The meaning and function of forgiveness are substantially different in each mode.

Forgiveness in the Workplace

The social sciences were, until recently, remarkably silent about forgiveness, but during the last decade no less than 200 papers have been published in scientific journals (DeShea, 2005). Interestingly, only a handful address forgiveness in the workplace (e.g. Aquino *et al.*, 2003; Bradfield and Aquino, 1999; Yamhure Thompson and Shahen, 2003). Because most people spend many of their waking hours in work organizations, the potential significance of forgiveness in the workplace is considerable. For example, forgiveness has been studied as a conflict resolution strategy (Butler and Mullis, 2001), a human resource strategy (Kurzynski, 1998), a means to rebuild cooperation (Bottom *et al.*, 2002), and as related to restorative justice (Bradfield and Aquino, 1999). Forgiveness is a means to repair workplace relationships (Aquino *et al.*, 2003), and when organizations require that people work interdependently, it can mitigate the occurrence of damaged connections. In addition, the costs of non-forgiveness, such as the seeking of revenge, incivility, and conflict are well known (Bies and Tripp, 1997; Andersson, 1999; Mikkelsen and Einarsen, 2002). If left unaddressed, such dysfunctional workplace relationships have a negative impact on the performance of organizations (Dutton *et al.*, 1997).

Studies have demonstrated several benefits of forgiveness. At the individual level, the biological effects of forgiveness include physiological and psychosocial healing, and reduced illness and stress. It is related to greater creativity and learning, enhanced cardiovascular fitness, emotional stability, happiness, and tolerance (Thoresen *et al.*, 2000; McCullough *et al.*, 2000b; Enright and Fitzgibbons, 2000; Exline and Baumeister, 2000). Those who have a forgiving disposition may have better social relationships, and greater life satisfaction and self-esteem (Cameron and Caza, 2002; Ashton *et al.*, 1998). An understanding of forgiveness in the workplace can only serve to enhance such benefits for employees and foster greater organizational performance (Cameron *et al.*, 2004). These benefits suggest that the propensity to forgive is central to the establishment, preservation and maintenance of effective interpersonal connections in organizations.

The Process of Forgiveness

Considerable debate has centered on the exact nature of the experience of forgiveness. Nearly all authors suggest that it has both intrapersonal and interpersonal components (Enright *et al.*, 1998; North, 1998; Temoshok and Chandra, 2000). The experience of forgiveness is apprehended at the individual level within a specific, interpersonal context (McCullough et al., 2000b; Baumeister *et al.*, 1997).

Forgiveness is generally understood as a process that unfolds in the aftermath of a perceived harmful event. While several authors have proposed variations on the key components of this process, we base our review on Yamhure Thompson and Shahen's (2003) model, which is specifically oriented toward forgiveness in the workplace and incorporates the salient features described by other authors. This view, summarized in Fig. 1, proposes that forgiveness unfolds through five phases. In the first phase, what we call the normative state, every person carries some set of deontological expectations and assumptions regarding appropriate activity in the social world. These norms might include ideas about the importance and roles of conflict, values, appropriate language, basic human rights, organizing practices, and so forth. So long as the social world continues to function in accordance with these norms, the normative state continues for this person.

Phase two, the offense, ensues when the person encounters an experience with another party in which normative expectations are

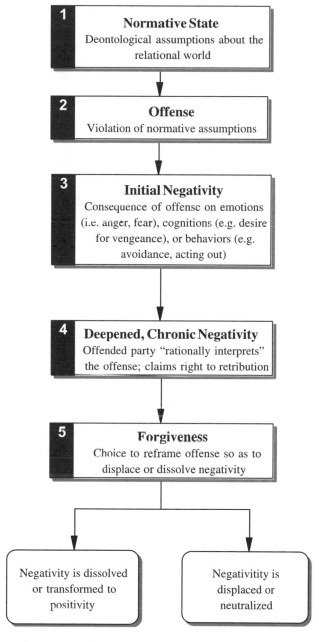

Fig. 1:   Five phase model of forgiveness. Based on Yamhure Thompson and Shahen (2003).

violated. This is the action of transgression, or perceived harm, and it causes the discomfiture of "dissonance and distress" (Yamhure Thompson and Shahen, 2003, p. 407; Janoff-Bulman, 1992).

As an immediate consequence of offense, the person experiences phase three, shown in Fig. 1 as initial negativity. Their reactions simultaneously occur in multiple dimensions, initiating emotional, cognitive, motivational, and behavioral/social responses. This initial reaction causes the person to "develop negative thoughts, feelings or behaviors" toward the offender and is associated with "negative attachment" (Yamhure Thompson and Shahen, 2003, p. 407).

In phase four, Yamhure Thompson and Shahen (2003) describe a deepened, chronic negativity that goes beyond the immediate negativity of phase three. The offended person relives the experience, using his or her normative lens to "rationally interpret" it (Enright and Fitzgibbons, 2000; North, 1998, 1987). Reflecting upon the transgression... typically elicits emotional responses (e.g. anger or fear), motivational responses (e.g., desires to avoid the transgressor or harm the transgressor in kind), cognitive responses (e.g. hostility toward or loss of respect or esteem for the transgressor), or behavioral responses (e.g. avoidance or aggression) that would promote the deterioration of good will toward the offender and social harmony. (McCullough and Worthington, 1999, p. 1142). Often, the harboring of these attachments is justified through the rationalization that the victim has a moral right to justice through retribution, vengeance, retaliation, etc. (Yamhure Thompson and Shahen, 2003; North, 1998; Enright and Fitzgibbons, 2000).

Finally, in phase five, some sort of transformation away from negativity occurs. For instance, arguing for the *neutrality* perspective, Tangney *et al.* (1999) describe forgiveness as the removal of oneself from the "victim" role, requiring merely a "cautiously neutral stance, respecting the humanity of the offender and keeping open the possibility of warmer feelings and connection." This is not coldness or detachment, but a "new sense of peace, free of anger and resentment." Aquino *et al.* (2003, p. 212) suggest that the forgiver must both "overcome negative emotions" and "abstain from acting out toward the perceived offender in retaliation".

From the *positivity* perspective, Augsburger (cited in Meek and McMinn, 1997) notes that, "Forgiveness happens as past resentments are owned, not disowned; are recognized, not repressed; are released, not retained; and are woven into new bonding relationships with others" (Meek and McMinn, 1997, p. 95). In this view, the "right" to retaliate, and the accompanying negativity that it justifies, is given away. Finally, the motivation for this "giving up" is done because of "beneficience," love and/or unconditional regard for the other (North, 1998, 1987; Enright and Fitzgibbons, 2000).

McCullough and Worthington (1999, p. 1143) attempt to find middle ground between the negativity and positivity perspectives, suggesting that "by forgiving, these negative emotional motivation, cognitive, or behavioral responses are modulated so that more prosocial, and harmonious interpersonal relationships can possibly be redeemed." This debate about the transformation of negativity in forgiveness is an important area for further consideration.

Forgiveness and Elevating Dynamics

It is interesting that the research interest in forgiveness has coincided with the emergence of Positive Psychology (Seligman and Csikszentmihalyi, 2000) and Positive Organizational Scholarship (Cameron *et al.*, 2003). The orientation in this research focuses on the study of "especially positive outcomes, processes, and attributes of organizations and their members ... to understand what represents and approaches the best of the human condition" (Cameron *et al.*, 2003, p. 4) or human flourishing (Keyes and Haidt, 2003).

A key hypothesis is that the dimensions of human experience include several qualitatively different conditions, as illustrated in Fig. 2 (Cameron, 2003). The lower end represents a condition of negative deviance, the middle — a condition of normality, and the upper end — a condition of positive deviance (Spreitzer and Sonenshein, 2003). Deviance in this sense is used to denote any variation from the forces of normativity that occur within people or organizations. Consider the study of mental health. At the lower end of the continuum, the concern is with mental illness and with the movement of healing or recovery

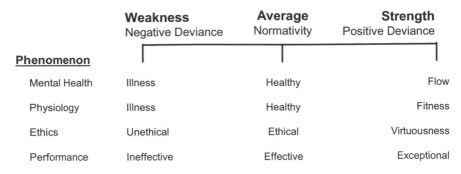

Fig. 2:   Continuum of positive and negative deviance in the human experience.

leading to normality. In contrast, the upper end of the continuum illustrates a concern with mental health beyond the norm, including such concepts as "authentic happiness" (Seligman, 2002) or "flow" (Csikszentmihalyi, 1990). A recent, substantial effort to define the terms associated with the upper-level dynamics has culminated in a categorization of human strengths and virtues, in which forgiveness is classed with other terms such as mercy, compassion, and generosity (Peterson and Seligman, 2004), thus fitting the positivity perspective above.

Much emerging research suggests that dynamics associated with each end of the continuum are quite different. For example, Fredrickson (1998) has demonstrated that positive emotions have a broadening effect on cognition whereas negative emotions have a narrowing effect. In other research, Losada and Heaphy (2004) show that high performing teams produce expansive interpersonal dynamics while low performing teams exhibit deflating interpersonal dynamics.

Moreover, the continuum suggests that the dynamics of intentional movement between these different conditions are quite different. The condition of normality, in human terms, is an average condition of equilibrium, and human and organizational forces tend to push behaviors toward the norm (Weick *et al.*, 1999; Spreitzer and Sonenshein, 2003). This implies that movement toward the right end of the continuum will be quite different, depending upon the point of origin. Below normality, any movement toward positive deviance will be *with* a natural tendency toward normality, whereas, movement toward positive deviance above the norm will be *against* any natural momentum. Movement from negativity to normality is about healing and repairing, a natural tendency. Movement from normality to a condition of positive deviance or excellence is about extending and elevating the best of the human experience, an *unnatural* tendency. From this perspective, it would be uncommon for people to find ways to extend forgiveness beyond the simple dissolution or displacement of negative feelings, attributions, and desires: the neutrality perspective.

Interestingly, most (if not all) research on forgiveness has focused on dynamics at the lower end of the human experience. As suggested earlier, nearly all definitions require offense as a pre-condition to forgiveness. The definitional debate about neutrality vs. positivity has predominantly favored the neutrality position. With a few exceptions, most researchers have resolved that forgiveness *at least* requires the intrapsychic neutralization of negativity (McCullough *et al.*, 2000a; Yamhure Thompson and Shahen, 2003; Tangney *et al.*, 2002). As a result, most work has focused on the potential of forgiveness as a healing and restorative mechanism, implying that it is a concept of importance only to the lower end of the human experience. The elevating potential of forgiveness, as implied by its consideration as a human strength (Peterson and Seligman, 2004), remains largely unexplored. Enright *et al.* (1998) argue that studies suffer from "definitional drift" when the positive swing of the person during the forgiveness process is minimized. While the positivity argument remains committed to a more rigorous definition, both positions in this debate concede that forgiveness may refer to dynamics beyond normality. However, neither the dimensions of neutrality and positivity have been adequately developed, nor have the factors that influence when one or the other may occur.

Thus, our task is to examine the meaning of forgiveness by exploring what people consider when they deliberate about how to react in the face of perceived offense. Yamhure Thompson and Shahen's (2003) phases of forgiveness imply that the violation of normative assumptions (phase 2) and initial negativity (phase 3) are often immediate and simultaneous. The propensity for people to react based on fight or flight response in the face of perceived threat is well established (Bion, 1959). However, the space between initial negativity (phase 3) and deepened, chronic negativity (phase 4) leaves open an opportunity for deliberation and willful choice. People frequently face "choice points" in which they can choose how to respond to situations that provoke significant emotional arousal (Enright and Fitzgibbons, 2000; Tangney, 2000; Glidewell, 1970). It is possible that a person, after experiencing his or her initial reaction to an event, is free to make intentional choices about a further response that may harbor and deepen the negativity at one extreme, neutralize it at a minimum, or transform it to positivity at the other extreme. An understanding of the cognitions a person invokes at this choice point should reveal the potential of forgiveness to be, not merely a neutralizing process, but also a process for building positivity.

Method

Because of the exploratory nature of the questions addressed in this article, the work is primary framed in the qualitative tradition of Grounded Theory (Glaser and Strauss, 1967; Strauss and Corbin, 1997), a methodology specifically suited to build theory.

Organization description and site selection

The focal organization, LTL Trucking,[2] is a freight shipping company with approximately 27,000 employees. Eighty percent of employees worked in one of 29 large "break-bulk" sites scattered across North America, ranging in size from approximately 250 employees at the smallest to about 1200 employees at the largest.

Union-management conflict had been typical in LTL's history; however, the organization was undergoing a massive change effort to improve interpersonal relations and performance. We chose three sites for the study, based on their differing degrees of experience in

---

[2] "Less-than-TruckLoad" is a reference to the size of freight handled, and seems an appropriate pseudoname for the organization. The company specializes in the shipment of freight that was too large to send via a small package carrier, but too small to require an entire trailer.

then-current organization change interventions.[3] These efforts have been demonstrated to create variance in the propensity toward forgiveness (Bright, 2005). Approximately 15–20 employees from the three sites were selected for an interview. At each site, the first author interviewed 4–7 dockworkers (front-line workers), 4–7 truck drivers, and 4–7 managers. Half of all interviewees were randomly selected from employee lists. The other half were selected based on their reported level of performance, targeted to include both high, average, and low performers. This selection process ensured variance in such a small sample. Overall, the first author interviewed 48 individuals, speaking with 17 dockworkers, 17 delivery truck drivers, and 14 local managers.

Interview procedure

The data were collected primarily through one-on-one interviews of approximately 60 min each. Respondents were asked to recount stories of "typical" and "exceptional" interpersonal experiences in the workplace. Forgiveness was not defined in the interview, because we wanted respondents to provide us with their own perspectives on its meaning. In part of the protocol, semi-structured questions included, "How forgiving are your peers of each other?" "How forgiving are you and your peers toward your supervisors?" and "How forgiving are your peers toward their supervisors?" Respondents were then asked "What did you think about when asked about forgiveness?" and "What does forgiveness mean to you, personally?" Respondents were encouraged to provide stories and illustrations to express their perspectives, including their observations about the degree of forgiveness exercised by others. A preliminary draft was tested with a cross-section of 10 employees at another, similar facility.

---

[3] The company was using the Appreciative Inquiry Summit methodology (Cooperrider and Srivastva, 1987; Cooperrider *et al.*, 2003; Ludema *et al.*, 2003) to foster an atmosphere of greater participation and launch multi-stakeholder change initiatives to improve operating margins.

Each interview was audio-recorded and then professionally transcribed. Forty-five of the 48 (94%) respondents provided usable statements about their perspectives on forgiveness in the workplace. ATLAS.ti (http://www.atlasti.com), a qualitative research software program, was used to tag all utterances related to the focal questions for ease of retrieval and analysis.

Analysis

We employed a mixture of guidelines for developing coding themes in qualitative data. The process involved several objectives: derive initial themes through "open" and "axial" coding (Strauss and Corbin, 1997), develop a codebook (Boyatzis, 1998), verify reliability and robustness of coding schema (Boyatzis, 1998), and analyze remaining data. The initial codebook identified three general categories of responses with respect to the meaning of forgiveness — *begrudgement, pragmatic, transcendent* — titles that conveyed the underlying structure of emerging ideas.

To explore the robustness of the initial themes, two blind coders were engaged to code a small sub-sample of data producing an initial inter-rater agreement[4] of 80% (Boyatzis, 1998) across the three categories. Feedback from the coders helped us to further refine the codebook. Then, the two blind coders coded an additional, randomly selected set of 50 utterances from the entire sample of data. Inter-rater agreement of presence[5] scores with Rater A were

---

[4] Percent Agreement = [Number of times coders agree] / [Total number of times coding was applied by either rater/2]. This approach assesses the overall agreement across all the codes. That is, how often coders ever agreed, no matter what code they applied (Boyatzis, 1998). It is a less stringent approach than the agreement of presence score used later.

[5] Percent Agreement on Presence = [2 × (the number of times both raters saw it)] / [(The number of times rater A saw it) + (The number of times rater B saw it)]. The inter-rater agreement on presence score is particularly appropriate in instances, such as this, where the presence of a theme does not necessarily equate to its absence (Boyatzis, 1998). For example, the fact that a respondent did not make statements commensurate with the transcendent mode does not mean that he or she does not ever draw on it.

transcendent = 0.79, *pragmatic* = 0.80, and *begrudgement* = 0.82, while the agreement scores with Rater B were *transcendent* = 0.70, *pragmatic* = 0.88, and *begrudgement* = 0.93.[6] The first author then proceeded to complete and cross-check the coding for all utterances across the entire sample.

Results: Three Responses to Offense

The analysis reveals that the term "forgiveness" indeed evokes a number of connotations when applied in the context of workplace interpersonal relationships. These are best described in three categories — *begrudgment, pragmatic,* and *transcendent.* Each type of response shapes how a person manages his or her emotions, cognitions, and behaviors in response to perceived interpersonal offenses. They each include distinct styles of justification for responding to perceived offenses.

Fig. 3 illustrates the distribution in our sample of these modes, described in more detail below. Each mode is counted only once per person, regardless of the total quantity of utterances from the individual that could be coded for a particular mode. The pragmatic response occurs with great frequency (91%) relative to begrudgement (26%) and transcendence (44%).

Theme 1: Begrudgement

Fourteen respondents (26%) made one or more statements that were conceptually consistent with begrudgement, a resentful condition dominated by negative emotions such as anger, frustration, and a desire for vengeance. In begrudgement, cognitions or stories are used to justify the harboring of these emotions. A desire for acting out or retaliating is rooted in these emotions and cognitions.

---

[6] We should also note that we did not provide the blind raters any training other than the written document provided in Appendix D. This is further evidence of robustness in the coding schema, because it implies that the code be understood and applied relatively easily by the novice coder.

Mode	N	%
Begrudgement Only	1	2%
Begrudgement & Pragmatic	9	20%
Pragmatic Only	15	33%
Pragmatic & Transcendent	16	36%
Transcendent Only	2	4%
Begrudgement & Transcendent	1	2%
All Modes	1	2%
TOTAL CODED =	45	100%
POSSIBLE N =	48	

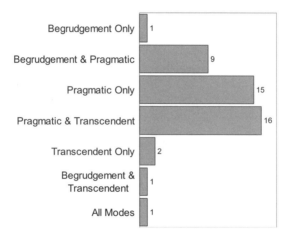

Fig. 3:   Frequencies and distribution in self-described modes of forgiveness.

Begrudgement is invoked by experiences in which "others" — either individuals or groups — are seen as perpetrating harm or offense against the victim(s). The begrudging victim makes little attempt to dispel these reactions, and may harbor them. The intention of begrudgement is to justify this harbored negativity toward the offensive party. To this end, the begrudger may deny any possibility of forgiveness. As a response mode, begrudgement is essentially *non-forgiving* and is associated with at least five indicators, described as follows.

Retaliation/desire for vengeance: in this category, the respondent describes a revengeful action or the desire to retaliate, in which the "victim" acts out against the perceived offender. These behaviors are often indicative of clear conflict.

> *I used to have real fits.* When I was first selected as a steward, for instance. The manager at the time ignored me.... But *I could yell louder than him, and everybody within 100 yards knew it. It became horrible for him. And me too.* I wasn't having any fun, but I wasn't giving up. (Driver and Union Steward, age 44; emphasis added)

In this instance, the manager had offended the steward by ignoring him, prompting the steward to retaliate. Such actions to lash out may be either overt or more subtle. For example, avoidance (e.g., "They're not talking anymore") could be considered as a vengeful action if it is intended to make a point. The key is that the desired action is or would be intended to perpetuate or express continued animosity/negativity toward the offender.

Harboring chronic negativity: some employees talked about moments in which spitefulness, "holding" grudges, harboring bad feelings, "not getting over it," or being unforgiving. These references clearly communicate the presence of chronic, negative emotions that are attributed to an offensive experience.

> One of the guys I work with, he got into it with a worker, *both of them under the circumstances were wrong in the way that they handled the situation.* And I was thinking in that instance that *the two of them are NEVER going to trust or forgive.* (Manager, age 33, emphasis added)

This "holding" of negativity could last for an extensive period of time: several days, months or years, though the amount of time is less important that the fact that a person intentionally fosters the negativity.

Judging others harshly: the respondent describes the "victim" as being highly attuned to possible offenses. "They" are easily offended, or they engage in "nitpicking." They might discuss the practice of "keeping score" — keeping track of moral slights in an effort to build up a case for retaliation against the perceived offender.

> *I don't have much patience with a guy who keeps screwing up*, I just don't.... when it comes to a head, *I get kind of out of control*...yelling and screaming.... I'll give you a good example. There's a kid who works on the dock ... he likes to screw off a lot. He likes to play pranks.... So *I made the mistake of talking to him* that day, just like I said three or four words to him. *He put a glue can underneath my dock plate*, so when I ran it over, it punctured the glue can and it shot up. *I let that slide*...[Then] he went over and *he pulled a [another] guy's pallet* out of his trailer and wrapped tape around it, wrapped it around a leg of a stand of his tray. The [other] guy comes back, he pulls the pallet and can't see the tape, his tray comes down and bills go flying all over the place.... Well there weren't any foremen around, and I got pissed off, so I grabbed hold of him and jerked him off his hyster, and basically shoved his head in the concrete and had a talk with him.... *he needed that*. (P&D driver, age 39, emphasis added)

In this story, the interviewee describes his process of building a case against the young offender: offending incidents have occurred previously — he "lets slide" the glue incident — but when he does something to another co-worker, the young worker has "gone too far. This was a typical pattern, in which workers might define, in terms of an ultimatum, lines of behavior that should not be crossed. If these behavioral lines were breached, offense or retaliation could justifiably ensue.

Telling negative stories: the telling of offensive incidents also occurred, particularly when employees described actions in others that were seen as morally illogical or unjustifiable. Stories recounted the details of an offensive set of actions as carried out by the perceived perpetrator. The accounts were nearly always filled with unflattering, negative attributions about the offender. These stories were often presented as evidence that it was justifiable to harbor negative feelings or attributions about perceived offenders. The retelling of such stories seemed to keep alive the experience of offense, refueling the initial negativity.

Disbelief in forgiveness: finally, in a few instances employees made statements that indicated skepticism about the existence of, possibility for, or utility of forgiveness.

> It's like a cat and a rat. Forever, forever enemies. That's just the way it is. When you hurt somebody, people here don't forgive that... *there is no forgiveness.* (Dockworker, age 55; emphasis added)

These statements implied that the idea of forgiveness is an illusion, or that forgiveness could result in the loss of relational power. Such remarks may indicate the pre-eminence of zero-sum assumptions about the relational world, in which the person is in repeated conflict and competition with others, and where there are always winners and losers.

Theme 2: The pragmatic response

In the pragmatic mode people actively and intentionally seek to manage their emotions and thoughts such that harbored negative resentment and related responses are untenable. However, in the pragmatic mode people are primarily concerned with *minimizing* the adverse consequences of harbored negativity. Workers see the consequences of not forgiving as highly undesirable and not in their self-interests. Their logic often includes deep descriptions of these potential, adverse consequences, which generates the mental and emotional energy required to "let it go." Thus, the most common rationale for seeking forgiveness has a *transactional* core: "it's not worth it" to "hold onto a grudge," to "harbor these feelings," etc. Forty-one respondents (91%) made statements that were conceptually *pragmatic*. Five basic ideas are associated with this response category.

Weighing the cost: this idea relates to transactional thinking. People compare the negative consequences of non-forgiveness to the benefits of minimal forgiveness, where they at least neutralize any perceived negativity.

> What happened yesterday is the past, I deal with what happens today. *I don't have time to dwell with negative feelings and emotions if I can help it.*" (Manager, age 40, emphasis added)

In this quotation, the worker makes clear that the "lost time" due to holding a grudge — implying lost investiture of attention, thought, and emotion — is clearly an unmerited opportunity cost. Many interviewees made similar statements such as "it's not worth it" to be unforgiving.

Focusing on practical compromise: a second idea is a focus on practical compromise, especially in the common interest of working together for the common good of each other and the company. Indeed, working together was an overarching, common goal that necessitated overcoming interpersonal negativity.

> *We got to try to keep the company going.* So we've got to learn to try to get along, and *we need to work together*.... I have to talk to these guys on a daily basis.... what happened in the past, ... we just put that in the background and move on.... It's hard sometimes, but you know, you have to keep going, and you have to keep the company going. (Dockworker, age 45, emphasis added)

The emphasis is on the exigency of interpersonal association: employees have to work together if they are to meet common objectives. In this sense, respondents frequently stated that there was "no time" for grudge-holding because "we have work to do."

Protecting self-interests: the pragmatic response is also associated with the protection of self-interests in relationships. While the interviewee may have discussed the need to overcome internalized negativity, he or she also acknowledges the need to "be smart" about maintaining self-protective measures — for example, avoiding offenders unless interaction was necessary:

> If somebody has screwed me in some way, or created subterfuge in some way, *I can forgive that*, but *[I'll] always be more cautious with that person....* I'm not going to associate with that person unless I have to. And to me it's not holding a grudge, *it's just being smart.* (Manager, age 40, emphasis added)

This example of avoidance is not "lashing out," as in the begrudging mode (i.e., acting by giving someone the "silent treatment"), but rather a pragmatic effort to avert future harm. Protecting oneself through what might be termed "smart remembering," was frequently cited as a challenge to the idea of "forgive and forget." When drawing on the pragmatic response mode, workers strongly suggested that forgetting, in a strict sense, was not a requirement of forgiveness.

Neutralizing negativity: finally, pragmatic thinkers actively addressed the negative emotions associated with discomfiting interpersonal experiences. They often described it, quite literally as "work" — as requiring effort. Specific references to "work out" or "let go" of the negativity were common. This activity included making sense of the experience in a way that allowed them to detach or suppress their emotions in the workplace. Common comments included such statements as, "It's just business, nothing personal (Manager, age 28)," or "I don't hold it against people if I have a run-in. I just consider that part of business" (Manager, age 55).

Theme 3: The transcendent response

The notion of transcendence refers to a style of proactive interpersonal engagement in which people seek to create substantive changes to extend or improve their social environment. This mode is particularly associated with dynamics of positivity in the human experience. When people use this frame they appear to be concerned with proactively encouraging learning, and developing others to exercise independent thought and action. It involves a tacit desire to be a positive influence, even in the midst of significant perceived negativity, to generate positivity and to reframe the apparent "given" reality of an initially negative response to offense into a more humane or life-giving form.

Individuals who drew upon transcendence described attempts to exercise choiceful control over their negative emotions, turning them to a useful purpose. They sometimes referred to their efforts to learn from difficult experiences, and they often portrayed a desire to help others learn, develop or improve. They also discussed their spiritual roots and experiences from which they derived strength and perspective. In the sample of 48 respondents, 20 (44%) made statements that were conceptually consistent with the transcendent category. At least four ideas were indicators for this theme.

Choosing to foster positivity: first, transcendence is associated with a choice to nurture positive emotions; an ability to manage or control one's emotions and thoughts:

> I'm not saying that it doesn't affect me sometimes — sometimes I get pretty stressful situations going on. I have to sit back, go do something, basically try to center myself. I'm not speaking religiously. I'm speaking mentally. I'm speaking emotionally. Try to *pull myself back into a good frame of mind*. I do it because *it's the most positive thing for me to do* emotionally and physically. (Manager, age 40; emphasis added)

In this example, the speaker conveys a belief that it is possible to choose to harbor positive emotions. He presumes that self-emotional control is not only possible but also essential. His last statement "it's the most positive thing for me to do" hints that he has specifically chosen to adopt a proactive social frame. Similar observations were often associated with stories about significant life experiences. For instance, earlier in the above interview, the respondent described his feelings of devastation when his wife suddenly left him alone to care for their children. He described his harbored, bitter feelings, and the day he realized, through what he described as a deeply spiritual moment, that there was "a way to forgive." From his perspective, the change became possible only after he specifically focused on creating positive feelings both within himself and in others in his life.

Elevating others: a second transcendent quality is a concern for the development or elevation of other people. Respondents suggested that, in the face of unpleasant interpersonal encounters, they regularly sought to create especially positive outcomes. The most common idea in these statements was a desire to learn, or to help others learn, from seemingly negative experiences:

> I try to stay calm and talk to the individual. I don't want to be little them, but I want them to see where they made the mistake, try to point it out to them, and at that point reach a common under-standing that "hey, you messed up, but *we can move on from this, we can both of us learn from this.* (Dock Supervisor, age 33; emphasis added)

Here, the worker described specific efforts and intentions to learn from conflicts and mistakes, and to develop others. In other cases, the interviewee depicted fellow employees as capable thinkers and actors. This reframing of offenders as capable individuals seemed to make a difference in the way that the actor was able to treat them in especially uplifting ways.

Seeking empathetic perspective: employees with a transcendent response expressed empathy, or the need to show it to others who may have offended them. They sought understanding not only to see others' perspectives, but also to reach out and connect to them by relating to their unique circumstances. The respondent might describe a search for understanding with the intention to help, rather than to "prove" a point or a position.

> I step back and start asking questions first versus reprimanding them first, and then asking questions second. It wouldn't make any sense

to reprimand him the way you would someone who knew and still made that mistake. (Dock Supervisor, age 33, emphasis added)

Comments such as this indicate that an empathetic concern for the offender allows for the development of a shared understanding that could serve as the basis for creating a mutually beneficial, social reality and experience.

Quick to forgive: other respondents talked about quickly forgiving or being slow to take offense, "You've got to have a short memory out there, to be a good supervisor. You gotta let it roll off your back (Dock Supervisor, age 30)." Still others suggested the need to choose an optimistic approach toward discomfiture, "You need to be happy, have a good attitude" (Driver, age 53). Again, the common underlying intent was the need for proactive choice in the management of one's emotions. Some respondents simply stated that they never experienced the emotions of offense (i.e., deep negativity), even though such reactions were typical or common in others.

Discussion

The key question for this paper has dealt with the considerations people make when they respond in the face of initial negativity. Researchers have generally defined forgiveness as a neutralizing activity. The potential for it to function as a true human strength, where it could foster positivity or positive deviance, has largely been ignored. The analysis confirms the view that forgiveness is associated with neutralizing negativity *and* that it also has the potential to foster positivity, perhaps at a previously underestimated level.

The three modes of response to the experience of offense provide evidence of a wide range in moral sensemaking during times of interpersonal conflict or organizational discomfiture, as illustrated in Fig. 4. The relationship between these responses and the decision to forgive suggest competing considerations regarding forgiveness.

For example, begrudgement is concerned with fierce self-protectionism, and the impulse to fight back, retaliate, or act out. Such

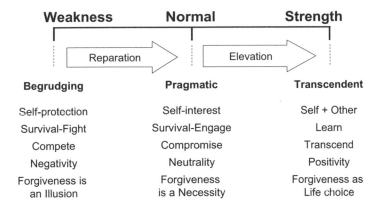

Fig. 4: Embedded assumptions in modes of forgiveness.

actions are commensurate with the perspective that every person has to "watch out" for him or herself, because the world is a competitive ground. People may see the world as a conflict in which some players have moral superiority over others. Reality as conflict extends to issues where combatants rhetorically fight for the moral high ground, from which they claim superiority over, or justification for action against others. Within such a reality, forgiveness could only be seen as a distant possibility, if not pure fantasy. The remembrance of conflict is key to one's identity in such a world, because it reignites emotions of hatred, bitterness, and vengeance toward others. It also justifies sharp divisions through ostracizing perceived offenders, and a heightened sensitivity to opportunities to be offended at the slightest misstep or miscue on the part of others. This propensity toward begrudgement has been characterized as a form of self-deception (Warner, 2001, 1982).

The pragmatic response is a mode of forgiveness, denoting a tempered interpretation of the world. It is necessary to acknowledge problems, and to develop practical efforts that foster minimally healthy levels of functionality. Interpersonal engagement with other people who may have differing views or motives is a necessity that calls for acknowledging challenges. Thus, the pragmatic mode fosters compromise, and is basically conciliatory. The dominant assumptions are highly utilitarian, where the ends of meeting job requirements are associated with and require the means of interpersonal association. The world of relationships might be in conflict, but compromise makes possible a focus on common aims. Defending oneself against the threats of others is still important, but forgiveness at a basic level of emotional self-control is viewed as an important, critical part of interpersonal exchange. A priority on preserving moral, mental and emotional health leads to assessing the costs of harbored negativity (to oneself and to the organization) as too great. Forgiveness, then, becomes a practical coping strategy, a means to self protect and to manage any day-to-day discomfitures in a manner that preserves one's own health and capacity to act.

The transcendent response promotes forgiveness because of its deontological force: forgiveness is fostered not merely for self-interest, but because it is the "right thing to do" and will have a worthy or virtuous impact on others. Transcendent thinking is often framed in moral terms as an expression of excellence in character and a quest for the best of both personal and common good. A transcendent moral system — as expressed through political philosophy, religion, or ethical beliefs — provides a rationale for forgiveness regardless of context. Forgiveness in this view is seen as a pro-active practice that brings benefit not only to self, but also to others, enabling thriving and fulfilling interpersonal relationships that may also have implications for how people connect.

Moreover, it would appear that the begrudging, pragmatic, and transcendent responses are conceptually commensurate with the conditions of negative deviance, normality, and positive deviance (Fig. 2), respectively. Begrudgement is negative deviance because healthy individuals, in general, do not harbor long-term, chronic negativity toward others (Witvliet *et al.*, 2001). At the same time, the transcendent form of forgiveness is grounded in the idea of extending or elevating one's relation with others. Both run counter to the normalizing influence in most organizations. A disproportional use of the pragmatic mode relative to begrudgement and the transcendent mode — a bell curve of sorts as shown in Fig. 3 — supports this conclusion.

Conclusion

The results and analyses in this article challenge and extend the dominant paradigm of research on forgiveness, which has focused on neutralizing negativity. Evidence shows that the enactment of forgiveness refers to a range of responses to perceived offense, each relating to a distinct strategy for forgiveness as operationalized through individual practice. Begrudgement represents a state of non-forgiveness, the pragmatic mode is associated with neutralized negativity as a response to perceived offense, and the transcendent mode is the proactive extension of positivity. Pure begrudgement and pure transcendence are both less common; however, they can often occur in combination with the pragmatic mode. The transcendent response has received relatively little attention as a viable form of forgiveness. These three categories of response — begrudgement, pragmatism and transcendence — provide insight that can be used in future work to explore the relevance of forgiveness in the workplace.

References

Andersson, LM (1999). Tit for Tat? The spiraling effect of incivility in the workplace. *Academy of Management Review*, 3, 452.

Aquino, K, SL Grover, R Goldman and R Folger (2003). When push doesn't come to shove: Interpersonal forgiveness in workplace relationships. *Journal of Management Inquiry*, 3, 209–216.

Arendt, H (1958). *The Human Condition*. Chicago, IL: University of Chicago Press.

Ashton, MC, SV Paunone, E Helmes and DN Jackson (1998. Kin altruism, reciprocal altruism, and the Big Five personality factors. *Evolution and Human Behavior*, 19, 243–255.

Baumeister, RF, JJ Exline and KL Sommer (1997). The victim role: grudge theory, and two dimensions of forgiveness. In *Dimensions of Forgiveness: Psychological Research and Theological Perspectives*, EJ Worthington, (ed.), pp. 79–105. Philadelphia, PA: Templeton Foundation Press.

Bies, RJ, and TM Tripp (1997). Revenge in organizations: the good, the bad, and the ugly. In *Dysfunctional Behavior in Organizations*, RW Griffin, A O'Leary-Kelly, and J Collins (eds.), Thousand Oaks, CA: Sage.

Bion, WR (1959). *Experiences in Groups*. New York, NY: Basic Books.

Bottom, WP, K Gibson, SE Daniels and JK Murnighan (2002). When talk Is not cheap: Substantive penance and expressions of intent in rebuilding cooperation. *Organization Science*, 5, 497.

Boyatzis, R (1998). *Transforming Qualitative Information*: Sage Publications.

Bradfield, M and K Aquino (1999). The effects of blame attributions and offender likableness on forgiveness and revenge in the workplace. *Journal of Management*, 25(5), 607–631.

Bright, DS (2005). *Forgiveness and change: begrudging, pragmatic, and transcendent responses to discomfiture in a unionized trucking company*. Cleveland, OH: Unpublished Dissertation, Case Western Reserve University: *Dissertation Abstracts International*.

Butler, DS and F Mullis (2001). Forgiveness: a conflict resolution strategy in the workplace. *Journal of Individual Psychology*, 3, 259.

Cameron, K and A Caza (2002). Organizational and leadership virtues and the role of forgiveness. *Journal of Leadership and Organizational Studies*, 9(1), 33–48.

Cameron, KS (2003). Organizational virtuousness and performance. In *Positive Organizational Scholarship: Foundations of a New Discipline*, KS Cameron, JE Dutton and RE Quinn (eds.), pp. 48–65. San Francisco: Berrett Koehler.

Cameron, KS, JE Dutton and RE Quinn (2003). Foundations of positive organizational scholarship. In *Positive Organizational Scholarship: Foundations of a New Discipline*, KS Cameron, JE Dutton and RE Quinn (eds.), pp. 3–13. San Francisco: Berrett Koehler.

Cameron, KS, DS Bright and A Caza (2004). Exploring the relationships between organizational virtuousness and performance. *American Behavioral Scientist*, 47(6), 766–790.

Cooperrider, DL and S Srivastva (1987). Appreciative inquiry in organizational life. *Research in Organizational Change and Development*, 1, 129–169.

Cooperrider, DL and M Avital (2004). Introduction: advances in appreciative inquiry — constructive discourse and human organization. In *Constructive Discourse and Human Organization*, DL Cooperrider and M Avital (eds.), pp. xi–xxxiii. Boston: Elsevier Ltd.

Cooperrider, DL, D Whitney and JM Stavros (2003). *Appreciative Inquiry Handbook: The First in a Series of AI Workbooks for Leaders of Change*. Bedford Heights, OH: Lakeshore Communications.

Csikszentmihalyi, M (1990). *Flow: The Psychology of Optimal Experience/Mihaly Csikszentmihalyi* 1st Ed. New York: Harper & Row.

DeShea, L (2005). *The Kentucky Forgiveness Collective*. World Wide Web, www.uky.edu/~ldesh2/forgive.htm. Access date: January 8, 2005.

Dutton, JE, SJ Ashford, EE Wlerba, R O'Neil and E Hayes (1997). Reading the wind: How middle managers assess the context for issue selling to top managers. *Strategic Management Journal*, 15, 407–425.

Dutton, JE, and ED Heaphy (2003). The power of high-quality connections. In *Positive Organizational Scholarship: Foundations of a New Discipline*, KS Cameron JE Dutton and RE Quinn (eds.), pp. 263–278. San Francisco: Berrett Koehler.

Enright, RD, and RP Fitzgibbons (2000). In *Helping Clients Forgive: An Empirical Guide for Resolving Anger and Restoring Hope* RD Enright and RP Fitzgibbons (eds.), Washington DC: American Psychological Association.

Enright, RD, S Freedman and J Rique (1998). The psychology of interpersonal forgiveness. In *Exploring Forgiveness*, RD Enright and J North (eds.), pp. 46–62. Madison, WI, US: University of Wisconsin Press.

Exline, JJ and RF Baumeister (2000). Expressing forgiveness and repentance: benefits and barriers. In *Forgiveness: Theory, Research, and Practice*, ME McCullough KI Pargament and CE Thoresen (eds.), pp. 133–155. New York, NY, US: The Guilford Press.

Fredrickson, BL (1998). What good are positive emotions? *Review of General Psychology*, 2, 300–319.

Glaser, B, and A Strauss (1967). *The Discovery of Grounded Theory*. New York: Aldine de Gruyter.

Glidewell, JC (1970). *Choice Points*. Boston, MA: The Colonial Press, Inc.

Janoff-Bulman, R (1992). *Shattered Assumptions: Towards a New Psychology of Trauma*. New York: The Free Press.

Keyes, CLM, and J Haidt (2003). *Flourishing: Positive Psychology and the Life Well-lived*, 1st Ed. Washington, DC: American Psychological Association.

Kurzynski, MJ (1998). The virtue of forgiveness as a human resource management strategy. *Journal of Business Ethics*, 1, 77–85.

Losada, M, and E Heaphy (2004). The role of positivity and connectivity in the performance of business teams. *American Behavioral Scientist*, 47(6), 740–765.

Ludema, JD, D Whitney BJ, Mohr and TJ Griffin (2003). *The Appreciative Inquiry Summit: A Practitioner's Guide for Leading Large-Group Change*. San Francisco: Berrett-Koehler.

McCullough, ME and EJ Worthington (1999). Religion and the forgiving personality. *Journal of Personality*, 67(6), 1141–1162.

McCullough, ME, WT Hoyt and KC Rachal (2000a). What we know (and need to know) about assessing forgiveness constructs. In *Forgiveness: Theory, Research, and Practice*, ME McCullough KI Pargament and CE Thoresen (eds.), pp. 65–88. New York, NY, US: The Guilford Press.

McCullough, ME, KI Pargament and CE Thoresen (2000b). The psychology of forgiveness: History, conceptual issues, and overview. In *Forgiveness: Theory, Research, and Practice*, ME McCullough KI Pargament and CE Thoresen (eds.), pp. 1–14. New York, NY, US: The Guilford Press.

Meek, KR and MR McMinn (1997). Forgiveness: more than a therapeutic technique. *Journal of Psychology and Christianity*, 16(1), 51–61.

Mikkelsen, EG and S Einarsen (2002). Basic assumptions and symptoms of post-traumatic stress among victims of bullying at work. *European Journal of Work & Organizational Psychology*, (1), 87–111.

North, J (1998). The "ideal" of forgiveness: a philosopher's exploration. In *Exploring Forgiveness*, RD Enright and J North (eds.), pp. 15–34. Madison, WI, US: University of Wisconsin Press.

North, J (1987). Wrongdoing and forgiveness. *Philosophy*, 62, 499–508.

Peterson, C, and MEP Seligman (eds.) (2004). *Character Strengths and Virtues: A Handbook and Classification*. New York: Oxford University Press.

Seligman, MP, and M Csikszentmihalyi (2000). Positive Psychology. *American Psychologist*, 55, 5–14.

Seligman, MEP (2002). *Authentic Happiness*. New York: Free Press.

Spreitzer, GM and S Sonenshein (2003). Positive deviance and extraordinary organizing. In *Positive Organizational Scholarship: Foundations of a New Discipline*, KS Cameron JE Dutton and RE Quinn (eds.), pp. 207–224. San Francisco: Berrett Koehler.

Strauss, A and J Corbin (1997). *Basics of Qualitative Research: Grounded Theory, Procedures, and Techniques*. London, UK: Sage Publications.

Tangney, J, AL Boone, R Dearing and C Reinsmith (2002). *Individual Differences in the Propensity to Forgive: Measurement and Implications for Psychological and Social Adjustment*. Working paper, George Mason University.

Tangney, J, C Reinsmith, R Fee, AL Boone and N Lee (1999). Assessing individual differences in the propensity to forgive. Paper presented at the annual meeting of the American Psychological Association, Boston, MA.

Tangney, JP (2000). Humility: theoretical perspectives, empirical findings and directions for future research. *Journal of Social & Clinical Psychology: Special Issue: Classical Sources of Human Strength: A Psychological Analysis*, 19(1), 70–82.

Temoshok, LR and PS Chandra (2000). The meaning of forgiveness in a specific situational and cultural context: persons living with HIV/AIDS in India. In *Forgiveness: Theory, Research, and Practice*, ME McCullough KI Pargament and CE Thoresen (eds.), pp. 41–64. New York, NY, US: The Guilford Press.

Thoresen, CE, AHS Harris and F Luskin (2000). Forgiveness and health: An unanswered question. In *Forgiveness: Theory, Research, and Practice*, ME McCullough KI Pargament and CE Thoresen (eds.), pp. 163–190. New York, NY: Guilford.

Warner, T (2001). Forgiving, forgoing, and living free. In *Bonds That Make us Free* T Warner (ed.), pp. 291–316. Salt Lake City, UT: Shadow Mountain.

Warner, CT (1982). Feelings, self-deception, and change. *AMCAP Journal*, 8(2), 21–31, 35.

Weick, K, KM Sutcliffe and D Dobsfeld (1999). Organizing for high reliability: processes of collective mindfulness. *Research in Organizational Behavior*, 21, 81–123.

Witvliet, CV, TE Ludwig and KL Vander Laan (2001). Granting forgiveness or harboring grudges: implications for emotion, physiology, and health. *Psychological Science*, 12(2), 117–123.

Yamhure Thompson, L and PE Shahen (2003). Forgiveness in the workplace. In *Handbook of Spirituality and Organizational Performance*, RC Giacalone and CL Jurkiewicz (eds.), pp. 405–420. New York: M.E. Sharpe.

Chapter Four

THE SPIRITUAL CHALLENGES OF POWER, HUMILITY, AND LOVE AS OFFSETS TO LEADERSHIP HUBRIS

Andre L. Delbecq

Santa Clara University

This chapter examines the failure of success, the corruption of triumph, and the danger of celebrity. It explains why the contemporary business press and academic studies are replete with examples of previously acclaimed leaders who slipped into situational narcissism leading to distorted decisions and subsequent public embarrassment. Every person playing a leadership role or attaining a position of notoriety is tempted by hubris, or the development of pride and dominance. The chapter explains why these outcomes are common and introduces the classic virtues of humility and love as offsets and counter-tendencies that can protect leaders from such falls from grace.

Contemporary business press and academic studies are replete with examples of previously acclaimed leaders who slip into situational narcissism leading to distorted decisions and subsequent public embarrassment. An examination of the classic virtues of humility and love in the spiritual traditions (little talked about in the world of "celebrity" leadership) will suggest how these spiritual gifts can protect executives from such a "fall from grace".

Prelude: Reflecting through the Lens of Your Life Experience

I frequently introduce the subject of leadership to executive audiences and MBAs with an exercise I learned from a wise management phenomenologist Melvin McKnight (1999). He taught me to begin the dialog by asking participants to list on the left-hand side of a divided sheet of paper (the "side of light") the positive characteristics of a leader they have admired for championing an important change. Next to ask participants to list on the right side of the page negative characteristics of the leader that decreased their potential as a collaborator ("the shadow side").

The results are quite invariant. It seems we have come to a shared cultural understanding of leadership. On the positive side typical items include the ability of the leader to envision and communicate a mission that serves a critical need of an important client, assistance in problem identification and solution development in order to design an unfolding course of action (inclusive of attention to efficiency, effectiveness and innovation), interpersonal support for followers helping them to engage and sustain the mission, and a sense of energy and timing in orchestrating the unfolding of the plan that balances urgency for action with stakeholder readiness. In all of this the leader is described with adjectives regarding a personal "presence" that is hopeful and energetic yet at the same time characterized by a relationship style that is open to others, inclusive of active listening, and supportive in times of difficulty. Likewise when the leader slips into the shadow side the descriptors are consistent. Words such as arrogant, impatient, insensitive, and punitive predominate.

I mention this exercise as a prelude to asking the readers of this reflection to also remain grounded in their experience and not to allow later theoretical and religious language to distance them from experiential knowledge. This essay encompasses a very familiar story of how leaders that we have admired during their terms of office slip into distortions associated with power. Nor does the story pertain only to a few political, corporate, or religious leaders who recently have fallen into scandal portrayed in national, local, or association press. Rather, we are dealing with a common aspect of human weakness that each of us has observed in daily organizational life. Indeed, if we are honest, some aspects of the story may have touched our own leadership history.

We should also read with compassion. Here we are not talking about "evil" individuals or "sociopaths." Rather we are seeking to understand why highly competent individuals rather unwittingly become distorted by positional power.

Leadership, like every calling, has its own particular set of subtle temptations that bring out the shadow side of gifted individuals. We have a sense of how careers are distorted in other callings. I am writing this reflection at the time of the steroid scandals in baseball. This is just the latest manifestation of a genre of temptations that talented athletics and coaches are subject to. Likewise from the press we are familiar with the temptations political leaders face, and those of actors and rock stars. My step-son is a sheriff's deputy working in the prisons of San Francisco. The temptations to hardness of heart, cynicism and brutality associated with custodial officers are well known and recently the military prison abuses are on the front pages of news reports. Even those not involved in "secular" callings do not escape particular temptations. Mystics are tempted by spiritual pride, and clerics by spiritual ambition.

Nor is the focus in this essay on totally "failed" leaders. I would posit every leader experiences each of the temptations we are about to deal with. I have certainly had occasions in my own career when I fell prey to these pitfalls. The MBAs I teach report they are subject to these distortions early in their career as team leaders, engineering design group managers, audit group managers, etc. Thus the argument made here is these temptations are endemic to the call to leadership. They are not simply associated with the senior level of leadership from which I will illustrate only because the temptations are more visible and more easily generalized at this level.

If you yourself have never experienced any of these dark holes in a serious way, the discussion will be forearming. If you fallen into one of the traps we will describe, the article will provide a stimulus to humility.

NASDAQ Executives Identify Hubris as the Key Leadership Temptation

The inspiration for this reflection was the identification of hubris as the great distortion associated with organizational leadership by NASDAQ CEOs several years ago. They had gathered at a Chief Executive Institute hosted by Professor Jeffrey Sonnenfeld. In a breakout session dealing with "executive legacy" I asked these CEOs what led to executive failure. In less than 12 seconds they identified as their top two distortions hubris and greed with hubris being the most serious. Although other issues were brought forth in a round robin nominal group process over the next hour, these NASDAQ CEOs never varied from this conviction (Chief Executive Leadership Institute, 1997).

Therefore, our attention in this article is on hubris. As understood by these executives hubris had two dimensions: "pride" often manifested as arrogance and "dominance", the tendency to seek subjection and to over-control others diminishing their freedom. We will examine these distortions and their causes, and then turn to the virtues of humility and love as offsets, particularly through the lens of the Christian tradition.

The First Dimension of Hubris: Arrogance

What are aspects of the leader's gifts that leave a thin barrier against arrogance? Reflect on what we admire leaders for.

Quickness of intellect and the ability to rapidly absorb and intuitively integrate complex information and chains of causation

High verbal facility allowing leaders to conceptualize compelling explanations and articulate convincing action paths

Visionary capacity to think "over the horizon" and link to the big picture avoiding being caught in parochial perspectives

Action orientation and risk taking propensity

It is these gifts that are associated with the visionary capacity we praise transformational leaders for (see for example Boal, 2004).

However, there is a dark side to these gifts. Almost without self-awareness, a talented leader can slip into arrogance in social interaction with subordinates and stakeholders precisely because of these gifts. A leader may begin to quickly trump the objections of others with articulate defense and justification of his position. Impatience with the less verbally facile and unwillingness to engage active listening can lead to overlooking non-confirming information, underestimating barriers, engaging in precipitous action before there is sufficient organizational readiness, and failing to build necessary coalitions among stakeholders. (Delbecq *et al.*, 2004)

There are excellent recent empirical summaries documenting these dysfunctional executive behaviors (Nutt, 2003; Finkelsetin, 2003). Spiritual perspectives of the distortion of pride are also readily available in classical spiritual writings (McIntosh, 2004). We are particularly concerned here with leadership failure in the orchestration of strategic decisions. The largest available data set suggests that more than half the time these distortions lead to strategic decision failure (Nutt, 2003).

Circumstances further seducing the leader toward arrogance

It is, of course, not simply the intellectual and verbal gifts of the leader that by themselves lead to distortion. In the Christian tradition such gifts are called "charisms"; spiritual gifts or capacities given to each individual to be used on behalf of others (Cantalamessa, 2003). Unfortunately, the circumstances of "office" add fuel to the smoldering fire of latent leadership vanity.

The prestige of the leadership role evokes deference from others, increasing their hesitancy to speak up in opposition to the leaders perceptual framework. There is also fear that the leader may engage in reprisals against those who seem to oppose the leader's favored course of action (however overestimated). Meanwhile, political sycophants create a chorus of non-representative acclamations of support for the leader's perceptual biases. These re-enforcers often cause a leader to assume there is greater agreement with his/her position than is in fact the case.

The trappings of power also symbolically reinforce the leader's "aura of superiority". These often include a physical office whose decoration, location, and furnishings set the leader apart; special privileges such as parking, private washrooms, personal administrative support, etc. Such symbols suggest to others (and soon subconsciously to the leader) that this person is exceptional. We can add florid introductions at receptions and gatherings and favorable seating at events when the leader is publicly "before" others. Then there are the economic "validations" of superiority (salary, stock options, bonuses, etc.) that in our contemporary society are both noticeable and increasingly differentiating. These economic advantages allow further distinctions in personal costume, housing, modes of travel, accommodations at conferences, etc.

Resulting temptation toward situational narcissism

How can we be surprised that such circumstances tempt the leader to slip into situational narcissism leading to arrogance? Clinical descriptions of narcissism include tendencies toward self-aggrandizement, bragging about personal accomplishments, and overestimation of personal abilities, self-absorption, and a sense of invulnerability. (DSMMD, 1994)

This is ritualized at the organizational level by self-flattering press, ego boasting rituals, and favorable corporate histories. More seriously these tendencies can lead to nonsensical acquisitions, excessive corporate architecture and furnishings, etc. (Brown, 1997). I remember during the dot com boom in Silicon Valley a wise venture capitalist who took his own personal measure of situational narcissism by quietly visiting both the corporate offices and the personal neighborhood of the entrepreneur seeking funding. He intuited that visible excess was one important measure of how "grounded" a leader was.

A correlate of all of this is the inability of leaders who succumb to situational narcissism to admit that unfavorable outcomes might be associated with any mistakes made by themselves or their associates. Instead, unfavorable events are attributed to unavoidable external circumstances or the behaviors of others (Rodewalt, 2001). Current financial scandals display leaders who hide embarrassing performance outcomes by financial manipulations in order to maintain the illusions of superiority.

Humility as the offset

What then might the spiritual traditions offer as an offset to the temptation to arrogance? They focus on a virtue that seems antithetical to the literature surrounding celebrity leadership — *humility*.

Many spiritual writers see humility as one of the two greatest spiritual gifts God grants, second only to the virtue of charity. Here are just a few quotations I have gathered over the years (regretfully without citations) from the spiritual traditions on the paradox of humility and power.

He hath put down the mighty from their seat: and hath exalted the humble and the meek.
   Magnificat —
   Book of Common Prayer

O God, make me live lowly and die lowly and rise from the dead among the lowly.
   Muslim Prayer of Mohammed

If you should ask me concerning the precepts of the Christian Religion, I should answer you, nothing but humility.
   St. Augustine of Hippo

To the truly humble man the ordinary ways and customs and habits of men are not a matter of conflict.
   Thomas Merton

Humility like darkness reveals the heavenly lights.
   Henry David Thoreau (Walden)

In the leadership role the testing of humility begins with the daily willingness to accept criticism and be open to modification of one's own thinking as one's concepts are subject to examination in exchanges with others. When employees speak of a leader as being "open to ideas" and a "good listener" they are not implying that this leader fails to offers ideas or challenge them by a new vision. Rather, they are saying that the appropriately humble leader is willing to admit that his/her initial conceptualizations are imperfect, subject to improvement, and at times even wrong. The ability to offer ideas tentatively, and to receive criticism is a hallmark of leadership humility that subordinates value. Such leaders create an atmosphere of inclusiveness in contrast to competitive "upstaging" that characterizes less constructive organizational cultures.

Here is an echo of this from the wisdom of the Tao:

The wise leader speaks rarely and briefly.

After all, no other natural outpouring goes on and on. It rains and then it stops. It thunders and then it stops.

The leader teaches more through being than through doing. The quality of one's silence conveys more than long speeches.

Be still. The leader who knows how to be still and feel deeply will be more effective.

Remember that the method is awareness of process.

Reflect.
Be Still.
What do you feel deeply?

(*Heider, 2003*)

The daily little humiliations of having your ideas sifted and winnowed through dialog prepare the leader for the larger humiliations associated with failures. These more serious errors require forthright admission as early as possible, resulting in quick redirection. By contrast cover-up and dissembling when uncovered destroys the perception of leadership integrity. Integrity is much appreciated by the market place, customers and employees (Kouzes and Posner, 1993).

The Second Dimension of Hubris: Dominance

Feeding off the evolving myth of self-importance and superiority a leader who is not self-aware experiences an increasing tendency toward dominance. The leader now becomes even more impatient with the need for consensus building, is even less willing to take time to inquire regarding stakeholder positions, and is even less willing to listen to challenging perspectives. As a result the leader fails to incorporate the insights of others into the decision strategy. This unwillingness to endure periods of uncertainty and constructive conflicts leads to self-belief that the correct course of action has been fully conceptualized and results in a drive for immediate gratification through action.

This increasing tendency toward dominance is not emotionally neutral. When the arrogant leader encounters subtle resistance because factual obstacles have been underestimated, he becomes frustrated and too often succumbs to the temptation to exercise raw power (both of personality and of office) to get "on with it" imposing his will in a manner that is harsh and judgmental of those who stand in the way of his preferred action.

In Silicon Valley my experience is that this hasty and domineering behavior is frequently publicly rationalized under the rubric of the need for speed and first mover advantage. This is a pattern of behavior spoken about over and over by my MBAs leading design and development efforts. When emerging obstacles are encountered that threaten design integrity or customer satisfaction, they often report that "top management" simply doesn't want to hear about the problems. Instead demanding and threatening memos amplified by new unrealistic deadlines come down. When such leaders seek to override the concerns of others by dominance, subordinates out of fear engage in political subterfuge and manipulation trying not to get caught in an unfolding potential failure. This further closes down effective problem solving.

Circumstances seducing the leader toward dominance

Again we can examine further reinforcements of leadership power that blow on the flames of dominance just as there were reinforcements that blew on the flames of initial arrogance.

As mentioned earlier, members of a small executive cadre often coalesce to reify the leader's point of view. This tendency for the leader's personal team to "agree" can be exacerbated if the leader's executive team possesses homogeneous demographics: similar training, educational background, age, and a shared perspective formed by the frequent closed interaction among themselves. Such a commonality of viewpoint leads to reinforcement of the belief that the problems associated with implementing a failed decision strategy are merely insufficient enthusiasm or compliance on the part of subordinates outside their inner circle.

Again a resulting comparison with situational narcissism

Once more we see in this evolving tendency toward dominance a pattern reflected in the literature of narcissism. The clinical literature speaks of denial, a primitive and unconscious method of coping with conflict and anxiety leading to a false confidence and feelings of invulnerability. It speaks of rationalization, attempts to justify or find reasons for unacceptable outcomes and to present choices in a form that is affirming of self, casting any negative consequences as failures of others. (Rodewalt, 2001; DSMMD, 1994)

Soon rhetoric and propaganda by the leader and corporate spokespeople are explaining away problems as temporary and unimportant while the real deep-seated issues that require revisiting and renewed problem solving are left unattended (Brown, 1997).

Perhaps most disturbing of all is the distortion evidenced in an increasing sense of entitlement by the leader and close associates even in the face of negative results; a lack of empathy that favors the leader's and close associates' personal interests over others as the problems of an ill-conceived strategy begin to take their toll.

Love as the offset

The virtue we examine as an offset here is Love (Charity). It is a central virtue in the religious and wisdom traditions. For example, in the traditions of Abraham (Jewish, Christian, Muslim) the "Great Commandments" center the tradition in love of God and Neighbor. Volumes have been devoted to the exploration of this keystone virtue (Brady, 2003). We have space to only briefly highlight aspects of the virtue relating to our immediate concerns.

A leader steeped in this virtue orients his/her life in service to God and neighbor. If all of life is seen as service, then leadership roles are a form of ministry, not a path to self-aggrandizement. "Servant Leadership" is not an empty phrase to such a leader (Delbecq and McGee, 2003; Delbecq, 2000).

This world-view leads to the leader's acceptance of individuals based on their "being", their deep and holistic self. There are two results. First, the leader is not be distracted by the imperfections of others. It is my experience of spiritually mature executives that they deal with their associates at work as "they are", not as they "wish their associates were". Second, they meet the whole person, not simply a "role actor," and are able to transcend preoccupation with restricted instrumental expectations. Instead they see each individual as a unique person with individual gifts able to contribute to the organizational mission in often surprising ways. They are able to respect and celebrate associates and have a desire for the their well-being and growth. This allows for fruitful mentoring and opens communication since the other person senses an acceptance of their real and total self.

This love of the other person in their wholeness (including imperfection and brokenness) is the prelude to giving up over-control of others with all its ego rewards. There is a fundamental respect for the freedom and dignity of the other. Forcing behaviors are let go of. This requires a higher plane of moral development (Zagano, 1999).

Love Enacted in Organizational Life

The expression of love is manifest in concrete ways that the leader structures organizational activity (Naughton, 2004). Some examples can be suggested.

Vision: a leader centered in love places human well-being first. Such a leader never loses sight of the ultimate purpose of all leadership acts, and the ultimate purpose of organizational life: (in the private sector) providing needed goods and services that benefit others. Even in the case of very technical products (e.g., hydraulic couplings, electronic chips) they understand that they contribute to a long chain of causation that serves humankind. Thus with a mystic's eye a executive in a micro-chip firm can envision the medical, education, pollution control, transportation and other end products his chips will enable. Through this broader vision leaders create a culture that is inclusive of but more than simply focused on efficiency, effectiveness, and profitability. The leader infuses the organizational purpose with larger human meaning that captures heart (Naughton, 2004).

Organizational structure: for leaders grounded in love, subsidiarity (decentralization and empowerment) is not simply a sociological construct. As already noted these leaders step away from undue centralization and undue bureaucratic over control because they respect the individuality and gifts of all associates in the organization. They create structures and processes that facilitate spontaneous vertical and horizontal communication because they enjoy and value the input from others. Believing in the spiritual dignity of each individual, where and when it is appropriate they decentralize initiatives because they perceive the Spirit is moving in the co-creative capacities of individuals at all organizational levels. They are present and available to teams at every stage of decision processes: problem formulation, solution development, and implementation. Rather than distancing themselves, they understand the criticality of presence but avoid dominance. They accept that collegial involvement of stakeholder voices will "muddy" the decision process, but understand this as a necessary part of a shared discernment protocol. They are also supportive of the disruptions that occur when associates seek to grow in their role through asking to shift their attention to new assignments. They accept this employee fluidity as another aspect of the movement of Spirit.

As a result there is, within the organization, a climate of openness, respect and trust that is not possible except in a context that is deeply respectful of individuals; a culture that is communal rather than individualistic and hyper-competitive.

All of this is not without cost. While we understand this type of organizational culture facilitates innovation, we also know there is a degree of greater chaos associated with greater degrees of human freedom and creative self-expression. In the midst of this more loosely coupled organizational setting there is greater confusion. Communication must increase, and leaders must be more available. Social distance between leader and follower must diminish. When failures occur, the leader and others must be able to admit and learn from experience without casting blame.

To sum up, love provokes the leader to exercise his/her own gifts in spheres of proper responsibility and grants the same freedom to others.

Some Closing Thoughts

The above reflections are not meant to imply that most leaders are clinically narcissistic. Instead, they suggest that narcissism is a situational neurosis that is seductive because it is born exactly out of the gifts of a charismatic leader. The seduction is especially strong in the American setting with its emphasis on individuality and the "great person" leadership myth with its superstitious tendency to ascribe organizational success to "a" leader rather than to all those who work to make an enterprise function well.

If avoiding the temptations to hubris were easy, from a spiritual perspective there would be no need for God, grace or spiritual enlightenment. There would be no such saying as "power corrupts."

There is no cure for temptations to arrogance and dominance as an affliction in the leadership suite any more then there is a cure for the common cold. The temptations will always be there, just as "sweets" are always in front of the dieter. Therefore, this reflection is offered so that we can be alert to the seductive dynamics and circumstances that lead into hubris. It is the role of the spiritual person to stand shoulder to shoulder with all individuals of good will in defense of a more human way of doing things (Lakeland, 2003).

I am reminded of a story told at a spiritual retreat for business leaders in which I recently participated.

> *His daughter who is asking a child's many questions pesters a father: "Why is the sky blue? How do birds fly?" Etc. Impatient, the father tears up a map of the world from his current newspaper and tells his daughter to put the world back together before asking more questions. In a very short time the child returns and asks: "Why do dog's have four legs?" The father is amazed that the child is back, and asked if and how she put the world back together so soon. She replied: "There was a picture of a person on the back of your puzzle. I simply put the person back together and the world fell into place."*

References

Boal, KB (2004). *Strategic Leadership, Organizational Learning and Network Ties.* Paper delivered at the International Institute for Management Development, Lausanne, Switzerland.

Brady, B (2003) *Christian Love.* Washington, D.C.: Georgetown University Press.

Brown, AD (1997). Narcissism, Identity and legitimacy. *Academy of Management Review*, 22(3), 643–686.

Cantalamessa, R (2003). *Come, Creator Spirit; Meditations on the Veni Creator.* Collegeville, MN: The Liturgical Press.

Cavanaugh, G, B Hanson, K Hanson and J Hinojoso, Toward a spirituality for the contemporary organization: implications for work, family and society. In *Spiritual Intelligence at Work: Meaning, Metaphor, and Morals.* ML Pava (ed.), pp. 111–138. San Francisco: Elsiver JAI Ltd.

Chief Executive Leadership Institute (May, 1997). Hosted by Professor Jeffrey Sonnenfeld, Mission Bay, Pebble Beach Ca: Yale University.

DSMMD-*Diagnostic and Statistical Manual of Mental Disorders* (1994). 4th ed. p. 308.8. Washington, DC: American Psychiatric Association.

Delbecq, AL (2000). Christian spirituality and contemporary business leadership. In *Work and Spirit: A Reader of New Spiritual Paradigms for Organizations.* J Bibberman and M Witty (eds.), pp. 175–180. Scranton, PA: University of Scranton Press.

Delbecq, AL and J McGee (2003). Business as a calling. In *Business, Religion and Spirituality: A New Synthesis,* OF Williams (ed.), pp. 94–110. South Bend, IN: University of Notre Dame Press.

Delbecq, AL, E Liebert, J Mostyn, PC Nutt and G Walter (2004). Discernment and strategic decision making, reflections for a spirituality of organizational leadership. In *Spiritual Intelligence at Work: Meaning, Metaphor, and Morals.* ML Pava (ed.), pp. 139–174. San Francisco: Elsevier JAI Ltd.

Delbecq, A (2004). Business executives and prayer: how a core spiritual discipline is expressed in the life of contemporary organizational leaders. Proceedings of CIRAN IV, Montreal CA [electronically published www.notreprojet.org].

Finkelsetin, S (2003). *Why Smart Executives Fail.* New York, Portfolio: Penguin Group.

Gregory The Great, ST (1978). *Pastoral Care.* Translated and annotated by SJ Henry Davis. Mahwah, NJ: Newman Press.

Haughey, SJ (2002). *Housing Heaven's Fire: The Challenge of Holiness.* Chicago: Loyola Press.

Heider, J (2003). *The Tao of Leadership.* New York: Bantam Books, p. 45.

Johnson, W (1995). *Mystical Theology: The Science of Love.* New York: Maryknoll.

Kouzes, JM and BZ Posner (1993). *Credibility: How Leaders Gain and Lose It, Why People Demand It.* San Francisco: Jossey Bass.

Lakeland, P (2003). *The Liberation of the Laity.* p. 247. New York: Continuum.

Mcintosh, MA (2004). *Discernment and Truth: The Spirituality and Theology of Knowledge.* pp. 82–124. New York: The Crossroads Publishing Co.

Mcknight, M (June 1999) *Conference on Executive Leadership.* Flagstaff Az: Northern Arizona University.

Naughton, M (2004). *Business as a Vocation,* St. Paul MN: University of St. Thomas [Electronically published papers from Protestant and Catholic Scholars available on the university web site of the John Ryan Institute of Catholic Social Thought; www.stthomas.edu].

Nutt, PC (2003). *Why Decisions Fail: The Blunders and Traps that Lead to Decision Debacles,* San Francisco, CA.: Barrett-Koehler.

Rohr, R (2003). *Everything Belongs: The Gift of Contemplative Prayer* (revised edition) New York: Crossroad Publishing Co.

Rodewalt, F (2001). The social mind of the narcissist: Cognitive and motivational aspects in interpersonal self-construction. In *The Social Mind: Cognitive and Motivational Aspects of Interpersonal Behavior.* JP Forgas K Williams and L Wheeler (eds.), pp. 177–198. New York: Cambridge University Press.

Santa Clara Conference (2004). Dialog between theologians, executives and management scholars on how a Christian organization would positively deviate from best practices.

Ware, BK (1979). *The Orthodox Way.* (Revised Edition). Crestwood, NY: St. Vladimir's Seminary Press.

Zagano, P (1999). Jean Vanier. *Twentieth-Century Apostles*, pp. 121–146. Collegeville MN: Liturgical Press.

Section Two

THE VIRTUOUS ORGANIZATION AND ORDINARY TIMES

Section Editor: Robert D. Marx

In this section, authors discuss the role of organizational virtues and virtuousness during ordinary times. At this point in our history, bombarded daily by instantaneous media coverage and global Internet accessibility one might wonder whether there remain moments which can truly be thought of as "ordinary". Ongoing terrorist attacks around the globe, seemingly random mass murders in homes, schools, and businesses, venues once thought to be safe havens, and increasing threats to the environment which supports our very life on this planet make it harder to maintain the stable rhythm and the daily routine of "ordinary times." And yet, despite reports of such alarming atrocities occurring every day somewhere in the world, we must still get up each morning, kiss our loved ones goodbye and continue to function within our own organizations. They are typically not in the crisis mode described in detail in the previous section, nor are they experiencing the bounty of exemplary times to be addressed in the following section, where there are more than enough exceptional opportunities to go around.

Sandwiched between crisis and exemplary times are the, often overlooked, ordinary times. How organizations take advantage of opportunities to employ virtuous behavior during ordinary times may significantly impact how effectively they will perform when they are faced with challenges of a crisis or flush with the abundance of exemplary times.

Each chapter in the ordinary times section views the role of virtuousness from a different perspective, from the individual to the organization and finally across cultures and toward resolution of global challenges.

Beginning with the individual, Manz, Marx, Neal and Manz examine the role of language in eliciting the private sources of virtuous behavior of individuals. Such sources often are based on religious, spiritual, or ethical traditions that have their own private, exclusive language. The authors discovered in their classroom testing ground that the language of virtues, for example courage and compassion, offered a more public, inclusive language that honored the individual origins of virtuousness, yet allowed for translation of these virtues into sources of action that can be implemented by the organization as a whole.

Youseff and Luthans then examine how to stem the doubts of researchers who question whether the presence of virtuousness in an organization can be assessed using the traditional measures of employee productivity. They introduce the concept of psychological capital as a resource developed during ordinary times which can be a catalyst for expressions of virtuousness especially during crisis situations.

Hofstede's paper expands on his well-known four dimensions of national culture and examines how a new dimension evolved when comparing Eastern cultures and religions with their Western counterparts. Western perspectives look for "Truth" as revealed by our religions and scientific frameworks which seek the best, or the correct answer. The Eastern perspective pursues "Virtue", which includes any methods that people can use to improve themselves, without requiring adherence to a single philosophy or religion.

The last two chapters entertain the enormous opportunities available to not-for-profit social sector firms and global multinationals to make positive contributions to society originating from organizational virtues.

In Joseph Maciariello's interview with Peter Drucker, the last published interview before his death in 2005, Drucker challenges social sector and not-for-profit organizations to improve their poor leadership and management practices which interfere with their efforts to engage in virtuous activities, while at the same time finding hope in the growing trend for "bright young person(s) on their way up" to engage in socially responsible volunteer activities.

In a fitting conclusion to the ordinary times section, Nancy Adler expands the reach of organizational virtue to the realm of global partnerships. In particular, she addresses the possible actions that private corporations can take to improve the conditions for finding global solutions to abuses of human rights, environmental protection, and ultimately creating world peace.

Taken together these essays make concrete recommendations for individuals and organizations to take advantage of ordinary times. In doing so, they may become better equipped at applying their virtuousness to the challenges that arise during a crisis, within the abundance of exemplary periods and throughout the relative stability of the daily routine of ordinary times.

Chapter Five

THE LANGUAGE OF VIRTUES: TOWARD AN INCLUSIVE APPROACH FOR INTEGRATING SPIRITUALITY IN MANAGEMENT EDUCATION

Karen P. Manz

Hartford Seminary

Robert D. Marx and Charles C. Manz

University of Massachusetts Amherst

Judi A. Neal

International Center for Spirit at Work

The virtuous organization is made up of people whose virtuous behavior emanates from a rich diversity of sources, each with its own language and beliefs. The language of virtues is suggested as a means to: (1) harness the power of each individual's unique reasons to act in a virtuous manner; and (2) translate these ideas into an inclusive public language that can be expressed in a public classroom or corporation. Tested in the classroom and the organization, virtues such as compassion, integrity, and courage offer terms that transcend source differences and help organizations discuss how the presence of such activity in the organization can support employee satisfaction and the bottom line. One activity found to be useful in making this transition is an exercise designed to show how spiritual or virtuous, values and business values can be reconciled.

The number of faculties and universities who have courses and programs on spirituality in the workplace has increased dramatically in the past few years. In 2002, there were over 44 universities documented to have spirituality in the workplace courses and/or programs in six countries (Neal, 2002). In 1999, the Academy of Management approved the formation of a new Interest Group called "Management, Spirituality, and Religion"; early 2008 membership stood at 686 members. This approval signals a dramatic shift in the field of management by legitimizing spirituality and religion as appropriate and valuable fields of study and teaching in relationship to management.

Scholastic inquiry and academic writing within management education has also evolved along similar lines. In 2000, the *Journal of Management Education* published a special issue on "Spirituality in Contemporary Work: Its Place, Space, and Role in Organization and Management" which focused on spirituality in management education (Dehler and Neal, 2000). Two special issues of the *Journal of Change Management* offered the latest thinking on empirical research on spirituality in organizations (Neal and Biberman, 2004). The *Journal of Management, Spirituality, and Religion,* posted its first call for papers in 2003 and published its first issue in 2004.

As the new field of spirituality in the workplace emerges, there is both creativity and chaos. Management educators who are incorporating concepts and practices related to spirituality in the classroom have few guidelines to follow. Many draw upon their own personal histories as a base for understanding, expressing and exploring the interface of spirituality and work. They may draw upon religious or philosophical traditions, personal experience (i.e., perceptual preferences, feelings, actual events which serve as filters for one's value system) as well as seek knowledge from other established fields where spirituality has been researched such as psychology (Emmons and Paloutzian, 2003; Miller, 2003); higher education (Astin and Astin, 1999; Tisdell 2003; Chickering *et al.*, 2005); and health/medicine (Koenig *et al.*, 2000; Chiu *et al.*, 2004). At the same time, educators recognize that a broad, open approach is necessary for discussing spirituality within the diverse audience that is frequently found in a classroom of a public college or university or in corporate training contexts.

The first key issue that management educators face when teaching about spirituality in the workplace is what language to use that will be inclusive of the personal perspectives on spirituality to be found in the typical classroom. Each of us has struggled with this issue in our own teaching over many years and across a vast array of teaching contexts including public and private institutions of higher education.[1] We will introduce the concept of "virtues" as an effective language for bridging the rich diversity of individual spiritual sources with the necessity of creating a collective, inclusive language that yields beneficial communications and ultimately meaningful organizational practices.

A simple model for extracting a public language and learning exercises we have found useful for discussing spirituality in the workplace will be presented. Finally, the implications of inclusive/bridging language will be considered in relation to the need for an expanded learning paradigm.

Defining Spirituality in the Workplace

Before the early 1990s, there were few publications in the management literature that mentioned spirituality in connection with work or business, except perhaps, the writings of Robert Greenleaf on Servant Leadership (cf. 1977, 1998). However, in the last 10 years or so with the dramatic increase in interest in the exploration of "spirituality" as an important variable in understanding management and organizations,

---

[1] Over approximately the past 10 years, members of this author team have developed course work in the emerging field of spirituality and work life and have presented it through the following formats: 1. modules within their undergraduate, MBA or doctoral courses (i.e., MBA Organizational Behavior, Leadership doctoral seminar); 2. undergraduate, MBA , MA and doctoral credit courses specifically in this field; 3. non-credit courses and workshops (including in-class, on-line and teleconference); and 4. presentations to executive, academic and general audiences throughout the United States and internationally.

attention has been focused towards identifying a standardized and operational definition.

The Latin origin of the word spirit is *spirare*, meaning "to breathe." In its most basic sense, spirit is the essence of our aliveness. Scott defines spirit as "That which is traditionally believed to be the vital principle or animating force within living beings; that which constitutes one's unseen intangible being; the real sense or significance of something" (Scott, 1994, p. 64).

Spirituality has been variously defined as: "the basic feeling of being connected with one's complete self, others and the entire universe" in a common purpose (Mitroff and Denton, 1999, p. 83); "an animating life force, an energy that inspires one toward certain ends or purposes that go beyond self" (McKnight, 1984, p. 142); and "a continuing search for meaning and purpose in life; an appreciation for the depth of life; the expanse of the universe, and natural forces which operate; a personal belief system" (Myers, 1990, p. 11).

Based on interviews and a survey, Mitroff and Denton (1999, p. 23) arrived at the following seven elements of spirituality:

1. Spirituality is highly individual and intensely personal. You don't have to be religious to be spiritual.
2. Spirituality is the basic belief that there is a supreme power, a being, a force, whatever you call it, that governs the entire universe. There is a purpose for everything and everyone.
3. Everything is interconnected with everything else. Everything affects and is affected by everything else.
4. Spirituality is the feeling of this interconnectedness. Spirituality is being in touch with it.
5. Spirituality is also the feeling that no matter how bad things get, they will always work out somehow. There is a guiding plan that governs all lives.
6. We are basically put here to do good. One must strive to produce products and services that serve all of humankind.
7. Spirituality is inextricably connected with caring, hope, kindness, love and optimism. Spirituality is the basic faith in the existence of these things.

All of the above definitions include references to either personal beliefs and feelings, world view statements (i.e., there is a supreme power that governs the universe), and/or references to meaning and purpose (i.e., we are put here to do good). The personal characterizations and broadness of concepts highlight the difficulties of generating a universal definition of spirituality.

"Spirituality in the workplace" is as ineffable and difficult to define as the word "spirituality." It is complex and multi-faceted. One definition attempts to describe several of these facets:

> Spirituality in the workplace is about people seeing their work as a spiritual path, as an opportunity to grow personally and to contribute to society in a meaningful way. It is about learning to be more caring and compassionate with fellow employees, with bosses, with subordinates and customers. It is about integrity, being true to oneself, and telling the truth to others. Spirituality in the workplace can refer to an individual's attempts to live his or her values more fully in the workplace. Or it can refer to the ways in which organizations structure themselves to support the spiritual growth of employees. (Neal, 1998)

Gibbons (1999, p. 14) in his critical analysis of the field of spirituality in the workplace used this definition: "A journey toward integration of work and spirituality, for individuals and organizations, which provides direction, wholeness and connectedness at work."

It is fairly common for people to interchange the terms "spirituality" and "religion." This often leads to resistance in discussions about spirituality in the workplace because some students fear that you are going to be talking about religion in the workplace. Hawley (1993) describes religion as institutional, based on a prescribed set of dogma and beliefs, and *collective* (our italics); spirituality is individualized.

Religion is an important source of spirituality for many people, but that it is not the only source. In a study of leaders in the spirituality in the workplace movement, Schaefer and Darling (1997) found that about 80% of the people who identified themselves as deeply committed to their spirituality were not aligned with any particular religion.

Creating an Inclusive Approach for Discussing Spirituality in the Management Classroom

Management educators who include the concept of spirituality and work in their academic courses and/or professional seminars face a significant obstacle. Spirituality as defined by Mitroff and Denton (1999) is "highly individual and intensely personal." How then, can the management educator acknowledge each idiosyncratic expression of spirituality elicited from class participants and yet discuss this topic in a language that is inclusive of all points of view?

We believe that it is necessary for each individual in the public classroom, including the instructor, to recognize his or her understanding of spirituality so that a more inclusive approach for discussing spirituality and "spirituality in the workplace" can be developed. This can be done through various learning exercises. In such exercises the instructor and students begin to become aware of how religious and/or philosophical tradition(s) have informed their world view and the contexts of spiritual language and its expression.

Students can become more cognizant of the strengths and profound experiences their faith tradition or life philosophy has provided for them. Also, they may become more sensitive to exclusionary beliefs or practices which may be mandated by a community of practice (i.e., family, workplace, religious) which can present impediments to the group if carried over into the learning arena of the public classroom.

There are several key considerations relating to language and the need for establishing an inclusive learning climate. As shown in Figure 1, we will begin our focus on the instructor's orientation, the student's personal language, and the need for an inclusive working definition for spirituality.

1. **The Instructor's Orientation**

   The instructor establishes and models an inclusive *openness* toward verbal expression of all perspectives about spirituality and *spirituality at work*.

2. **The Students' Personal Language**

   The instructor facilitates a discussion with students that recongnises personal (private) language by

   A. Eliciting, recognizing and honoring individual definitions and understanding of spirituality;
   B. Giving attention throughout this process to the public/private and inclusive/exclusive context dimensions of language about spirituality and spirituality at work.

3. **An Inclusive Working Definition of Spirituality**

   The instructor develops from class input (or provides depending upon time constraints) an inclusive working definition of spirituality (acknowledging and accommodating) for the purpose of classroom discussion.

Fig. 1: Establishing an inclusive environment for discussing spirituality and spirituality at work in the management classroom.

We suggest that the management educator in a public classroom considers these distinctions if a discussion of spirituality at work is to yield meaningful learning and organizational outcomes.

The instructor's orientation

Before a fruitful discussion of spirituality at work can take place, the instructor must have a clear orientation from which to work. First, the instructor should be able to recognize the unique language that each student employs to describe his or her spiritual sources. This would include religious dogma, rituals, and practices that form the basis of many persons' spiritual identities. For others, there are spiritual, but not religious-based, sources such as nature, medita-tion, pacifism — all of which inspire spiritual thought and language. Many students may subscribe to a combination of religious and spir-itual sources. Finally, there are those who reject any claim to spiri-tuality as a driving force and base their philosophy of life on the tenets of ethics, economics, science, humanism, and other concep-tual frameworks operating outside of the realm of spirituality as defined above.

The instructor's orientation needs to honor the private language used by each student to describe one's spiritual and/or non-spiritual life experiences. Acknowledging and accommodating the personal language used by individuals to express their spiritual origins is an essential prerequisite, we believe, for evolving the language to an inclusive perspective for class discussion.

An inclusive orientation is characterized by acknowledgment of diverse perspectives on spirituality regardless of the origin or source. It emphasizes the unique language of a religious, spiritual, or philo-sophical source. Lastly, it embraces the detail that comprises any per-sonal spiritual language, ritual or practice.

The students' personal language

For many students in management classes and corporate seminars, the connection of spirituality to the workplace is an unusual and some-times uncomfortable alliance. Long-standing American norms about the "separation of church and state" as well as perceived conflicts between different religious and spiritual traditions can dampen efforts to converse openly about such issues in a public forum such as a class or seminar.

The language employed to facilitate such conversations must be carefully chosen to accomplish the ultimate goal of enhancing positive workplace actions. When the instructor can make the case that one's personal spiritual, religious, or philosophy of life values and beliefs can transcend the personal/private world of the individual and be brought to bear on the problems facing modern organizations, the initial hesitation of participants can be softened. Therefore, it is also important to consider the ground rules for the conversation.

When the instructor can elicit numerous examples of participants' personal/private sources in their own words, the first step toward evolving a public, inclusive language has occurred. At this point there is no attempt to evaluate, diminish, promote, or marginalize any specific sources of beliefs and values. As these personal/private sources are uttered in the public forum of the classroom or seminar, the diversity of the language used by the students can be examined for religious, spiritual, and scientific or philosophical origin.

The management classroom, with a few exceptions, is likely to include some individuals with strong religious backgrounds which have a profound influence on their perceptions of spirituality and how it might be interpreted and applied in life and at work. For example, a highly religious individual who bases his or her behavior on a religious source may or may not accept individual religious or life philosophy differences in others (classmates or co-workers). There is no attempt to hide the source of one's beliefs and values nor does one dismiss the sources of the others in the class. For the management educator as well as the students who have a religious-based spirituality, the issue of authenticity is at stake. Religious exclusive language speaks to activities that are both solitary and communal which comprise the religious experience including prayer, celebration, holidays, and service. It is in the details and connections between these activities that the religious exclusive bond is shared by like-minded members. At the same time, the religious exclusive language may not so much concern itself with ecumenical consensus but rather reflect an inward focus as a religion of choice for a particular individual or group. This exclusivity is understood as appropriate and necessary in the life of individuals as they learn and repeat the activities that help give meaning to their lives.

The instructor who has met the challenge of including the language of many religious-based notions of spirituality must then be prepared to include with equal voice the numerous varieties of non-religious spiritual sources. The diverse management classroom is typically comprised of both individuals whose spirituality is rooted in a belief in God and religion, and others who embrace spiritual sources that are inspired by a cause or philosophy such as preservation of the planet or contemplative practices.

As with religious sources of spirituality, the roots may run deep with the lifestyles of individuals tightly connected to a spiritual concern (i.e., meditation, ecology, world peace, or reducing racism) and that may contain exclusive components when enacted with others who share the same purpose. These perspectives also need to be transitioned toward inclusiveness to affect a consensus with other non-religious as well as with the earlier mentioned religious sources of spirituality.

Religious and non-religious exclusive language is appropriate and useful in some educational settings such as parochial schools where participants have chosen to focus exclusively on a single way of expressing their religiosity or an analogous institute which teaches from a doctrine based upon respect for nature. In most classroom and workplace settings, however, such an exclusive stance is more effective in private or in public with others of the same spiritual or religious emphasis.

An inclusive working definition of spirituality

The issue of inclusiveness has many points of juncture in the classroom and requires an openness to other perspectives and the "personal/public" language issues around beliefs, values and expression of the instructor and students. The personal language issue, however, is only partly addressed unless an inclusive working definition of spirituality is offered for use in the class discussions. Thus a key step can be to create a working definition based on class members' input as indicated in the following classroom exercise.

Brainstorming the relationship between spirituality and religion: the purpose of this exercise is to make language the first issue of any discussion about spirituality in the workplace, and to explore the shared meanings of words like "spirituality" and "religion," as well as to make it safe to have different viewpoints, values, and beliefs. This exercise is often used just before a lecture on the emerging field of spirituality in the workplace.

To create an open and inclusive context, it is helpful to preface the lecture by saying that even if the students do not have a personal interest in the topic, they should know that about 25% of the workforce considers themselves spiritual (Ray and Anderson, 2000), and that more than 95% of Americans believe in God or the transcendent (Conlin, 1999), which underscores that this is an important issue for management.

The instructor begins by stating to the class that there is some confusion in organizations about spirituality in the workplace because many people are concerned that we are talking about religion. So, it is important to understand the differences in terms. The word "Spirituality" is written on one blackboard or flip chart, and the word "Religion" on another; brainstorming can then begin. As each person calls out a word or phrase, ask which column it goes in to. At first the words appear quite clear, but quickly words that are not so clearly delineated, like "community" or "love" may begin to arise. Allow ample time for clarification. Students should be encouraged to discuss and debate these words to find out what people mean. Usually someone will say, "I think they go in both columns." So then a third category of terms is created that fits both spirituality and religion. By the end of this brainstorming exercise, people are more comfortable with the idea of spirituality, because they have helped define it. Then a discussion can begin on what spirituality in the workplace might mean, and what it might look like.

Students and workshop participants get very engaged in the brainstorming, and the energy tends to be pretty high and positive. Frequently, following this exercise, students will say something like, "You know, I was really worried when I heard we were going to be talking about spirituality in the workplace. I was afraid this was going to be some kind of proselytizing session. Now I see that this is a very worthwhile topic, and I would like to learn more."

This exercise has been used in undergraduate and graduate courses on management, leadership, diversity, and current issues. It has also been used in executive retreats and at business and academic conferences.

Another alternative to brainstorming for a definition is to draw from published (and validated) research definitions which allow the instructor to continue modeling an inclusive stance in perspective and language. An example could be the following definition of spirituality: "Spirituality is the personal quest for understanding answers to ultimate questions about life, about meaning, and about relationship to the sacred or .... transcendent, which may (or may not) lead to or arise from the development of religious rituals and the formation of community" (Koenig *et al.*, 2000, p. 18).

The objective is to find a definition that allows for a broad context (i.e., including questions about life) with a broad focus (e.g., addressing meaning and relationships) which gives space for individual characterization (is inclusive) and which has an open-ended foundation based on "sense making." That is, the individual can "fill in the blanks" from his or her own life experience including whether it is religiously informed by a community of practice, or not.

Definitions alone, however, will not be sufficient to help well-intended faculty or consultants traverse the delicate minefield of mis-cues that threaten to sabotage the potentially positive outcomes of including the topic of spirituality at work in the management class-room. Care also needs to be given so that the non-spiritual class member is included as a full participant in any consensus that is reached and not feel marginalized by an instructor who has introduced the concept of spirituality at work because he or she feels it has some potential to improve workplace effectiveness. The experiences of individuals who do not espouse spiritual sources for their workplace behavior need to be legitimized (as they may comprise a significant portion of the group).

We have found it useful to engage many in this category by shifting the focus to different values or virtues that may be expressed in the work-place, but may also be seen as originating for the individual from an ethical/legal/scientific source rather than primarily a spiritual one. Thus the organizational outcomes that are agreed upon by a consensus of participants can be based on both spiritual and non-spiritual origins.

Spirituality at Work and Virtues

Kinjerski and Skrypnek (2004) identify alignment as one of the characteristics of spirituality at work as measured by descriptions from professionals in the field. "Alignment refers to the fit or congruity among our values and beliefs with the work we do, the people we work with, and ultimately the organization we work for."

In an organization that encourages the expression of spirituality, the private spiritual sources may be extremely diverse, but their public expression is aligned to the "common good through the expression of positive outcomes, creativity, honesty, trust, personal fulfillment, and commitment" (Krishnakumar and Neck, 2002). Once we enter the workplace there is a necessity to move from the exclusivity of one's spiritual roots to the inclusivity of "encouraging people to speak openly about their spiritual ideas but then helping them relate these ideas to the company's values" (Thompson, 2000). The following classroom exercise is offered to help students envision the connection between their spirituality and their work places.

Spiritual lifeline: one of the ways to create an inclusive environment and to help students feel more comfortable using their own personal language around spirituality is to offer them the opportunity to tell stories about their lives. The spiritual lifeline exercise asks students to reflect on significant events in their spiritual life and their work life (Neal, 1997). Often these two parts of life are kept separate. By doing this exercise and then talking about it with a small group of people, students begin to see the relevance of their own personal and spiritual experiences for their work and career.

By creating both a spiritual path and career path lifelines students are enabled to study how these parts of their lives may overlap. The exercise requires one large sheet of flip chart paper and at least 5–6 different colored magic markers or crayons for each person. It normally takes 1–2 hours, depending on the size of the group and the amount of time allowed for processing, roughly divided up as follows:

a)   Ten minutes for a brief lecturette on the stages of the spiritual journey at work (for example, see Neal *et al.*, 1999).

b)   Twenty-five minutes for each person to symbolically portray, on a lifeline, the critical spiritual events and critical work events in their lives. Students are asked to use only symbols rather than words. (Note: artistic ability can actually be a hindrance in this exercise, because artists may spend too much time on the aesthetics instead of their own unfolding life story.) Symbols should be kept simple and identifiable enough to know what significant event they stand for. If there is time, students can also portray where they think their spiritual path and career path may be going in the future. (Note: this part of the exercise works best when people can go to someplace where they can be quietly reflective and alone, ideally in or near nature).

c)   Twenty-five minutes to more than an hour for group sharing. If the group is small, every one can share their drawings with the entire group. Create an environment of deeply respectful listening. If the group is large, ask people to form groups of 2–3 people and allow them at least 20–25 minutes to share their drawings with each other. At the end of this time, ask for two or three volunteers to share their drawings with the whole group.

The spiritual lifeline exercise has been used with undergraduate and graduate students, and it tends to work better with older, more mature students who have had some working experience. Younger undergraduates tend to be more uncomfortable talking about their spiritual experiences in the classroom setting. It is best to use this exercise after some level of trust and openness has been created in the classroom, perhaps mid-semester or later.

Management educators can begin to take advantage of the positive impact that the introduction of spirituality at work can have on organizational productivity and individual well-being by emphasizing the delicate process of relating individual spiritual engagements to aligned organizational outcomes and avoiding the extremes of trivializing spirituality on the one hand and dictating spiritual practices on the other.

One way to accomplish these ends is by connecting with individual and organizational values. For example, organizations have long recognized the central role of business values such as profitability, efficiency, and control. By introducing "spirituality at work" into the classroom the related concept of virtues (e.g., transcendent values such as compassion and integrity) can serve as a potent bridge for inclusive public discussion of both business and spiritual concerns.

Recent research, writing, and teaching have specifically explored the role of virtues in organizational contexts for establishing a more balanced and holistic orientation toward work life (Marx *et al.*, 1999; Manz *et al.*, 2001; Cameron *et al.*, 2003; Neal and Biberman, 2004; Kessler and Bailey, 2007). A virtues "lens" offers promise for counterbalancing the more usual dominant focus on profit, efficiency, and rationality as illustrated in the next classroom exercise.

Linking spiritual virtues with business values: this exercise evolved naturally from a common theme that emerged from class discussions about virtues (Marx *et al.*, 1999). While virtues offer a blueprint for ideal ethical and moral workplace conduct, the realities of the market are often largely in opposition to these lofty intentions. For example, performance and the bottom line can conflict with integrity and compassion. This consistent pattern enabled us to design this exercise to help participants explore these issues, and then experiment with ways to reconcile them.

First, participants are asked to identify a virtue that has proven particularly problematic for them to enact in their own work setting. Six posters, each naming one of a core set of virtues (for example, compassion, justice, or wisdom) are affixed to the walls of the room in different physical locations. Participants gather near the virtue of their choice and are asked to form a subgroup to discuss their personal examples with one another and create a five-minute role play which clearly depicts an example of the dilemma posed by business values in conflict with their chosen virtue. Their role play can be an adaptation of one of the individual examples or an amalgamation of several. In small classes participants are asked to choose a "second choice" virtue so that no group has less than three role players.

Each group performs their role play for the other virtue groups and then facilitates a discussion among the remaining participants focused on how their selected virtue and business value might be reconciled. The exercise concludes with each group performing a revised version of their role play that includes ways organizations might modify their behavior to infuse virtuousness into their practices.

This exercise has the advantage of examining the integration of individual values with organizational outcomes. Motivation to behave in virtuous ways can emanate from religious and/or philosophically based perspectives. This is an important consideration for helping many to move beyond a legal or policy enforcement climate as the primary impetus for motivating and sustaining ethical behavior in organizations.

The role-plays are clearly understood by participants even though in their attempt to be theatrical they tend to exaggerate the behavior of targeted individuals and company policies. Because the feedback about the role plays and the recommendations for enhancing organizational virtuousness come from informed employees of the organization and tend to be realistic for the company's culture, the potential for follow-through is high.

This exercise has also been effective in the brief workshop format, where time constraints make it impossible to examine individual differences in definitions of spirituality. By immersing participants immediately into organizational realities through the inclusive and bridging language which is used to describe the expression of virtues at work, the facilitator can take advantage of the perceived tension between the perception of real vs. ideal expression of virtues at work. Invariably, this activity engages participants so that when further sessions on this topic are scheduled, motivation is high to reveal the more private, personal definitions of spirituality which motivates the diversity of individuals who comprise an organization.

This exercise has been used effectively in corporate and academic settings and in numerous formats from two-hour seminars to 14-week semester-long courses. It has been most effective in professional development programs where all participants are employed in the same organization. When used with undergraduates, they might be asked to think about a part-time job that they held over a period of time or a job they held briefly which seemed lacking in virtuous behaviors.

Virtues in Organizations

One of the most notable recent developments in the pursuit of better understanding of management and organizational knowledge is the area of Positive Organizational Scholarship (POS) (Cameron *et al.*, 2003). This new movement was inspired by pioneering work in the field of psychology under the umbrella term "Positive Psychology." Essentially this perspective calls for a shift away from focusing on what is wrong with people — neurosis, psychosis, and various other forms of psychological dysfunction — toward studying and learning from what is right with people. By examining strengths, capabilities, healthy and functional attributes and behavior the potential is established for learning what might be pursued, emulated, and developed as opposed to avoided, treated, and attacked.

This shift represents a dramatic departure from the norm. Indeed, Seligman (2002) estimated that over the last half century 99% of research in psychology focused on dysfunction and attempts to establish normal function. Under the leadership of prominent psychologists such as Seligman and Csikszentmihalyi (2000) positive psychology has emerged as a reaction to the preoccupation with what is wrong with people. Similarly, organizational research has largely focused on attempts to study and correct manager, human resource, and organizational weaknesses (Luthans *et al.*, 2002).

By extrapolating the logic of positive psychology to the organization sciences the possibility of learning important positive factors and principles for guiding effective organizational behavior and management practice is created. For example, some of the more interesting recent POS research has examined organizational virtuousness, a concept that we believe gets at the heart of workplace spirituality. According to Cameron *et al.* (2004) virtuousness relates to what organizations and people strive to be when they are "at their very best." Marcic (1997) argues that virtues form the philosophical and spiritual underpinnings for many of the concepts in the new paradigm of management. Virtuousness has been connected in the literature to a variety of concepts such as meaning, purpose, ennoblement, flourishing and even health and happiness (Becker, 1992; Lipman-Blumen and Levitt, 1999; Myers 2000a, b). Further, Cameron *et al.* (2004) conducted a study of 18 organizations and found significant relationships between virtuousness in organizations, which they concluded created buffering effects against trauma as well as positive amplifying effects of desirable attributes, and perceived and objective measures of performance.

The implications of POS for what goes on in the management classroom are immense. It provides a potent perspective that is consistent with much of the emphasis of workplace spirituality without religious or exclusionary overtones. It can mean the difference between students solely focusing on analyzing theories and cases to determine what is wrong with an organization and its various elements to eliminate or fix them, as opposed to also studying, discussing and exploring virtuous aspects of organizations and focusing on what is desirable, healthy and effective and should be honored, nurtured, and supported. Instead of centering learning predominantly on solving problems (and learning what not to do) the focus would shift to what is exceptional, optimal and worthy of emulation. Outstanding organizations and leaders who exemplify these principles are the focus of the next classroom exercise.

Role models/cases: public leaders and spirituality at work: use written cases and/or videos that center on visible leaders and how their leadership represents spiritual virtues at work. The compelling story of Aaron Feuerstein, owner of the fire ravaged Malden Mills, who paid his employees salaries and benefits even though many could not work, is a case in point (Manz *et al.*, 2001).

While much of Feuerstein's largesse was rooted in his adherence to Orthodox Judaism, which requires owners to treat their workers fairly, he never imposed his private religious dogma on his employees. What was essential in his dealings with employees was the outcome (humane and generous treatment) not the religious or philosophical source of the behavior. To put it simply, Aaron Feuerstein, an orthodox Jew who prays several times a day in Hebrew, the language of his faith, appears at his factory daily with a spiritual mandate to treat his workers with generosity and respect. His language is exclusive at home and inclusive at work. His behavior is consistent. He is authentic in his honoring of his religious traditions but he is inclusive in not imposing the specifics of his faith on his company. Management educators must examine this distinction with great care lest they create an atmosphere of exclusivity rather than inclusivity in the educational setting.

A variety of other cases, such as CEO's and companies in the mold of Herman Miller or Timberland, can be obtained from broadcasts and publications. Other sources for identifying exemplary leaders or organizations include recipients of the International Spirit at Work Award (www.spiritatwork.org) or companies that are profiled by the Social Venture Network or Businesses for Social Responsibility.

The role model/video case has been an excellent exercise for beginning an introduction to spirituality, virtues and work, whether it be a short, half-day seminar or a semester-long course (Marx *et al.*, 2008). News broadcasts or feature films that showcase individuals who are able to acknowledge their own spiritual origins and yet be inclusive of the spiritual sources of others in their organization seem to provoke the most interesting discussions. Video clips or written cases offer participants concrete examples that students can respond to initially without revealing much about their own spiritual sources. The case/clip also works well with large audiences where participants can first "observe" an example. When followed by a small group discussion eliciting their reaction to the case, participation is likely to be high. Large group report out can both demonstrate the diversity of perceptions that people in the small groups have regarding this concept as well as represent some commonality in opinion to build upon. When the clip is properly chosen, it can energize subsequent activities by beginning to define the characteristics of spirituality at work but leaving the door open for further elaboration as more examples are encountered.

Ultimately, management education should address both solving problems and learning from what is right about organizations and its members. To date, however, the focus appears to have been predominantly on the former. We believe that POS offers a viable and important means for helping to create a perspective and practice of greater integrity in the workplace.

Conclusions and Implications

There is an increasing recognition that spirituality and one's aligned values are important variables in organizational life, and in the study and practice of management. As a result, a growing number of management educators are incorporating discussions of spirituality in the workplace into their classrooms. Because of the newness of this field and the lack of experience with teaching about this topic, it is very important for the management educator to pay attention to issues of language when dealing with spirituality.

In classroom and corporate programs, we have observed the versatility of the language of virtues to be inclusive of the many constituencies that comprise the management classroom. In several years of working with virtues as a public expression of personal sources of positive organizational activity, we found it to be inclusive of nearly all religious, spiritual and other philosophical (i.e., scientific or economic) private language sources.

Part of the challenge that the emerging area of spirituality in the workplace brings to contemporary business thinking and learning is to consider ways that more traditional business values can be reconciled with spiritual virtues without excluding students based on differing backgrounds and beliefs. Studying and reflecting on the possible contribution of more fully emphasizing virtues at work — or in the language of POS, what is right in the workplace — provides a rich context for learning in the management classroom. POS provides an inclusive lens for considering many management and organizational issues and it offers potential for not only furthering management thought but ultimately contributing to the quality of work life for organization members and employee and organizational effectiveness.

In light of the above and as management educators, we believe there is a great need to focus pedagogical thinking in several new areas. Some key questions come to mind. What if we believed that the concept of "spirituality" really added value to our understanding and practice of management? How might our approach to teaching change? Would the content be different? The process? What would we do to nurture the spirits of our students, or our own spirit for that matter? If we truly take a Positive Organizational Scholarship approach to management education, what kind of case studies would we write? How would our lectures change? If we focused more on the acknowledgement and development of virtues in students, how would we evaluate them — or would we? We are moving toward a paradigm of management education that values the whole person — body, mind, and spirit — and we believe it will call for a new model of transformative learning.

References

Astin, A and H Astin (1999). *Meaning and Spirituality in the Lives of College Faculty: A Study of Values, Authenticity, and Stress.* University of California, Los Angeles: Higher Education Institute.

Becker, LC (1992). Good lives: Prolegomena. *Social Philosophy and Policy*, 9, 15–37.

Cameron, KS, JE Dutton and RE Quinn (2003). *Positive Organizational Scholarship: Foundations for a New Discipline.* San Francisco: Berrett-Koehler.

Cameron, KS, D Bright and A Caza (2004). Exploring the relationships between organizational virtuousness and performance. *American Behavioral Scientist*, 47, 766–790.

Chickering, AW, JC Dalton and L Stamm (2005). *Encouraging Authenticity and Spirituality in Higher Education.* San Francisco: Jossey Bass.

Chiu, L, J Emblen, L Hofwegen, R Sawatzky and H Meyerhoff (2004). An integrative review of the concept of spirituality in the health sciences. *Western Journal of Nursing Research*, 26, 405–428.

Conlin, M (1999). Religion in the workplace, *Business Week*, November 1, p. 150+.

Dehler, G and J Neal (eds.), (2000). Spirituality in contemporary work: its place, space, and role in organization and management. *Journal of Management Education*, 24, 5.

Emmons, RA and RF Paloutzian (2003). The psychology of religion. *Annual Review of Psychology*, 54, 377–402.

Gibbons, P (1999). Spirituality at work: a pre-theoretical view, Unpublished masters thesis, University of London.

Greenleaf, RK (1977). *Servant Leadership: A Journey into the Nature of Legitimate Power and Greatness.* Mahwah, NJ: Paulist Press.

Greenleaf, RK(L Spears ed.), (1998). *The Power of Servant-Leadership.* San Francisco: Berrett-Koehler.

Hawley, J (1993). *Reawakening the Spirit at Work: The Power of Dharmic Management.* San Francisco: Berrett-Koehler.

Kessler, E and J Bailey (eds.), (2007). *Handbook of Organizational and Managerial Wisdom.* Los Angeles:Sage.

Kinjerski, V and B Syrypnek (2004). Defining spirit at work: finding common ground, *Journal of Organizational Change Management.* 17, 26–42.

Koenig, H, M McCullough and D Larson (eds.), (2000). *Handbook of Religion and Health.* New York: Oxford University Press.

Krishnakumar, K and C Neck (2002). The "what", "why", and "how" of spirituality in the workplace. *The Journal of Managerial Psychology,* 17, 153–164.

Lipman-Blumen, J and HJ Leavitt (1999). *Hot Groups: Seeking Them, Feeding Them, and Using Them to Ignite Your Organization.* New York: Oxford University Press.

Luthans, F, K Luthans, RM Hodgetts and BC Luthans (2002). Positive approach to leadership (PAL): implications for today's organizations. *The Journal of Leadership Studies*, 8, 3–20.

Manz, C, K Manz, R Marx and C Neck (2001). *The Wisdom of Solomon at Work: Ancient Virtues for Living and Leading Today.* San Francisco: Berrett-Koehler.

Marcic, D (1997). *Managing With the Wisdom of Love: Uncovering Virtue in People and Organizations.* San Francisco: Berrett-Koehler.

Marx, R, C Manz, K Manz and C Neck (1999). Teaching with the wisdom of Solomon: Helping to reconcile business values with spiritual virtues in the management classroom. The Organizational Behavior Teaching Conference, Las Cruces, NM.

Marx, R, C Manz, K Manz and C Neck (2001). The challenges of going public with spirituality in the management classroom. A workshop presented at the Academy of Management annual meeting, Washington, DC.

Marx, R, J Neal K Manz and C Manz (2008). Teaching about spirituality and work: Experiential exercises for management educators. In *Spirituality in Business: Theory,*

Practice and Future Directions. J Biberman and L Tischler (eds.), New York: Palgrave Macmillan.

McKnight, R (1984). Spirituality in the workplace. In *Transforming Work.* J Adams (ed.). Alexandria, VA: Miles River Press.

Miller, J (2003). *Incorporating Spirituality in Counseling and Psychotherapy:Theory and Technique.* Hoboken, NJ: John Wiley and Sons.

Mitroff, I and E Denton (1999). *A Spiritual Audit of Corporate America: A Hard Look at Spirituality, Religion, and Values in the Workplace.* San Francisco: Jossey-Bass.

Myers, JE (1990). Wellness through the lifespan, *Guidepost,* 5, 11.

Myers, DG (2000a). The funds, friends, and faith of happy people. *American Psychologist,* 55, 56–67.

Myers, DG (2000b). *An American Paradox: Spiritual Hunger in an Age of Plenty.* New Haven, CT: Yale University Press.

Neal, J (1997). Spirituality and career development: a lifeline exercise, A workshop presented at the Academy of Management annual meeting, Boston, MA.

Neal, J (1998). Teaching with soul: support for the management educator, *Journal of Management Systems,* 10, 73–90.

Neal, J (2002). Spirituality in the workplace in higher education: a global phenomenon, A presentation at the Spirit in Business Conference, New York, NY. April.

Neal, J and G Biberman (2004). Research that matters: helping organizations integrate spiritual values and practices. *Journal of Organization Change Management,* 17, 7–10.

Neal, J, B Lichtenstein and D Banner (1999). Spiritual perspectives on individual, organizational, and societal transformation. *Journal of Organizational Change Management,* 12, 3.

Ray, P and S Anderson (2000). *The Cultural Creatives: How 50 Million People are Changing the World.* New York: Harmony Books.

Schaefer, C and D Darling (1997). Does spirit matter? A look at contemplative disciplines in the workplace. *Spirit at work newsletter.* East Haven, CT: July.

Scott, G (1994). *The Empowered Mind: How to Harness the Creative Force Within You.* Englewood Cliffs, NJ: Prentice-Hall.

Seligman, MEP (2002). Positive psychology, positive prevention, and positive therapy. In *Handbook of Positive Psychology.* CR Snyder and SJ Lopez (eds.), pp. 3–9. New York: Oxford University Press.

Seligman, MEP and M Csikszentmihalyi (2000). Positive psychology: an Introduction. *American Psychologist,* 55, 5–14.

Thompson, WD (2000). Can you train people to be spiritual? *Training and Development,* 54, 18–19.

Tisdell, E (2003). *Exploring Spirituality and Culture in Adult and Higher Education.* San Francisco: Jossey-Bass.

Chapter Six

LEVERAGING PSYCHOLOGICAL CAPITAL IN VIRTUOUS ORGANIZATIONS: WHY AND HOW?

Carolyn M. Youssef

Bellevue University

Fred Luthans

University of Nebraska

Psychological Capital is introduced as an important asset that can be leveraged to enhance the virtuousness of organizations. Psychological capital is defined as a state of development characterized by self-efficacy, optimism, hope and resilience, though there are many other similar resources. The authors examine empirical studies showing promise that psychological capital can be translated from moral goals to bottom line results. It is proposed that the relative stability and certainty of ordinary times offer the optimal conditions for developing psychological capital that can enhance the virtuousness of the organization when circumstances are less predictable.

Traditionally, the term "capital" has been most often associated with economics, finance or accounting when referring to a firm's assets that are held out of consumption in order to make more money, a profit. Thus, when used in conjunction with virtuous organizations, the use of capital at first glance appears almost sacrilegious, or at least the antithesis of what is good, right, and virtuous about organizations. However, in recent years, a broader definition of capital beyond mere physical and financial assets to include human, social, and now psychological capital has emerged. After briefly defining what is meant by virtuousness and psychological capital, the purpose of this chapter is to answer the why and how questions concerning our proposal that psychological capital can be leveraged to enhance the positive, but challenging to measure and develop, virtuousness of organizations. In particular, we attempt to address some of the lingering doubts and questions concerning the acknowledged value and righteousness of virtuous organizations, versus the more pragmatic, realistic need for performance impact, and in the private sector, bottom-line profits and competitive advantage.

What is Virtuousness?

As with all concepts in the social sciences, the definition of virtuousness is far from being consensual. However, most positive psychologists and positive organizational scholars would agree with the following dimensions of what is meant by virtue (see Cameron *et al.*, 2003; Peterson and Seligman, 2004). First, virtue must have some inherent terminal value, rather than merely being a means toward other ends. Second, there is a sense of "fulfillment" associated with virtues. This fulfillment results in the terminal value of virtues beyond any other intrinsic or extrinsic rewards. Third, the practice of virtue requires conscious choice and the investment of effort. Fourth, at a "high-enough" level of abstraction, there are indeed some universal virtues that cross the lines of time and place. Fifth, although virtues are not easily created, they still can be enabled, developed or hindered by the larger context within which they exist. Finally, individual and organizational level virtues may be related, but the dynamics are far more complex than what can be interpreted through simply adding together individuals to form the collective or to determine causal relationships.

Although these dimensions of virtues are interesting from a philosophical, humanistic perspective, and are difficult to refute, they have nevertheless alienated some researchers and practitioners that require more pragmatism and measurable performance impact. Such doubters of the value of virtues when applied to organizations argue that economic returns may be the only value-added to consider and appreciate, especially where decision making prudence is primarily assessed through quantitative measures. Although they may not publically admit it, in these scholars' and practitioners' view, money may become the only real virtue. If the reader of this book on virtuous organizations considers this statement to be exceptionally inflamatory or outdated, we recommend revisiting the above dimensions, replacing the word "virtue" with the word "money" every time it appears. In other words, there may still be many individuals and organizations for which money has terminal value, and making money provides a sense of fulfillment or accomplishment.

Material wealth cannot be easily created, but it can be increased through making the "right" choices, investing adequate amounts of time and effort, or simply luck. It can also be lost through poor choices or negative situational events. Furthermore, money does seem to have universal motivational value. As Kets de Vries (2007, p. 232) recently noted, "It's easy to say that money isn't everything as long as we have enough of it. Unfortunately, though, the typical scenario is that the more money we have, the more we want." Finally, although individual and organizational material wealth may be related, the relationships are far from being straightforward.

At this point, the controversies emanating from the above statements about money may tempt some readers, particularly those predisposed to virtuousness, to move on to the next chapter. However, before you do so, please take comfort in our assurance that this chapter, too, is about virtuous organizations. However, we offer what we feel is an often overlooked, but still needed, approach to help begin to answer the questions and stem the doubts about the linkage between virtuousness (the pursuit of what is positive, extraordinary, excellent, benevolent, and meaningful) and performance (assessed through traditional measures of employee productivity and corporate profitability). Our thoughts expand on the ideas of leading positive organizational scholars such as Kim Cameron (e.g., Cameron, 2003; Cameron and Levine, 2006) and positive psychologists such as

Christopher Peterson (e.g., Park and Peterson, 2003; Peterson and Seligman, 2004), Barbara Fredrickson (2001), and others. In this chapter, we will propose that our recently emerging theory and research on psychological capital may begin to bridge the gap between the idealism of virtuous organizations and desired pragmatic performance outcomes.

What is Psychological Capital?

Drawing from positive psychology (Seligman and Csikszentmihalyi, 2000; Snyder and Lopez, 2002), several years ago Luthans introduced positive organizational behavior (Luthans, 2002a, b). This positive organizational behavior or simply POB was defined as "the study and application of positively-oriented human resources that can be measured, developed, and effectively managed for performance improvement in today's workplace" (Luthans, 2002b, p. 59; also see Luthans and Avolio, 2008; Nelson and Cooper, 2007; Wright, 2003). Then a couple of years later, based on POB and as a way to apply, develop, and manage a positive approach to the workplace, we introduced psychological capital or simply PsyCap (Luthans *et al.*, 2004; Luthans and Youssef, 2004).

To be included in PsyCap, a positive psychological resource had to meet the criteria inherent in the definition of POB (i.e., based in theory, research and valid measurement, state-like and open to development, and demonstrated performance impact). We determined four positive psychological resources, that, at least initially, best met these POB inclusion criteria and thus we defined psychological capital or PsyCap as "an individual's positive psychological state of development that is characterized by: (1) having confidence (self-efficacy) to take on and put in the necessary effort to succeed at challenging tasks; (2) making a positive attribution (optimism) about succeeding now and in the future; (3) persevering toward goals and, when necessary, redirecting paths to goals (hope) in order to succeed; and (4) when beset by problems and adversity, sustaining and bouncing back and even beyond (resiliency) to attain success" (Luthans *et al.*, 2007b, p. 3).

These four psychological resources of efficacy, optimism, hope, and resilience are not intended to be the only ones included in PsyCap (e.g., we have recently identified and assessed individual-level wisdom, courage, creativity, authenticity, spirituality, gratitude, forgiveness, flow, humor, and emotional intelligence for potential inclusion, see Luthans *et al.*, 2007b), but for the purposes of this chapter on the role that PsyCap may play in virtuous organizations we will focus on just the four.

Specifically, we define self-efficacy as "one's conviction (or confidence) about his or her abilities to mobilize the motivation, cognitive resources, and courses of action needed to successfully execute a specific task within a given context" (Stajkovic and Luthans, 1998b, p. 66). Hope is defined as "a positive motivational state that is based on an interactively derived sense of successful (1) agency (goal-directed energy) and (2) pathways (planning to meet goals)" (Snyder *et al.*, 1991, p. 287). The optimism psychological resource in PsyCap represents positivity-oriented future expectancies (Carver and Scheier, 2002), as well as an attributional style that interprets positive events through personal, permanent and pervasive causes, and negative events through external, temporary and situation-specific ones (Seligman, 1998). PsyCap resiliency is defined as "the capacity to rebound or bounce back from adversity, conflict, failure, or even positive events, progress, and increased responsibility" (Luthans, 2002a, p. 702). These four positive psychological resources have been demonstrated conceptually (Luthans and Youssef, 2007; Luthans *et al.*, 2007b) and empirically (Luthans *et al.* 2007a) to be a higher-order, core construct that is related to performance and satisfaction (Luthans *et al.*, 2007a) and can be developed (Luthans *et al.*, 2008b).

Why is PsyCap Relevant to Virtuous Organizations?

Using the above meaning of virtuousness and psychological capital (PsyCap) as the point of departure, we proposed that PsyCap is not only relevant to virtuous organizations (especially, but also, for-profit business organizations, which is implied in the discussion throughout this chapter), but can be leveraged to resolve the dilemma between ideal goodness/righteousness and pragmatic development/perform-ance. The starting point of answering the relevancy question is whether the individual level PsyCap can even be applied to organiza-tional level virtues.

Positive psychologists are faced with the same question of whether their individual-level strengths, traits and values can be taken to the organization level. For example, Park and Peterson (2003, p. 37) asked the question: "What do we mean by organizational level virtues?" The guidelines they provide for attempting such a challeng-ing endeavor fall primarily along two important assumptions. First, organizational virtues must transcend its individual members. Second, organizational virtues must incorporate moral goals that go beyond "bottom line" oriented measures.

While we would agree with Park and Peterson's (2003) first proposition, we find the second one to be more problematic. We believe that cultivating and nurturing organizational culture can indeed allow some organizational traditions, rituals, and especially values to transcend the individuals who created them. For example, after a brief analysis, Park and Peterson (2003) conclude there appears to be at least five widely valued organizational-level virtues: purpose, safety, fairness, humanity, and dignity. On the other hand, the Values in Action (VIA) classification of strengths (see Peterson and Seligman, 2004) also includes some virtues that may not be as applicable at the organizational level as they would be at the individual level, at least in today's environment. For example, wisdom and knowledge have been studied and applied both at the individual (e.g., knowledge, skills and abilities or KSAs, competencies, work experience) and organizational levels (e.g., organizational learning). Similarly, justice has been exten-sively researched and practiced at both the individual and organiza-tional levels. On the other hand, the organizational level research and practice on courage, love, temperance and transcendence is at a much earlier stage of understanding and development. While there is cer-tainly potential for these latter virtues to apply across levels, their rel-evancy at the organizational level needs much more research.

To further illustrate the challenges in applying character strengths and virtues at the organizational level, we expand on Park and

Peterson's (2003) so-called "death-bed test." While individuals may be able to come to grips with what they truly value by asking themselves, on their death beds, what they would have spent more time doing, this may be inadequate as a litmus test for virtues applicable to the organizational level for at least two reasons. First, agency theory would posit that the decision makers (e.g., senior management) of organizations would be the ones to answer such a question, and that their interests would likely conflict with those of their principals (e.g., shareholders). This conflict would defy the purpose of the exercise, namely finding a unified set of organizational virtues. Second, even if we operate under the assumption that virtuous organizations are exceptionally good at aligning the goals of their participants (principals, agents, employees, and even suppliers and customers), an economic perspective is likely to prevail. After all, unlike individuals, at least business organizations were "born" to create economic value (i.e., make a profit) and promote their stakeholders' financial interests (e.g., stock values, wages, prices), so why wouldn't it be acceptable for these firms to "die" in pursuit of their most significant purpose?

Our intent with such questions is certainly not to discount or discourage the importance of organizational virtuousness or the growing scholarly activity leading to its better understanding and application. To the contrary, we use the above questions and challenges, also recognized by the very same positive organizational scholars cited earlier, as a form of devil's advocacy and springboard in our attempt to show how PsyCap may be able to provide answers to some of these questions and practical approaches toward furthering organizational virtuousness. Specifically, Fig. 1 graphically depicts our proposed contributions that PsyCap can make virtuous organizations to depend on the context ranging from crises to ordinary or exemplary times.

Organizational Virtuousness and PsyCap During Crises

As shown in the bottom, left section of Fig. 1, and in line with existing research findings, organizations that are high on virtuousness can outperform their less virtuous counterparts during times of crisis,

Fig. 1:   Virtuousness, Psychological Capital (PsyCap) and performance at various times.

such as during a major downsizing (Cameron, 2003; Cameron and Levine, 2006). This positive impact on performance can be accomplished through the "amplifying" and "buffering" mechanisms of virtuousness (Cameron, 2003; Cameron and Levine, 2006). This simply means that in virtuous organizations the positive effects are magnified and spiral upward, while the negative aspects are thwarted and a hardiness is developed. These mechanisms are conceptually related to Fredrickson's (2001) broaden-and-build model, where positive emotions broaden thought-action repertoires, and build human, social and psychological resources that replace or "undo" the negatives.

We propose that organizations that channel their virtuousness toward the development of their managers' and employees' PsyCap (i.e., their confidence, hope, optimism, and resilience) are likely to realize even higher performance during crises. In other words, as shown in Fig. 1, highly virtuous organizations that leverage their members into high PsyCap will have higher performance outcomes than highly virtuous organizations with low PsyCap members or low virtuous organizations. Although at this point such proposed relationships remain empirical questions, however, for now we can draw from Park and Peterson's (2003) conceptualization of "the good workplace" as an example. Virtuous workplaces provide their members with a well articulated moral goal or vision that they can embrace, and it can also be practical enough to guide their everyday actions. The virtuous organization treats members in an equitable manner. It gives them autonomy but holds them responsible for their actions. It allows them to be creative and to act as individuals, rather than gears in a machine. It places them in jobs that fit their skills, abilities and interests and allows them to do what they do best every day. And finally, it openly and honestly communicates with them and follows through on its commitments to them.

As indicated in Fig. 1, the virtuous organization as described above will have higher performance than those without such characteristics, and beginning research supports this assertion (Cameron, 2003; Cameron and Levine, 2006). However, as shown, being a virtuous organization alone may not be enough for maximum performance. We would argue that organizational virtuousness must touch participants at a very deep, personal level, in order for its impact to materialize into more tangible performance outcomes. We propose this can occur through PsyCap development and management. For example, when a virtuous organization builds its managers' and employees' self-efficacy regarding moral behavior, they are likely to exhibit more virtuous behaviors at the individual level, especially during times of crisis when they may feel tempted, encouraged, or even coerced to act unethically (Youssef and Luthans, 2005a). Furthermore, PsyCap hope can provide managers and employees in a crisis with the willpower to stay on course and stick to the values that their virtuous organization instilled in them, even when such virtues do not seem to "pay off" in the short run. A high level of hope can also provide them with the "waypower" or the ability to develop multiple creative, yet morally sound pathways to overcome obstacles, without having to resort to "questionable" approaches and behaviors to achieve their goals. Moreover, PsyCap optimism can help managers and employees see "the light at the end of the tunnel" during crises. Finally, PsyCap resiliency can equip managers and employees with the ability and patience to weather the storm (Park and Peterson, 2003), bounce back, and even grow and learn from crises.

Again, we emphasize that we do not intend to offer PsyCap as a substitute for organizational virtuousness, but rather a catalyst in times of crisis for the manifestation of the characteristics of virtuous organizations as well as take advantage of the heightened psychological resources of its individual participants, resulting in performance improvement. The mechanisms and processes described earlier can align individual goals and psychological resources to those of the virtuous organization. This alignment can facilitate the expression of virtuousness beyond just forgiving the organization for the crisis or having compassion for its decision makers, although these virtues are indeed important and can be impactful compared to organizations without such virtues (Cameron, 2003; Cameron and Levine, 2006). On the other hand, we propose that PsyCap can additionally allow both managers and employees to believe in themselves, develop more stamina and independence, build a more positive outlook, and grow through crises. High PsyCap members of a virtuous organization can be more equipped to anticipate, prepare for, and deal with uncertainty and a crisis. In other words, while virtuousness may facilitate a "back to normal" or gradual recovery, and certainly have a greater impact on performance than those without such virtuousness, highly virtuous organizations that also have members with high PsyCap may actually view a crisis as an opportunity for growth and development and result in high performance impact. For example, those with high PsyCap resilience in a crisis, instead of asking themselves "why me?" will react with "why not me?" and "what can I learn from this adverse situation?" (Coutu, 2002).

Organizational Virtuousness and PsyCap in Ordinary Times

We propose that both virtuousness and PsyCap are also necessary for maximum performance impact in ordinary times, and not just during crises. Again in line with Park and Peterson's (2003) descriptions of virtuous organizations, considerable organizational research over the years supports that organizations that effectively manage perceptions of equity and justice, and that promote high quality goal-setting processes, emphasize employee safety and welfare, and utilize high performance work practices in placement and enriched job designs, are likely to outperform their non-virtuous counterparts (e.g., see Greenberg, 2007; Judge and Hurst, 2007). As depicted in the middle section of Fig. 1, virtuous and non-virtuous organizations may be at completely different, unrelated levels of performance. Left unchallenged (during ordinary times), non-virtuous organizations may continue to survive and perform at adequate levels, but they are less likely to reach their full potential.

On the other hand, we propose that virtuous organizations that also emphasize the development of their participants' PsyCap during ordinary times are likely to realize the highest performance gains, for several reasons. First, ordinary times are characterized by relative stability and certainty. Constant, or at least predictable, streams of resources may accelerate the proactive investment in people, including the deliberate development of human capital (e.g., through training and development programs) and through the natural course of events also social capital (e.g., through team work and networking) and psychological capital resources (enhanced confidence, hope, optimism, and resilience), leading to excellence and competitive advantage. It is during such ordinary times that these human, social and psychological capital resources are built, previously drained resources (e.g., due to previous crises and the aftermath) are replenished, or existing resources are refined. For example, the development of self-efficacy can be best accomplished through mastery experiences (Bandura, 1997). The practice-to-perfection that precedes mastery is more likely to occur in ordinary times than during crises. Similarly, the positive, or at least non-negative, emotions experienced during ordinary times are likely to afford managers and employees broader thought-action repertoires (Fredrickson, 2001), and building more hope pathways. Ordinary times also offer opportunities for new goals to be set and achieved, and old ones to be inventoried and reassessed, which helps rekindle hope and optimism. Even resilience, which tends to be reactive in nature and thus more relevant for times of crisis, may be refined and perfected during ordinary times, as day-to-day challenges, minor setbacks, and windows of opportunity present themselves and allow organizational participants to build their personal assets to later draw from when adversity strikes.

Our recent empirical research supports the performance impact of PsyCap in the workplace, mostly in ordinary times. For example, findings to date provide considerable support for individual components and overall PsyCap to be positively related with objectively measured performance, job satisfaction, organizational commitment, and organizational citizenship behaviors, and negatively related to cynicism, turnover intentions, absenteeism, and others (e.g., Avey *et al.*, 2006, Avey *et al.*, 2008b; Luthans *et al.*, 2007a, 2005, 2008c; Youssef and Luthans, 2007). These findings also aligns with Park and Peterson's (2003, p. 39) assertion that "a good organization is one that enables the good life for its members." Perhaps the most directly related research is our recent finding that employees' PsyCap mediated the relationship between a supportive organizational climate and their performance (Luthans *et al.*, 2008b). Although the measure of supportive climate in this study did not incorporate all the richness of a virtuous organization, it does provide at least preliminary support for our proposal concerning the positive influence that PsyCap in conjunction with a virtuous organization may have on maximizing performance impact (see Fig. 1).

Our broader perspective on what constitutes the outcomes of positivity also aligns with the emphasis of positivity scholars on a more holistic perspective that goes beyond immediate productivity and profit measures, to also account for indirectly related outcomes such as attitudes, behaviors, and behavioral intentions that are likely to ultimately impact the long term survival and performance of an organization (Harter *et al.*, 2002, 2003; Luthans and Youssef, 2007; Roberts, 2006; Youssef and Luthans, 2007, 2008). Finally, there is both conceptual and empirical support for the applicability of individual components or overall PsyCap and its favorable impact on organizational outcomes across cultures (Luthans *et al.*, 2008a, 2005, 2004, 2006b; Luthans and Ibrayeva, 2006; Youssef and Luthans, 2006). This cross-cultural work supports our emphasis on PsyCap development and management with the potential universal nature of some virtues.

Organizational Virtuousness and PsyCap During Exemplary Times

At least in the economic, business context, we interpret exemplary times to be relatively brief periods when a firm is presented with exceptional opportunities such as a breakthrough in product or service innovation that can be turned into areas of long term core competence, and consequently a source of sustainable competitive advantage. The more effective the organization's structure, culture, strategies and processes are in capitalizing upon the full potential of an exceptional opportunity, the more likely it is to realize the involved gains, financial or otherwise. On the other hand, an organization may also fail to recognize the opportunity, or it may recognize something has occurred but undervalue its worth, or it may just choose a wrong direction in taking advantage of what has happened. These faulty responses to an opportunity may lead to less positive outcomes that may range from only partially realizing the potential gains, to possibly even exposing the whole organization to threats that may jeopardize its survival. In other words, it takes an exemplary organization to fully capitalize upon exemplary times, and since excellence is not an all-or-none type of outcome, varying degrees of excellence may ensue.

As shown in the rightmost section of Fig. 1, we propose a unique, counterintuitive perspective on the relationships between virtuousness, PsyCap and performance in organizations in exemplary times. At first glance, positive organizational scholars may disagree with what we are proposing. However, we feel with explanation there is some consistency in our proposed relationships and existing positivity research. First, we suggest that in exemplary times, virtuous organizations may consciously make choices that could potentially lead to lower profits, at least in the short term. For example, in good times a virtuous organization may realize higher than usual profits, but choose to spend this profit windfall on costly philanthropic activities, or to greatly increase compensation and benefits to employees, or make excessive expenditures on technology and buildings. Another example would be a virtuous organization experiencing unusually high profit but choosing not to pursue a business-sense opportunity with somewhat questionable ethics, such as driving a competitor out of business or entering into a merger that results in a close-to-monopoly situation. Still another example would be the virtuous organization that chooses to recall a product based on only a very slim chance that there may be a problem.

In all these examples, their non-virtuous counterparts would tend to make more economically-oriented choices, with the possible outcome that the virtuous organization is at a disadvantage. However, there are likely long-term goals also being pursued, including higher levels of virtuousness and resulting in high performance at both the organizational and the individual levels. Suffice it to say at this point that while the results will obviously vary, as shown in Fig. 1, at least in the short term, the virtuous organization with low PsyCap members may actually experience a negative impact on performance.

In exemplary times, a less virtuous organization may capitalize on what appears to be an opportunity that makes good business sense, even if there are ethical dilemmas and moral challenges involved. As a result, unless exposed, substantial short-term profits may be realized by less virtuous organizations during exemplary times. There are many real-world examples of this scenario (e.g., Enron, Tyco, WorldCom, and Arthur Anderson come quickly to mind). The case of "questionable" business opportunities go beyond "creative" accounting practices, to also include the use of sweatshops, outsourcing of services involving confidential personal information (e.g., tax preparation), industrial espionage, intellectual property violations and piracy in countries with lax legal standards, and others. In most, if not all these cases, there are likely additional short-term returns involved, and those returns may lead even the most prudent investors or other stakeholders to believe that a non-virtuous organization is more effective than a virtuous one.

We propose PsyCap is a potential solution for this possible dilemma facing virtuous organizations. Armed with confidence, determination, willpower, optimism, and resilience (i.e., high PsyCap), members of a virtuous organization may enhance their firm's chances of realizing performance gains experienced during an exemplary time, without jeopardizing its virtuousness. More importantly, being involved and able to see the "big picture," they can also facilitate the realization of those potential opportunities for organizational virtuousness to be exhibited, instead of focusing on the short term returns. For example, confident about their own and their organization's capabilities, self-efficacious employees are likely to view the situation as a worthwhile strategic choice that their virtuous organization has made. These high efficacy employees are able to mobilize a substantial amount of effort, motivation and cognitive resources to overcome, or at least work around, any potential short-term profitability decreases.

Besides the positive impact of high PsyCap efficacy in virtuous organizations during exemplary times, the same can be said of the other psychological resources. For example, believing in and buying into (i.e., psychologically owning, Avey *et al.*, 2008a) the organization's virtuous goals, those with high hope are likely to be more determined to do the right thing, and to creatively and proactively find alternative pathways to maintain reasonable short-term profitability levels. These high hopers' ability to see the value, significance and priority of virtuous goals and actions is also likely to promote more positive thoughts and optimistic expectancies regarding future profitability. On the other hand, those with neutral or low hope would more likely focus on blaming themselves or the organization for not taking advantage of immediate opportunities. Finally, their resiliency is likely to help them bounce back from temporary, short term setbacks, learning from them, and using them as springboards for future growth and building competitiveness to new heights. Again, highly resilient members of virtuous organizations may not just bounce back to normal or equilibrium. Instead, because they have the support of their virtuous organization, they may have the potential to bounce back and beyond to extraordinary levels of performance. In addition, collective levels of PsyCap, that go beyond the additive sum of the organization members' individual PsyCap levels, may also develop. Examples include collective efficacy (Bandura, 1997) and organizational level resiliency (Sutcliffe and Vogus, 2003; Youssef and Luthans, 2005b).

To further illustrate the contribution of PsyCap, it may be helpful to also portray a virtuous organization that does not develop participants' PsyCap to a high level. Although it may be difficult to imagine, at least over time, a virtuous organization without high PsyCap members, for the sake of argument, would indicate that this organization has hopeless, pessimistic, and non-resilient managers and employees. Thus, even though the organization may have purpose, compassion, forgiveness, and so forth, the associates could still have a short-term focus, an externalized perspective, and a very low tolerance for the ambiguities often involved with being different, let alone being virtuous. They may find it difficult to believe in their own and their organization's abilities to overcome any temporary setbacks associated with virtuousness. They may lack the motivation or the creativity to find ways to meet virtuous goals, and may therefore desire to just work for an organization that stays within the status quo, rather than one that seems to be going against the flow or trying to change the world. As a result, they may get discouraged when short term results do not seem to match those of competitors, and may choose to leave and work for one of those non-virtuous firms showing higher short term profits (e.g., Enron was swarmed with applicants during its run-up).

How Can PsyCap Be Developed and Managed in a Virtuous Organization?

Unlike virtuousness, which can be enabled or hindered over time but may be very difficult to create, develop or manage through the relatively brief interventions common in today's workplace, PsyCap has been shown to be readily developmental through very short interventions of 1–3 hours (Luthans *et al.*, 2006a, 2008b, 2007b). This can be done through the development of each positive psychological resource independently, or through an integrated PsyCap development intervention. Below are some practical guidelines for PsyCap development:

- Some of the most common approaches to developing self-efficacy can be drawn from the extensive work by Bandura (1997) and include: (a) mastery experiences, in which an individual is provided with opportunities to experience success in a given task, (b) vicarious learning, in which relevant role models are observed to succeed in a similar task, (c) social persuasion, in which the individual is convinced about his or her ability to succeed by relevant and respected others, and (d) physiological and psychological arousal, in which general physical and psychological health can reflect on one's levels of self-efficacy at work. Meta-analytical findings indicate a highly significant positive correlation between self-efficacy and work-related outcomes that is higher than other constructs and approaches (Stajkovic and Luthans, 1998a). Thus, developing efficacy should be given a high priority in today's virtuous organizations intending to maximize their performance impact.

- Drawing from Snyder's (2000) considerable clinical work, hope can be developed through (a) effective goal setting, (b) using "stepping" or breaking down large goals into smaller, more manageable ones, (c) effective contingency planning, and (d) learning to "re-goal" or shift to other goals to avoid false hope when situational factors or new information clearly render a goal to be faulty or in need of updating (also see Luthans *et al.*, 2006a; Luthans and Youssef, 2004).

- Drawing from the work of Schneider (2001), an optimistic explanatory style can be developed through (a) leniency for the past, in which individuals learn to identify, evaluate, challenge, and discount any inaccurate self-defeating beliefs they may be holding onto, and replace them with more accurate or less damaging ones, (b) appreciation for the present, including taking credit for positive situations, and (c) opportunity-seeking for the future, by creating positive expectations based on perceptions of permanence and pervasiveness of past and present positive events. Critical for optimism to be effective, especially in the business context, is realism. In this approach, an optimistic explanatory style is merged with prudence and responsibility for one's actions, as well as flexibility, in which both optimistic and pessimistic explanatory styles are learned and adapted depending on the needs of the situation (Peterson, 2000; Schneider, 2001).

- Although more complex and thus difficult, Masten (2001) has determined that resilience can be developed through (a) asset-focused strategies, in which assets such as human and social capital are developed, for example through cross-training, (b) risk-focused strategies, in which risks such as stress, conflict, or various asset deficiencies are anticipated, prevented, mitigated or managed, and (c) process-focused strategies, in which various mechanisms and processes are developed and employed for the effective allocation of one's assets toward handling various risks.
- Finally, the core construct of overall PsyCap can be developed as an integrated set of positive psychological resources. Using experimental designs, broad cross-sectional samples, and training programs for specific companies, our recent studies (Luthans *et al.*, 2006a, 2008b) support the impact of short training interventions.

These PsyCap programs can be delivered both face-to-face and online, and have been found so far to increase PsyCap by about 1.5–3 percent over a 1–3 hour session (Luthans *et al.*, 2006a, 2008b). Utility analysis has found over a 200 percent return on investment on such PsyCap development (Luthans *et al.*, 2006a, 2007b).

Conclusion

In today's environment, not only shareholders and employees, but also customers, suppliers and various community stakeholders are powerful, knowledgeable and informed decision makers. In such an inclusive and accountable environment, it becomes critical for organizations to consistently maintain and communicate a clear value system in crises, ordinary and exemplary times. Other chapters in this book clearly indicate the nature and importance of virtuous organizations. Our purpose was to propose a role that positive psychological resources represented by our recent work on psychological capital (PsyCap) may play, especially in relation to the performance of virtuous organizations. We hope that we have began to answer the why and how questions and have also stimulated future research on our proposals for the relation of PsyCap to the performance of virtuous organizations under crises, ordinary and exemplary times.

References

Avey, JB, BJ Avolio, CD Crossley and F Luthans (2008a). Psychological ownership: theoretical extensions, measurement, and relation to work outcomes. *Journal of Organizational Behavior*.

Avey, JB, JL Patera and BJ West (2006). Positive psychological capital: a new approach for understanding absenteeism. *Journal of Leadership and Organizational Studies*, 13, 42–60.

Avey, JB, TS Wernsing and F Luthans (2008b). Can positive employees help positive organizational change? Impact of psychological capital and emotions on relevant attitudes and behaviors. *Journal of Applied Behavioral Science*.

Bandura, A (1997). *Self-efficacy: The Exercise of Control*. New York: Freeman.

Cameron, K (2003). Organizational virtuousness and performance. In *Positive Organizational Scholarship*, KS Cameron, JE Dutton and RE Quinn (eds.), pp. 48–65. San Francisco: Berrett-Koehler.

Cameron, K, J Dutton and R Quinn (eds.), (2003). *Positive Organizational Scholarship*. San Francisco: Berrett-Koehler.

Cameron, K and M Levine (2006). *Making the Impossible Possible*. San Francisco: Berrett-Koehler.

Carver, CS and MS Scheier (2002). Optimism. In *Handbook of Positive Psychology*, CR Snyder and SJ Lopez (eds.), pp. 231–243. Oxford, UK: Oxford University Press.

Coutu, DL (2002). How resilience works. *Harvard Business Review*, 80(5), 46–55.

Fredrickson, BL (2001). The role of positive emotions in positive psychology: The broaden-and-build theory of positive emotions. *American Psychologist*, 56, 218–226.

Greenberg, J (2007). Positive organizational justice: from fair to fairer — and beyond. In *Exploring Positive Relationships at Work*, JE Dutton and BR Ragins (eds.), pp. 159–178. Mahwah, NJ: Erlbaum.

Harter, J, F Schmidt and T Hayes (2002). Business-unit-level relationship between employee satisfaction, employee engagement, and business outcomes: a meta-analysis. *Journal of Applied Psychology*, 87, 268–279.

Harter, J, F Schmidt and C Keyes (2003). Well-being in the workplace and its relationship to business outcomes: a review of the Gallup studies. In *Flourishing: Positive Psychology and the Life Well-Lived*, C Keyes and J Haidt (eds.), pp. 205–224. Washington, DC: American Psychological Association.

Judge, TA and C Hurst (2007). The benefits and possible costs of positive core self-evaluations. In *Positive Organizational Behavior* DL Nelson and CL Cooper (eds.), pp. 159–174. Thousand Oaks, CA: Sage.

Kets de Vries, M (2007). Money, money, money. *Organizational Dynamics*, 36, 231–243.

Luthans, F (2002a). The need for and meaning of positive organizational behavior. *Journal of Organizational Behavior*, 23, 695–706.

Luthans, F (2002b). Positive organizational behavior: developing and managing psychological strengths. *Academy of Management Executive*, 16(1), 57–72.

Luthans, F, JB Avey, BJ Avolio, SM Norman and GJ Combs (2006a). Psychological capital development: toward a micro-intervention. *Journal of Organizational Behavior*, 27, 387–393.

Luthans, F, JB Avey, R Clapp-Smith and W Li (2008a). More evidence on the value of Chinese workers' psychological capital: a potentially unlimited competitive resource? *International Journal of Human Resource Management*.

Luthans, F, JB Avey and JL Patera (2008b). Experimental analysis of a web-based training intervention to develop positive psychological capital. *Academy of Management Learning and Education*.

Luthans, F and BJ Avolio (2008). The 'point' of positive organizational behavior. *Journal of Organizational Behavior*.

Luthans, F, BJ Avolio, J Avey and S Norman (2007a). Psychological capital: Measurement and relationship with performance and satisfaction. *Personnel Psychology*, 60, 541–572.

Luthans, F, BJ Avolio, FO Walumbwa and W Li (2005). The psychological capital of Chinese workers: exploring the relationship with performance. *Management and Organization Review*, 1, 247–269.

Luthans, F and ES Ibrayeva (2006). Entrepreneurial self-efficacy in Central Asian transition economies: quantitative and qualitative analyses. *Journal of International Business Studies*, 37, 92–110.

Luthans, F, K Luthans and B Luthans (2004). Positive psychological capital: going beyond human and social capital. *Business Horizons*, 47(1), 45–50.

Luthans, F, SM Norman, BJ Avolio and JB Avey (2008c). The mediating role of psychological capital in the supportive organizational climate-employee performance relationship. *Journal of Organizational Behavior*.

Luthans, F, R Van Wyk and FO Walumbwa (2004). Recognition and development of hope for South African organizational leaders. *Leadership & Organization Development Journal*, 25, 512–527.

Luthans, F and CM Youssef (2004). Human, social and now positive psychological capital management: investing in people for competitive advantage. *Organizational Dynamics*, 33, 143–160.

Luthans, F and CM Youssef (2007). Emerging positive organizational behavior. *Journal of Management*, 33, 321–349.

Luthans, F, CM Youssef and BJ Avolio (2007b). *Psychological Capital: Developing the Human Competitive Edge*. Oxford, UK: Oxford University Press.

Luthans, F, W Zhu and BJ Avolio (2006b). The impact of efficacy on work attitudes across cultures. *Journal of World Business,* 41, 121–132.

Masten, AS (2001). Ordinary magic: resilience process in development. *American Psychologist,* 56, 227–239.

Nelson, D and CL Cooper (eds.), (2007). *Positive Organizational Behavior.* Thousand Oaks, CA: Sage.

Park, N and C Peterson (2003). Virtues and organizations. In *Positive organizational scholarship,* KS Cameron, JE Dutton and RE Quinn (eds.), pp. 33–47. San Francisco: Berrett-Koehler.

Peterson, C (2000). The future of optimism. *American Psychologist,* 55, 44–55.

Peterson, C and M Seligman (2004). *Character Strengths and Virtues: A Handbook and Classification.* New York: Oxford University Press.

Roberts, LM (2006). Shifting the lens on organizational life: the added value of positive scholarship. *Academy of Management Review,* 31, 292–305.

Schneider, SL (2001). In search of realistic optimism. *American Psychologist,* 56, 250–263.

Seligman, MEP (1998). *Learned Optimism.* New York: Pocket Books.

Seligman, MEP and M Csikszentmihalyi (2000). Positive psychology. *American Psychologist,* 55, 5–14.

Snyder, CR (2000). *Handbook of Hope.* San Diego: Academic Press.

Snyder, CR, L Irving and J Anderson (1991). Hope and health: measuring the will and the ways. In *Handbook of Social and Clinical Psychology,* CR Snyder and DR Forsyth (eds.), pp. 285–305. Elmsford, NY: Pergamon.

Snyder, CR and SJ Lopez (eds.), (2002). *Handbook of Positive Psychology.* Oxford, UK: Oxford University Press.

Stajkovic, A and F Luthans (1998a). Self efficacy and work related performance: a meta-analysis. *Psychological Bulletin,* 44, 580–590.

Stajkovic, AD and F Luthans (1998b). Social cognitive theory and self-efficacy: going beyond traditional motivational and behavioral approaches. *Organizational Dynamics,* 26, 62–74.

Sutcliffe, KM and T Vogus (2003). Organizing for resilience. In *Positive organizational scholarship,* KS Cameron, JE Dutton and RE Quinn (eds.), pp. 94–110. San Francisco: Berrett-Koehler.

Wright, TA (2003). Positive organizational behavior: an idea whose time has truly come. *Journal of Organizational Behavior,* 24, 437–442.

Youssef, CM and F Luthans (2005a). A positive organizational behavior approach to ethical performance. In *Positive Psychology in Business Ethics and Corporate Social Responsibility,* R Giacalone, C Jurkiewicz and C Dunn (eds.), pp. 1–22. Greenwich, CT: Information Age.

Youssef, C and F Luthans (2005b). Resiliency development of organizations, leaders & employees: Multi-level theory building for sustained performance.

In *Authentic Leadership Theory and Practice: Origins, Effects and Development (Monographs in Leadership and Management, Vol. 3)*, W Gardner, B Avolio and F Walumbwa (eds.), pp. 303–343. Oxford, UK: Elsevier.

Youssef, CM and F Luthans (2006). Positivity in the middle east: developing hopeful Egyptian organizational leaders. In *Advances in Global Leadership* (Vol. 4), W Mobley and E Weldon (eds.), pp. 283–297. Oxford, UK: Elsevier Science/JAI.

Youssef, CM and F Luthans (2007). Positive organizational behavior in the workplace: the impact of hope, optimism, and resilience. *Journal of Management*, 33, 774–800.

Youssef, CM and F Luthans (2008). An integrated model of psychological capital in the workplace. In *Handbook of Positive Psychology and Work*, A Linley (ed.), New York: Oxford University Press.

Chapter Seven

EUROPE VERSUS ASIA: TRUTH VERSUS VIRTUE

Geert Hofstede

University of Tilburg

University of Maastricht

When examining the four dimensions of national culture from an Asian perspective, Hofstede expands on his well-known measure of comparative cultural values and emerges with a new dimension unrelated to results from questionnaires designed by Western scholars. This new dimension emphasizes a Long-Term versus a Short-Term Orientation in Life. The author explores the religious and philosophical origins of these two approaches and illustrates how each views the concept of virtue differently with Western ideas of virtue tied closely to Truth, while Eastern ideas of virtue are not attached to any particular version of Truth. The implications of these differing ways of thinking on scientific inquiry, forms of government, and ways of managing are considered.

Science and technology are products of human ingenuity, and as such they are cultural phenomena: products of human culture. Values also belong to culture, but to a different kind of culture. The word "culture" is used in two meanings, but in discussions people often do not realize this. There is culture in the narrow sense, let us call it "culture one", which stands for civilization and its products; and there is culture in the wider, anthropological sense, "culture two", which means patterns of thinking, feeling and acting that differ from one group of people to another. Values belong to culture two, not to culture one. My research has been on values, that is culture two, and I will compare values in Europe and in Asia.

Several studies have been devoted to differences in values among similar people from different countries. I compared people working for the same multinational organization in the same jobs, but in more than 50 different countries, using a questionnaire developed for comparing departments within this organization. My Hong Kong colleague Michael Bond compared psychology students in ten different countries, using the Rokeach Values Survey (RVS), a questionnaire developed for comparing individuals within the U.S.A., which Bond extended with a few questions about issues he missed. We both found that the differences in the values of our respondents reflected four dimensions of national culture, and across the countries covered by both studies, each of the four dimensions in Bond's study was significantly correlated with a corresponding dimension in mine. My four dimensions were described as follows:

(1) *Power Distance*, or the extent to which the less powerful members of institutions and organizations within a country expect and accept that power is distributed unequally: from relatively equal to extremely unequal.

(2) *Individualism*, or the degree to which people in a country have learned to act as individuals rather than as members of cohesive groups: from collectivist to individualist.

(3) *Masculinity*, or the degree to which values like assertiveness, performance, success and competition, which in most cultures are traditionally considered the domain of men, prevail in a country over values like the quality of life, maintaining warm personal relationships, service, care for the weak, and solidarity, which in most cultures are considered to be more the domain of women: from tender to tough.

(4) *Uncertainty Avoidance*, or the degree to which people in a country feel threatened by uncertain or unknown situations: the

extent to which they reject those who do not think, look and act like themselves, and believe in one single Truth; from relatively flexible to extremely rigid.

All countries I studied could be located on these four dimensions. European countries varied widely among each other and so did Asian countries; there was no common European or Asian pattern, except for the dimension of Individualism where European countries scored more individualist and Asian Countries more collectivist.

The fact that Michael Bond and I had obtained similar results in two completely different studies was, of course, extremely supportive of the universality of our conclusions. Yet we were puzzled about the meaning of what we had found. Both Bond's and my questionnaire had been products of Western minds. In both cases respondents, not only in Western but also in Nonwestern countries, were asked to answer questions formulated by Western researchers. Some of these may have been less relevant to them, but were answered anyway; other issues more relevant in the Nonwestern countries than in the West may not have been included. To what extent could the categories we found have been in our minds rather than in those of our respondents?

Bond, a Canadian who lived and worked in the Far East since 1971, found a creative solution to the Western bias problem. He asked a number of Chinese social scientists from Hong Kong and Taiwan to prepare in Chinese a list of basic values for Chinese people. Thus he introduced a deliberate Nonwestern bias, in this case a Chinese culture bias. Like in the previous study, he extended the original list with a few items he missed. The new questionnaire was called the *Chinese Value Survey* or *CVS*. It was translated from the original Chinese into a number of other languages. It was administered to 50 male and 50 female students in 23 countries around the world.

A statistical analysis of the CVS results from the 23 countries produced again four dimensions: one of them was significantly correlated with my dimension of Power Distance, one with Individualism, and one with Masculinity. These three dimensions were common to the Chinese Value Survey and the two Western studies. They all refer to expected social behavior: toward seniors or juniors, toward one's in-group, and as a function of one's gender. These represent cultural choices so fundamental to any human society that they were found regardless whether the questions asked were designed by Eastern or by Western minds.

One dimension from the Western studies was missing in the CVS results. None of the CVS factors was correlated with Uncertainty Avoidance. I associate this dimension with man's search for Truth with a big T. It seems that for the Chinese minds which composed the Chinese Value Survey questions related to Truth were not relevant enough to include them in their questionnaire.

Instead of Uncertainty Avoidance, the students' worldwide answers to the Chinese questions revealed a fourth dimension, unrelated to anything found through Western-designed questionnaires. It refers to a Long Term versus a Short Term Orientation in life. It deals with values which the Western mind will clearly recognize, but which were not considered important by the designers of Western questionnaires.

The questions that composed the new dimension, both on the Long Term and on the Short Term pole, were inspired by the teachings of Confucius. Confucianism is not a religion but a set of pragmatic rules for daily life derived from what Confucius, a Chinese philosopher who lived around 500 BC, saw as the lessons of Chinese history. The new dimension contrasts one group of Confucian values to another. On the "Long Term Orientation" pole we find the values of persistence (perseverance), of ordering relationships by status and observing this order, of thrift (saving), and of having a sense of shame. On the opposite, "Short Term Orientation" pole we find the values of personal steadiness and stability, of protecting one's "face", of respect for tradition, and of reciprocation of greetings, favors, and gifts.

East-Asian countries were the top scorers on the Long Term pole: China, Hong Kong, Taiwan, Japan and South Korea. Singapore was in the ninth position. China, Confucius' homeland, is a case apart. The other five countries are known as 'The Five Dragons' because of their surprisingly fast economic growth over the past decades. Because of this, it should be no surprise that the "Long Term

Orientation" Index across all 23 countries was strongly correlated" with the economic growth data published by the World Bank for the past 40 years.

East Asian entrepreneurship does not seem to be based only on the values of the entrepreneurs themselves. The way the Chinese Value Survey scores were found, by surveying student samples, suggests that the decisive values are held broadly within entire societies, among entrepreneurs and future entrepreneurs, among their employees and their families, and among other members of the society.

The values that together form the dimension Long Term versus Short Term Orientation have sometimes puzzled Western readers. Their amazement is not surprising, because the dimension is composed precisely of elements that Western questionnaires had not registered. A Westerner would not normally find them important.

Eastern and Western minds tend to think differently: Eastern minds think in terms related to the dimension of Long or Short Term Orientation, Western minds think in terms related to the dimension of strong or weak Uncertainty Avoidance. Uncertainty Avoidance ultimately deals with a society's search for Truth. Strongly uncertainty avoiding cultures foster a belief in an absolute Truth, and uncertainty accepting cultures take a more relativistic stance. Long Term Orientation can be interpreted as dealing with a society's search for Virtue. It is no accident that this dimension relates to the teachings of Confucius. Confucius was a teacher of practical ethics without a specific religious content. He dealt with Virtue but he left the question of Truth open.

Eastern religions — Hinduism, Buddhism, Shintoism and Taoism — are separated from Western religions — Judaism, Christianity and Islam — by a deep philosophical dividing line. The three Western religions are based on a revealed Truth which is accessible to the true believers. All three have a Book. In the East, Confucianism, which is a nonreligious ethic, but also the major Eastern religions, are not based on the assumption that there is a Truth which a human community can embrace. They offer various ways in which a person can improve him/herself but these do not consist in believing but in ritual, meditation, or ways of living. This is why a questionnaire invented by

Western minds led to the identification of a fourth dimension dealing with Truth; a questionnaire invented by Eastern minds found a fourth dimension dealing with Virtue.

The Western concern with Truth is supported by an axiom in Western logic that a statement excludes its opposite: if "A" is true, "B" which is the opposite of "A" must be false. Eastern logic does not have such an axiom. If "A" is true, its opposite "B" may also be true, and together they produce a wisdom which is superior to either "A" or "B". People in East- and South-East Asian countries can rather easily adopt elements from different religions or philosophical systems, or adhere to more than one religion at the same time. In countries with such a philosophical background a practical nonreligious ethical system like Confucianism can be a cornerstone of society. In the West, ethical rules tend to be derived from religion: Virtue from Truth.

During the Industrial Revolution which originated in the West 200 years ago, the Western concern for Truth was first an asset. It led to the discovery of the laws of nature which could then be exploited for the sake of human progress. It is surprising that Chinese scholars despite their high level of civilization never discovered Newton's laws: they were simply not looking for laws. The Chinese script also betrays this lack of interest in generalizing: it needs some 5000 different characters, one for each syllable, while by splitting the syllables into separate letters Western languages need only about 30 signs. Western thinking is analytical, while Eastern thinking is synthetic.

By the middle of the 20th century the Western concern for Truth gradually ceased to be an asset and turned instead into a liability. Science may benefit from analytical thinking, but management and government are based on the art of synthesis. With the results of Western, analytically derived technologies freely available, cultures that can practice Virtue without a concern for Truth have a strategic advantage.

References

Hofstede, G (2001). *Culture's Consequences: Comparing Values, Behaviors, Institutions and Organizations across Nations.* 2nd Ed., Thousand Oaks, CA: Sage.

Hofstede, G and GJ Hofstede (2005). *Cultures and Organizations: Software of the Mind.* Revised and expanded 2nd Ed. New York, USA: McGraw Hill.

Hofstede, G and MH Bond (1984). Hofstede's culture dimensions: an independent validation using Rokeach's value survey. *Journal of Cross-Cultural Psychology*, 15, 417–433.

Hofstede, G and MH Bond (1988). The Confucius connection: from cultural roots to economic growth". *Organizational Dynamics*, 16(4), 4–21.

The Chinese Culture Connection (a team of 24 researchers coordinated by MH Bond) (1987). Chinese values and the search for culture-free dimensions of culture. *Journal of Cross-Cultural Psychology*, 18, 143–164.

Chapter Eight

PETER F. DRUCKER ON MISSION-DRIVEN LEADERSHIP AND MANAGEMENT IN THE SOCIAL SECTOR: INTERVIEWS AND POSTSCRIPT[1]

Joseph A. Maciariello

Claremont Graduate University

Peter Drucker, one of the great visionary management thinkers, shares his thoughts in his last published interview before he died in 2005. He credits social sector and nonprofit organizations in the U.S. for keeping the government out of their governance as much as possible and, unlike their European counterparts, utilizing volunteers. Yet Drucker criticizes this sector for focusing primarily how much money is raised while paying inadequate attention to mission and results. Another hurdle to virtuous activity in this sector is poor succession planning and professional management competencies. He ends with the possibility for mega-churches as well as hospitals and

[1] This dialogue is first an extension of an interview with Peter F. Drucker on February 11, 2005, for the 15th Anniversary Commemorative Book: *Shine a Light*, for the Leader to Leader Institute. A follow-up interview was conducted on June 6, 2005, for a special issue of the *Journal of Management, Spirituality and Religion*, Vol. 3, Issues 1&2, 2006.

The original interview was published as "Managing for Results, Planning for Succession," An interview with Peter F. Drucker by Joseph Maciariello, in *Shine a Light*, Leader to Leader Institute, April 2005, pp. 15–19 (John Wiley & Sons). It is used here as revised and amended by permission of Peter F. Drucker, Joseph A. Maciariello, and Leader to Leader Institute.

charities to have a greater impact on society when they solve the aforementioned administrative problems and focus more on virtuous behavior.

There may be no more powerful avenue for the expression and implementation of positive contributions to society originating from virtues in organizations than in the social sector. In the following rare interview with Peter Drucker on the subject he shares his wisdom and insight on the social sector and nonprofit organizations.

Joseph Maciariello (JM): Peter, why is the social sector and nonprofit organizations so important in America?

Peter Drucker (PD): Nonprofits are characteristic of American society. We are a society of volunteers. In 2003 there were approximately 1.4 million social sector institutions, including charities, religious organizations and advocacy groups. Almost half of all adult Americans participate as volunteers in these organizations.

A friend of mine, the head of a major business, is an active member on boards of seven nonprofit institutions. The same man in the same position in Europe sits on five or six company boards but on the boards of only a few state institutions. And on these boards, he serves in an advisory capacity. Government governs. But, in America we expect people to take on community responsibilities including managing nonprofits. That is why we can keep government limited. We expect the community to supply the leadership and the money.

The major tasks nonprofits perform in America are performed on the continent of Europe and in England by governments. For example, churches on the European continent are state institutions. Hospitals are also state institutions. In Europe, government runs all of the major churches and the great bulk of education and healthcare. These institutions, churches and hospitals, are amongst the biggest nonprofits in America.

It is the unique character of American society that social tasks are not all governmental. We are trying to keep government out of social tasks and in government tasks, "in governing" rather than "in doing." We are trying to, sometimes not successfully, but by-and-large quite successfully. Call it privatization. But, this is the unique characteristic of American society and the resultant leadership demands and leadership opportunities.

That is why the social sector is so important in America.

JM: What makes the management of social sector organizations so much more difficult than the management of private sector organizations?

PD: The bottom line is not an adequate definition of results in business but it is a parameter restraint. And it is a very sensitive thermometer. Nonprofits do not have such a sensitive thermometer for results. As a result they are more vulnerable than businesses. Nonprofits can get off course for a long time without noticing it. And they are by-and-large poorly managed.

Nonprofits, at least the ones I have worked with, are exceedingly conscious of how much money they have raised. But they often pay inadequate attention to mission and results. They neither define their mission adequately nor do they define results. Therefore, the important and very unpopular question for nonprofits is, "How do we define results?"

The critical issues I am up against all the time in nonprofits is that they are not results focused. They are budget focused. Their mistake; their measure of success is how much money they have raised. They think results come from the Good Lord. And the other critical mistake is that they believe their mission is forever. This is precisely because they do not have the discipline of the bottom line.

And so in nonprofits you have the added challenge of the definition of results and the revision of results. And then sometimes when you attain them you become obsolete and you have to think through results again and that is very unpopular and very painful.

This is what makes their management more difficult than business. And that is how I first came to see that mission and the definition of results are so much more important, and difficult, in nonprofits than in business.

JM: Peter, many executives of major nonprofits will be retiring in the next five years. Little seems to have been done to groom successors, the pipeline of leaders seems sparse. Isn't this a very serious problem?

PD: One major challenge in institutions as you point out will be in leadership changes and we are not as prepared in the social sector for succession as we are in business. We are at the stage now that business was when we began executive development in business.

The present non-profit executives came into management about the time of the Vietnam War, when they were in their thirties. And they are now moving out. And few nonprofit organizations have work going on preparing their successors. A great many nonprofits have yet not developed professional management.

It's going to be rough. Very few of these people have thought through the succession questions: "What kind of people do we need to succeed us? What kind of background should they have? How do we train them? How do we test them? How do we screen them?" The way we pick them now is to have the board get on the telephone and ask various people, "Do you know somebody?"

This morning I got first a fax and then a phone call from an organization that I have never heard about. It turns out to be a fairly large organization, affiliated with a major Catholic diocese, but not itself a religious organization. This organization is focused on first generation immigrant children and their mothers, providing them community — a very successful organization.

A Catholic priest, whom I've known for many years, runs the very large charitable programs of this very large diocese. He has done it for 25 years and he is now 78. He intends to live out his remaining years as pastor in his own parish no longer in the diocese as number two man.

I asked, "Father, Who's going to take over your job?" He said, "That is for the bishop to decide." But that bishop has 2800 women volunteers to deal with in the charity.

The questions I ask non-profit organizations looking for successors are "What are results in the job? What competences do you need? What experiences do you need?"

JM: How then would you propose training new leaders? How would you develop new leaders?

PD: In the social sector, you need three things: you need professionals, you need community leaders, and you need volunteer leaders. For the professionals, today we have a fairly substantial body of educational programs, some of them excellent and some of them so-so. But there is no shortage today of professionals.

I regularly call up my previous students and ask them, "What are you doing?" And I have concluded that there is no shortage of able people who usually, in their second or third job, can go into management in the social sector.

We have well-developed hospital management programs and are beginning to develop good church management programs. Some Catholic universities are doing a very good job. And social sector management is being taught now in a great number of management schools.

Within the last few weeks, again and again, I have people call me and say, "We need a person who can take over our organization in five years. I would like to discuss our candidates."

Take a Catholic parish, a large parish; the bishop happens to be a former student of mine when I was in New York. And I had to tell this bishop to bring in a layperson as an administrator. She has experience in a non-religious organization. She has just left her job as administrator of the business side of the hospital and medical programs of a very large metropolitan area institution. That type of experience qualifies her even though she has never worked in a religious organization.

I had to tell the bishop that work in a religious organization is not part of the qualifications. She is succeeding somebody who has built this organization. And the bishop had not thought through what is needed. He was looking to place a priest, who is a failure as a priest, and whom he had to place. He was looking for the absence of negatives. He had a big problem and had to think it through or he would make mistakes.

Finally, in large companies in particular, we are making social responsibility a criterion for leadership. Different people in business take social leadership differently. But, it is becoming increasingly common in businesses to expect that a "comer," a bright young person on the way up, spend a part of his/her time in the social sector, as a volunteer in community leadership. You expect it now.

It is nearly unique that in this country we expect, encourage and support executives who volunteer in the non-profit sector. In the rest of the world, a business executive is either not allowed to do any work in the social sector, for example, in Japan. Or while it does not harm a person in business to participate in a non-profit as a volunteer, it does not help either. In Europe he is likely to be told in his annual review, "stick to your last." And the result is the social sector has to be governmental, bureaucratic, top down.

These are some of the ways of training and developing future leaders for the social sector in America.

JM: Peter, doesn't this succession problem also create real opportunities?

PD: It does indeed! There is part of the social sector that is not volunteer and the succession crisis creates leadership opportunities. And for the part that is volunteer it creates opportunities for parallel careers.

Here is a fellow from business who at age 43 has become a controller of a small division of a large company. Basically, he has reached his terminal job. Only one of 40 controllers will become the chief financial officer of the company.

He may make it from a small division to a large division. But he is in his terminal job. His opportunities for leadership, for growth, for stimulation, are in the social sector. Either as a second career or as a parallel career.

The social sector is full of leadership challenges creating new opportunities for first, second and parallel careers.

JM: In closing Peter, you have said,

> "The most significant sociological phenomena of the second half of the 20th century has been the development of the large pastoral church."

And you have said that this phenomenon of the mega-church is due in part at least to the "emergence of the knowledge society today." This group of well educated, busy professionals appears to be exactly the group that Saddleback Community Church, and Rick Warren, is engaging.

But how did you come to see the connection between the knowledge society and the emergence of the mega-church?

PD: Because the knowledge society is creating a new and different constituency which the likes of Rick Warren, Senior Pastor of Saddleback Community Church, and Bill Hybels, Senior Pastor of Willow Creek Community Church, recognized and organized. All I had to do was to take a look.

Joseph Maciariello: Thank you Peter Drucker for giving us still more insight into the problems and enormous promise of the social sector in America.

Postscript

The mega-church is another example of Peter Drucker's ability to "see the future that has already happened." He was the first to observe the emergence of an educated, knowledge society, over 50 years ago as a result of the passage of the G.I. bill after World War II. Similarly in his book *Concept of the Corporation* (1946), Drucker was the first to identify and describe the emergence of the large corporation as a major institution of society, a distinct social entity, and a legitimate subject of inquiry.

Now, with the emergence of the large pastoral church, he has identified still another institution that is making a significant impact upon our society and because of its global reach upon the world. It too is a distinct social entity and a legitimate subject of inquiry for management scholars.

For example, Saddleback Community Church in Lake Forest, California itself looks like a management marvel and its architect, Rick Warren, cites the importance of the mentoring of Peter Drucker to its development.

Rick Warren's book *The Purpose Driven Church* (Zondervan, 1995) offers a management system for balancing the purposes of social sector organizations, around its mission, while constantly focusing upon results. Warren provides a prototype organization that has widespread applicability to the leadership and management of mission-driven, social sector organizations.

In the words of Rick Warren,[2] "At Saddleback we align everything we do around the mission. We budget on purpose, we structure on purpose, we staff on purpose, we schedule on purpose, we program on purpose, we plan on purpose, we group on purpose, I preach on purpose. Everything is purpose driven, because Peter taught me that it starts with a mission. You have got to know what your mission is."

The new PEACE Plan recently announced by Warren is breathtaking in scope. Using the combined resources of Saddleback's network of churches, of global executives, and of governments, the PEACE Plan is addressing the major ills of society:

- Preventable childhood diseases,
- Illiteracy,
- Poverty,
- Egocentric leaders, and
- Spiritual blindness on a global basis.

---

[2] Excerpt from the Keynote Speech, Alumni Day, Peter F. Drucker/Masatoshi Ito Graduate School of Management, Claremont Graduate University, November 2004.

Warren is following Drucker's advice on innovation, by first piloting the PEACE program. The first country in which the program is to be implemented is Rwanda, with the full support and backing of the country's current president.

In conclusion, Rick Warren and The Purpose Driven Church address all of the problems involved in leading and managing social sector organizations that Peter Drucker identified in these interviews. The management genius that is Warren's is a reflection of the management genius Peter Drucker.

Chapter Nine

CORPORATE GLOBAL CITIZENSHIP: SUCCESSFUL PARTNERING WITH THE WORLD

Nancy J. Adler

McGill University

Global corporations have become more and more powerful over the past 50 years, yet CEOs of the world's largest corporations have not risen to the challenge to leverage their money and influence to perform in virtuous ways such as becoming role models for engaged global citizenship. Even worse, many of these organizations consider commitment to societal well-being to be a drain on their profits. Adler illustrates with several powerful examples how virtuous corporations can effectively partner with government, communities and other corporations to "reduce poverty, wage peace, and enhance environmental quality while making a profit." She encourages leading thinkers to create partnerships that include the business sector.

Corporations have frequently been demonized for their many real and assumed damaging impacts on the world. By contrast, this chapter focuses on the private sector's real and potential contributions to society's betterment — in this case, world peace and security. It emphasizes business's role as an agent of world benefit. To achieve such contributions, companies and the individuals who lead them must alter not only their behavior, but, more fundamentally, they must alter their perspective. Such a shift is determined by managers and executives ability to shift from a focus on success to a focus on significance.[1]

"Remember your humanity, and forget the rest."

Joseph Rotblat, Nobel Peace Prize Laureate[2]

"That victory never leads to peace is not a theoretical affirmation, but an empirical statement."[3] Fifty years ago, led by Albert Einstein and Bertrand Russell, 11 of the world's most eminent scientists issued the Russell–Einstein Manifesto, warning of the dire consequences that would ensue if the world continued attempting to resolve its most complex and contested issues through war:

> *"We have to learn to think in a new way. We have to learn to ask our-selves, not what steps can be taken to give military victory to whatever group we prefer, for there no longer are such steps; the question we have to ask ourselves is: what steps can be taken to prevent a military contest ... [knowing that it would end disastrously for] all parties?"*[4]

As we enter the 21st century, physicist and Nobel Peace Prize Laureate Joseph Rotblat, at 97 the only living signatory of the Russell–Einstein Manifesto, sagely reminds us what such new thinking entails: "Throughout the centuries we have tried to ensure that we have peace by preparing for war. And throughout the centuries we had war. ... It is of the utmost importance to recognize the folly of

---

[1] The remaining text of this chapter was originally published in Gabriele Suder (Ed.) (2006). *Corporate Strategies Under International Terrorism and Adversity*, Chapter 11, pp. 177–195, Cheltenham, U.K.: Edward Elgar Publishing, used with permission.

[2] Nobel Peace Prize recipient Joseph Rotblat citing the admonition included in the 1955 Russell–Einstein Manifesto as reported in Rotblat (2005). Rotblat, then 97, passed away in September 2005.

[3] Raimon Panikkar as cited in Franck *et al.* (2000); as published in the original edition: Nyack, NY: Circumstantial Productions Publishing, 1998, p. 89.

[4] 1955 Russell–Einstein Manifesto as cited in Rotblat (2005).

this policy and adopt a new policy: ...If you want peace, prepare for peace."[5]

If You Want Peace, Prepare For Peace

In a post-9/11 world focused on creating security in the midst of terrorism, what does it mean to "think in a new way"? What does it mean to prepare for peace?[6] The Norwegian Nobel Committee, in choosing whom to award the Nobel Peace Prize to each year, has progressively embraced new ways of thinking about peace. Over the years, the Committee has broadened its definition of peace-makers from limiting it to those engaged primarily in ending wars after they have broken out, to including those involved in reducing the probability of violent conflicts ever occurring in the first place. The Committee has expanded its list of Peace Prize recipients which formerly included only political leaders and diplomats courageously negotiating resolutions to end raging conflicts, by adding people and organizations involved in creating and maintaining the preconditions for peace. These preconditions include: establishing democracy in place of totalitarian regimes, broadening human rights, promoting ecologically sustainable development that supports a flourishing natural environment, and eliminating poverty and extreme inequities in income distribution so that every person on the planet can have adequate access to life's necessities.

Preconditions for Peace

Democracy and human rights

In 2003, the Nobel Committee explicitly recognized human rights and democracy as preconditions for peace when it chose to award the

---

[5] Joseph Rotblat as cited in Franck *et al.* (2000) as published in the original edition: Nyack, NY: Circumstantial Productions Publishing, 1998, pp. 73–74.

[6] For a thorough and up-to-date discussion of the complex causes of security and insecurity in the world today, see The Worldwatch Institute's *State of the World 2005: Redefining Global Security.*

Nobel Peace Prize to Iranian lawyer Shirin Ebadi for her work supporting "democracy and human rights", and especially for her advocacy for women's and children's rights.[7]

The Committee emphasized its reasons for giving the Nobel Peace Prize to Ebadi, the first woman from the Muslim world ever to be so honored, and explained why it was particularly important to make the award now, at the beginning of the 21st century:

> *All people are entitled to fundamental rights, and at a time when Islam is being demonized in many quarters of the western world, it was the Norwegian Nobel Committee's wish to underline how important and how valuable it is to foster dialogue between peoples and between civilizations.*[8]

In offering its reasons for selecting Ebadi, the Committee stressed that whereas there have been several long-running themes in the 102-year history of the Nobel Peace Prize, "In the last few decades, the most distinct ... has ... been the increasing emphasis ... placed on democracy and human rights."[9] Ebadi, a conscious Muslim,

> *"sees no conflict between Islam and fundamental human rights. Islam is a diverse religion. How the message of justice is to be realized in practice and how human integrity is to be preserved is an essential issue for Muslims of today. ... [W]omen have an important role to play; no longer is it for elderly men to interpret the message... .*

---

[7] "The Nobel Peace Prize for 2003" speech given by The Chairman of the Norwegian Nobel Committee Ole Danbolt Mjøs in Oslo, Norway on December 10, 2003 announcing Shirin Ebadi and the 2003 Nobel Peace Prize recipient. As cited at http://www.nobel.no/eng_lect_2003a.html.

[8] Ibid.

[9] Ibid. Some of the Nobel Peace Prize Laureates who received their awards primarily for their human rights and democracy work include Albert Lutuli of South Africa in 1960. Martin Luther King in 1964, Andrei Sakharov in 1975, Amnesty International in 1977, Lech Walesa in 1983, Desmond Tutu in 1984, Aung San Suu Kyi in 1991, Rigoberta Menchu in 1992, and Nelson Mandela in 1993.

"Those who kill in the name of Islam... violate Islam", says Shirin Ebadi. We know that human rights are being violated not only in Muslim countries. It happens whether regimes are religious or secular, nationalistic or Marxist."[10]

Ebadi emphasizes that dialogue among the world's wide range of cultures must be founded on the values that some of the seemingly most divergent cultures hold in common. One of those values is democracy, and "[o]ne of the most certain findings of modern political science is ... that democracies do not go to war against each other."[11] Ebadi recognizes, for example, that there "... need be no fundamental conflict between Islam and Christianity. That is why Ebadi was pleased that the Pope was among the first to congratulate her on the Peace Prize."[12] Ebadi profoundly understands the importance of democracy and human rights as preconditions for peace.

Sustainable development and a flourishing environment

Again choosing to highlight people who create the preconditions for peace rather than those working to resolve conflicts after they have erupted into war, the 2004 Nobel Committee chose to honor Wangari Maathai, a Kenyan woman who has worked her entire life creating conditions for peace. For the first time in the Prize's more than 100-year history, the Committee decided to broaden its thinking and embrace a definition of peace-making that encompasses the health of the natural environment. In announcing Maathai, a lifelong advocate of sustainable development, as the 2004 recipient of the Nobel Peace Prize, the Committee signaled its change in thinking:

"Peace on earth depends on our ability to secure our living environment. Maathai stands at the front of the fight to promote ecologically

---

[10] "The Nobel Peace Prize for 2003" speech given by The Chairman of the Norwegian Nobel Committee Ole Danbolt Mjøs in Oslo, Norway on December 10, 2003 announcing Shirin Ebadi and the 2003 Nobel Peace Prize recipient. As cited at http://www.nobel.no/eng_lect_2003a.html.

[11] Ibid.

[12] Ibid.

viable social, economic and cultural development in Kenya and in
Africa. She has taken a holistic approach to sustainable development
that embraces democracy, human rights and women's rights in partic-
ular. She thinks globally and acts locally."[13]

Wangari Maathai, unlike the majority of her Nobel-laureate pred-
ecessors is not an international diplomat; she is a planter of trees.
Maathai founded the Green Belt Movement. For nearly 30 years, she
has mobilized poor women to plant trees — over 30 million trees.[14]
Because of its departure from previous definitions of peace-making,
the Nobel Committee explicitly explained the reasons for its
expanded appreciation of what leads to peace:

In recent decades, the Nobel Committee has made human rights a cen-
tral element of the definition of peace. There were many warnings
against such a broadening of the concept of peace. Today there are few
things peace researchers and other scholars are readier to agree on
than ... that democracy and human rights advance peace. ... This year,
the Norwegian Nobel Committee has ...broadened its definition of
peace still further. Environmental protection has become yet another
path to peace.[15]

What is the relationship between peace and the environment? As
the Nobel Committee explained:

Most people would probably agree that there are connections between
peace on the one hand and an environment on the other in which scarce

---

[13] Norwegian Nobel Committee (2004) in their press release announcing Wangari
Maathai as the recipient of the 2004 Nobel Peace Prize (as cited at Nobelprize.org at
http://nobelprize.org/peace/laureates/2004/press.html). The arguments focusing
on environmental degradation leading to the extinction of society are also expressed
in Jared Diamond's book *Collapse* (2005).
[14] Ibid.
[15] December 10, 2004 speech by Wangari Maathai accepting her Nobel Peace Prize
in Oslo, Norway (as cited at Nobelprize.org at www.nobel.no/eng_lect_2004b.
html).

resources such as oil, water, minerals or timber are quarreled over. The Middle East is full of disputes relating to oil and water. Clearly, not everyone outside the region has appreciated the importance to Arab-Israeli relations of the conflicts over the waters of the Jordan, Litani, Orontes and other rivers. Competition for minerals has been an important element of several conflicts in Africa in recent years. Competition for timber has figured prominently in Liberia, Indonesia, and Brazil.[16]

But where does tree-planting come in?

When we analyze local conflicts, we tend to focus on their ethnic and religious aspects. But it is often the underlying ecological circumstances that bring the more readily visible factors to the flashpoint. Consider the conflict in Darfur in the Sudan. What catches the eye is that this is a conflict between Arabs and Africans, between the government, various armed militia groups, and civilians. Below this surface, however, lies the desertification that has taken place in the last few decades, especially in northern Darfur. The desert has spread southwards, forcing Arab nomads further and further south year by year, bringing them into conflict with African farmers.[17]

In the Philippines, uncontrolled deforestation has helped to provoke an uprising against the authorities. In Mexico, soil erosion and deforestation have been factors in the revolt in Chiapas against the central government. In Haiti, the Amazon, and the Himalayas, deforestation and the resulting soil erosion have contributed to deteriorating living conditions and caused tension between population groups and countries. In many countries deforestation, often together with other problems,

---

[16] Nobel Peace Prize Presentation Speech by Professor Ole Danbolt Mjøs, Chairman of the Norwegian Nobel Committee, Oslo, December 10, 2004 to Wangari Maathai as reported at: http://nobelprize.org/peace/laureates/2004/presentation-speech.html.

[17] For a fuller understanding of the situation in the Sudan, see Kakutani (2005) and Caputo (2005).

*leads to migration to the big cities, where the lack of infrastructure is
another source of further conflict.*[18]

The relationship between inadequate and inequitably-distributed
resources and conflict are powerful, direct, and devastating in their
consequences. With her profound understanding of such relationships, Maathai summarizes:

> *"We are sharing our [planet's] resources in a very inequitable way. We
> have parts of the world that are very deprived and parts of the world
> that are very rich. And that is partly the reason why we have conflicts.
> Wars and conflicts certainly have many other causes, too. But who
> would deny that inequitable distribution, locally and internationally,
> is relevant in this connection? I predict that within a few decades, when
> researchers have developed more comprehensive analyses of many of the
> world's conflicts, the relation between the environment, resources, and
> conflict may seem almost as obvious as the connection we see today
> between human rights, democracy and peace."*[19]

The Nobel Committee concluded its 2004 Peace Prize presentation by emphasizing the need for cooperation; the need for all parties
to learn how to cooperate with each other on a global basis:

> *[S]ooner or later, in order to meet environmental problems, there will
> have to be international cooperation across all national boundaries on a
> much larger scale than we have seen up to now. We live on the same globe.
> We must all cooperate to meet the world's environmental challenges.*[20]

Considering the global experience and structures needed for such international cooperation, one is struck by the more extensive and integrated

---

[18] Mjøs (2004).

[19] Mjøs (2004).

[20] Norwegian Nobel Committee (2004) in their press release announcing Wangari
Maathai as the recipient of the 2004 Nobel Peace Prize, as cited at Nobelprize.org at
http://nobelprize.org/peace/laureates/2004/press.html.

global experience of most multinational corporations as compared with the more discrete, geographically-defined experience of most countries and governments.[21] In determining which organizations should be involved in delivering global solutions to global problems, it is incumbent on the world community to more seriously consider the potential contributions of all sectors, including the private sector.

Health, poverty reduction and an equitable income distribution

Democracy, human rights, and environmental sustainability are preconditions for peace, but they are not the only preconditions. Experts have also added health, poverty reduction, and a more equitable income distribution to the list of necessary conditions for global security and sustainability. The Executive Director of the World Health Organization, Gro Harlem Brundtland, a medical doctor and former Prime Minister of Norway, was one of the first to prominently label poverty as the leading cause of illness. At the opening of the 21st century, in her 2000 BBC Reich Lecture, Brundtland explained the connections between illness and poverty,

"I feel it is necessary to re-establish in people's minds ... the fact that it is not only... that poverty leads to ill health, but ...ill health also leads to poverty.... I [therefore] want the fight against poverty to be our global cause as we straddle the millennium. Our goal must be to create a world where we all can live well fed and clothed, and with dignity. We must do this without undermining future generations' ability to do the same."[22]

---

[21] For a fuller discussion contrasting the geographically local (domestic) structures of most governments and the multi-domestic structures of most international organizations (such as the United Nations) versus the more globally integrated strategies and structures of most multinational and global companies, see Adler (1994) and Adler and Ghadar (1993, 1990).

[22] Gro Harlem Brundtland's 2000 Reich Lecture on the BBC program Talking Points on January 16, 2001 as found at http://news.bbc.co.uk/1/hi/talking_point/1108388.stm.

In the world today,

About three billion people live on less than two dollars a day. ...That means that 3 billion people live in such poverty that they cannot afford proper housing, proper health care and proper education for their children. Almost half of those people live on less than one dollar per day. That means more than a billion people not having enough to eat every day and at constant risk of malnutrition. ... [Such extreme] poverty has a woman's face; of the 1.3 billion poorest, only 30 percent are male. ...Women from poor households are more than a hundred times more likely to die as a result of childbirth than their wealthier counterparts.[23]

According to Brundtland, many of the conflicts in the world "are not so much territorial disputes as they are rooted in general misery, the aftermath of humanitarian crises, shortages of food and water and the spreading of poverty and ill-health."[24] In the wake of governments' attempts to ameliorate the crises, the situation, instead of improving, often grows worse. As long as such poverty continues, the world cannot hope for peace, security, or an end to terrorism. As long as we continue to rely on previously tried, and all too often failed, solutions driven primarily by governmental and intergovernmental agencies, we cannot hope to improve the situation.

Poverty is now not only understood to be a leading cause of illness, but also beginning to be understood as a leading cause of conflict and global insecurity. In the 21st century's globally interconnected society, illness in one part of the world leads to a lack of security worldwide. Health crises originating in the world's poorest countries no longer remain local, but, as we have seen with SARS, AIDS, TB, and a list of other feared diseases, often rapidly spread worldwide. As Brundtland describes,

"Diseases cannot be kept out of even the richest of countries by rearguard defensive action. The separation between domestic and international

---

[23] Ibid.
[24] Ibid.

health problems is no longer useful, as people and goods travel across continents. Two million people cross international borders every single day, about a tenth of humanity each year. And of these, more than a million travel from developing to industrialized countries each week."[25]

Such globally interconnected patterns are fundamentally changing leaders' appreciation of what matters in the world, even from the perspective of the world's wealthiest peoples, nations, and companies.

"Health security", as Brundtland labels it, is now "as important as national security. Threats to health undermine... the world's 'human security'. Illness experienced by most of the world's people threatens [not only their own] countries' economic and political viability: [it]... affects [the] economic and political interests of all ...countries. Several countries — including the United States — [along with the United Nations] now recognize that improving international levels of health is neither solely a domestic health issue nor an act of charity, but rather a matter of national security."[26]

Unfortunately, similar to the management of other preconditions for peace and security, past approaches that have relied primarily on programs led by governments, international agencies, and non-governmental organizations (NGOs), have failed so far to successfully address the most crucial issues.

"Over the past few years, the human development index has declined in more than 30 countries. Almost one third of all children are under-nourished. The average African household consumes 20 percent less today than it did 25 years ago! And development assistance is falling too. Only a few countries have fulfilled past commitments to provide 0.7 per cent of their GDP for development assistance. In actual fact the world average is now closer to 0.2 percent.[27]

---

[25] Ibid.

[26] Ibid.

[27] Ibid.

Many world leaders are now urgently calling for new approaches, including the unorthodox recommendation that alliances be formed between industry and international agencies to address society's most pressing and important challenges. What is — and more importantly — what could be the role of the private sector in addressing these challenges and establishing global security? What hope do we have that the private sector will play the constructive role that the world needs it to play?

Global Security, Peace-Making and the Private Sector

Clearly, strides have been made in the world's understanding of what constitutes peace-making.[28] To succeed as a global civilization in the 21st century, however, our ways of thinking about global security and peace-making need to expand once again; this time to more prominently and explicitly include the private sector. This is not because the private sector has better values than the other sectors — it doesn't — but because of the private sector's global prominence and its worldwide structures and processes. For the first time in history, answers to questions of societal well-being — including questions of war and peace and of terrorism and security — may well be more in the hands of business people than in those of political, diplomatic, military, or humanitarian leaders.

Over the past 50 years, power has shifted dramatically from the public to the private sector. Today, 49 of the 100 largest economies in the world are multinational companies, not countries.[29] Due to this shift in power, traditional perspectives that assumed government and intergovernmental agencies could or would take care of society's welfare are no longer relevant either for society or for the

---

[28] For a discussion on women leaders' actual and potential contributions to peace-making, see Adler (1998). Also see the 2005 initiative to get 1000 women from around the world collectively nominated for the 2005 Nobel Peace Prize (see "1000 Women for the Nobel Peace Prize 2005 at http://www.1000peacewomen.org/).

[29] As cited in the October 8, 2003 report of the Aspen Institute and the World Resource Institute ranking business schools on their social impact.

economy; this applies to both the richest and the poorest nations and peoples.

Wal-Mart, for example, is now the 19th largest economy in the world, with sales exceeding $250 billion.[30] If it were a country, Wal-Mart would be China's eighth largest trading partner.[31] Wal-Mart's single-day revenue is larger than the annual gross domestic product of 36 independent countries.[32] With over 1.3 million employees, Wal-Mart is now the world's largest employer. The company has more people in uniform than the entire United States Army.[33] What Wal-Mart does in the world matters, not only to its own employees, customers, and suppliers, but also to the global economy and society within which all companies operate and all people live. Global solutions cannot be conceived of or implemented without taking companies such as Wal-Mart into account.

Business's contribution: Are CEOs missing in action?[34]

United Nations' Secretary General Kofi Annan has challenged businesses to become co-creators of society's success and security:

> *"Let us choose to unite the power of markets with the strengths of universal ideals...let us choose to reconcile the creative forces of private entrepreneurship with the needs of the disadvantaged and the requirements of future generations."*[35]

---

[30] Mau *et al.* (2004, p. 128).

[31] Friedman (2005b, c).

[32] Wal-Mart's 2002 revenue on the day after U.S. Thanksgiving was almost $1.5 billion, as cited in Mau *et al.* (2004, p. 128).

[33] Mau *et al.* (2004, p. 128).

[34] Friedman (2005a).

[35] Speech given by U.N. Secretary General Kofi Annan at the World Economic Forum in Davos, Switzerland in 1999 which initiated the Unites Nations Global Compact, see http://www.aiccafrica.com/PDF%20files/Global%20Compact%20Handout.pdf.

Many, however, rightfully question the role that business has taken. Simultaneously recognizing the importance of business's increasing influence and society's wariness at how CEOs have used that influence, World Economic Forum president Klaus Schwab confronted the world's top business leaders as they convened in Davos, Switzerland:

> *"In today's trust-starved climate, our market-driven system is under attack ... large parts of the population feel that business has become detached from society, that business interests are no longer aligned with societal interests. ... The only way to respond to this new wave of anti-business sentiment is for business to take the lead and to reposition itself clearly and convincingly as part of society."*[36]

Enlightened 21st century pleas for corporate global citizenship recognize that without the private sector, no attempt to create and maintain a peaceful, prosperous, equitable, and sustainable society can succeed. They also acknowledge that much of the private sector will have to rethink its role if it is to contribute in more than narrowly defined, self-interested ways.

Are CEOs rising to the challenge and becoming co-creators of the type of global society that the Nobel Committee, the United Nations, and the World Economic Forum aspire to? Many observers bluntly say no. Whether they cite corporate greed and corruption — as brilliantly demonstrated in recent years by Arthur Andersen, Enron, Health South, Tyco, and WorldCom, among many others — or other forms of corporate malfeasance, the private sector is rarely perceived as a primary contributor to global society's security and success.[37]

New York Times editorial writer Thomas Friedman suggests that the private sector's crime is not simply behavior that is ultimately

---

[36] Klaus Schwab's remarks as reported in *Newsweek* (Schwab, 2003).

[37] Among many other articles, see Sorkin (2005) on the Tyco convictions, McLean and Elkind (2003) for a through description of the Enron scandal, Scott (2005) on the initial Enron convictions, Creswell (2005a) for Citigroup's $2 billion payment for its involvement in the Enron scandal, and Creswell (2005b) for J.P. Morgan Chase's $2.2 billion payment to its investors for its involvement in the Enron scandal.

exposed as criminal, but rather CEOs' lack of constructive engagement with the world's most serious problems. As he labels it, many CEOs are simply "missing in action."[38] Equally seriously, many of these missing-in-action CEOs still view commitment to societal well-being not as a strategy for superior performance — both fiscal and societal — but rather as a net drain on their companies' revenues and profits. Locked in an overly narrow definition of free enterprise, they continue to adhere to classical economist Milton Friedman's dictum that the only "social responsibility of business is to increase its profits."[39]

Peace, Security & Economic Prosperity

Whereas "missing-in-action" might reflect the behavior of far too many CEOs, it does not accurately describe either all business leaders or all business approaches. Contributions to societal well-being that some companies are making through their core business strategies and processes are so extraordinarily innovative and effective that the Nobel Committee may need to consider expanding its candidate pool for future Nobel Peace Prize recipients to include private-sector initiatives. Perhaps the next Nobel Peace Prize will be offered to a global company, rather than to a diplomat or a tree-planter. Some of the most interesting private sector strategies include business efforts to reduce poverty, to "wage peace", and to enhance environmental quality — all while making a profit.

Bottom-of-the-pyramid business strategies: Reducing poverty and creating fortunes

According to management professors C.K. Prahalad and Stuart Hart, "Low-income markets present a prodigious opportunity for the

---

[38] Friedman (2005b).

[39] See Milton Friedman's classic 1970 article "The Social Responsibility of Business Is to Increase Its Profits," explicitly stating that the role of business is to make a profit; nothing more and nothing less (Friedman, 1970).

world's wealthiest companies to seek their fortunes and bring prosperity to the aspiring poor."[40] Taking a novel approach to bringing private sector expertise to solving some of the world's most crucial problems, Prahalad and Hart guide multinationals on how to reduce extreme poverty — and by extension global instability — while simultaneously earning significant profits. Prahalad and Hart advise global companies to "see" a market that was previously invisible to them — and remains invisible to most of their competitors.[41] That market is the four billion people who earn less than $1500 annually. Global business strategists Prahalad and Hart dispel the illusion that the world's poorest people do not constitute a market, that they do not posses buying power, and that there are not significant profits to be earned by the companies serving them. By giving the world's poor access to better and more reasonably priced products and services — most of which would not be possible without today's advanced technological design capabilities — bottom-of-the-pyramid strategies offer the possibility of reducing the risk of disease, terrorism, and insurgence caused by poverty. Prahalad and Hart explain that

> *"Although complete income equality is an ideological pipe dream, the use of commercial development to bring people out of poverty and give them the chance for a better life is critical to the stability and health of the global economy and the continued success of Western MNCs."*[42]

Such strategies unambiguously work to the mutual benefit of business and society.

A number of companies are already using bottom-of-the-pyramid strategies to create wealth, reduce poverty, and thus increase global

---

[40] Prahalad and Hart (2002, p. 2).

[41] For a fuller and more in-depth discussion of bottom-of-the-pyramid strategies processes, and approaches, see the recently released books by Hart (2005) and Prahalad (2005), along with their articles on the topic, including Prahalad and Hart (2002), Hart and Christensen (2002), and Prahaland and Hammond (2002), among others.

[42] Prahalad and Hart (2002, p. 4).

security. Examples include Hindustan Lever (HLL), which created a new detergent, called Wheel, which now has 38 percent market share in a market that Unilever, the parent company, never realized existed.[43] Using a new business model that emphasizes volume rather than high profit margins, Wheel

> *"...was formulated to substantially reduce the ratio of oil to water in the product, responding to the fact that the poor often wash their clothes in rivers and other public water systems. HLL decentralized the production, marketing, and distribution of the product to leverage the abundant labor pool in rural India, quickly creating sales channels through the thousands of small outlets where people at the bottom of the pyramid shop. HLL also changed the cost structure of its detergent business so it could introduce Wheel at a low price point.*

In its first five years on the market, Hindustan Lever enjoyed "a 20 percent growth in revenue and a 25 percent growth in profits per year."[44] Prahalad and Hart warn that "the strategic challenge for managers is to visualize an active market where only abject poverty exists today. It takes tremendous imagination and creativity to engineer a market infrastructure out of a completely unorganized sector."[45]

Other bottom-of-the-pyramid strategies are found, for example, in the area of micro-lending. Companies choosing to embrace micro-lending strategies are making a profit by giving the poor access to reasonable borrowing power, and thus access to buying power.

> *"According to the International Labor Organization's World Employment Report 2001, nearly a billion people—roughly one-third of the world's work force—are either underemployed or have such low-paying jobs that they cannot support themselves or their families. Helping the world's poor elevate themselves above this desperation line is a business opportunity to do well and do good."[46]*

---

[43] Opt cit., p. 5.
[44] Ibid.
[45] Prahalad and Hart (2002, p. 6).
[46] Ibid.

The business opportunity comes from the fact that, under the current system, money lenders in the poorest areas charge as much as 20 percent per day interest. Micro-lenders can charge much less and still make a substantial profit. Whereas the Grameen Bank, founded by Bangladeshi economist Muhammad Yunus, is the highly successful pioneer in this field, micro-lending — offering very small loans at reasonable interest rates and within structures that are accessible to the poor — is now a thriving business for the largest banks in a number of countries. "At the 1999 Microcredit Summit, the United Nations, in conjunction with several major MNCs, such as Citigroup Inc. and Monsanto Company, set a goal of making basic credit available to the 100 million poorest families in the world by the year 2005."[47] Whereas they have yet to achieve their goal, progress is being made.

Other examples of bottom-of-the-pyramid strategies include Honeywell's interest in offering micro-turbines as small-scale distributed energy solutions to extremely poor communities; The Body Shop's policy, led by founder and former CEO Anita Roddick, of trade-not-aid; and Starbucks' (together with Conservation International's) strategy to eliminate intermediaries from its business model and source coffee directly from farmers in Mexico's Chiapas region, thus enabling the company to provide coffee farmers with a reasonable standard of living and the company with a respectable profit.

As Prahalad and Hart help individual companies embrace these new, highly profitable bottom-of-the-pyramid business strategies, they remind the entire private sector that:

> *"It is tragic that ... Western capitalists ... have implicitly assumed that the rich will be served by the corporate sector, while governments and NGOs will protect the poor and the environment. This implicit divide is stronger than most realize. Managers in MNCs, public policymakers, and NGO activists all suffer from the historical division of roles. A huge opportunity lies in breaking this code—linking the poor and the rich across the world in a seamless market organized around the concept of sustainable growth and development.*

---

[47] Prahalad and Hart (2002, p. 8).

Collectively, we have only begun to scratch the surface of what is the biggest potential market opportunity in the history of commerce. Those in the private sector who commit their companies to a more inclusive capitalism have the opportunity to prosper and share their prosperity with those who are less fortunate. In a very real sense, the fortune at the bottom of the pyramid represents the loftiest of our global goals.[48]

Giving peace a chance: Industrial parks as tools for peace

Bottom-of-the-pyramid strategies are by no means the only noteworthy approaches that businesses are successfully employing to enhance societal well-being and the possibilities for peace. Industrialist Stef Wertheimer, founder, former CEO, and Chairman of the Board of ISCAR Ltd., a $1 billion-a-year metal-tool-cutting business, offers a very different, yet compelling approach. Now over 75 years old, this Israeli entrepreneur has expanded his vision beyond profits to include peacemaking. Wertheimer has taken on one of the toughest problems in the world, Middle East peace.

In his and many others' opinions, diplomatic efforts to foster peace in the Middle East have failed. Wertheimer now offers an alternative, the Tefen Model, a unique business-based, cross-culturally integrated industrial-park approach that "stresses creativity through an unusual combination of aims: providing high quality products to a global market, advancing entrepreneurial education and industrial training, fostering new indigenous industries, and showcasing art and culture. To these ends, the [industrial] parks in Israel, Jordan, and Turkey all have incubator spaces, educational and training facilities, museums, and sculpture gardens."[49]

---

[48] Prahalad and Hart (2002, p. 14).

[49] Statement by Stef Wertheimer, Chairman, Board of Directors, ISCAR, Ltd. at the June 24, 2002 Hearing of the United States House Committee on International Relations, as found at http://www.israelnewsagency.com/stefwertheimer.html. For a further discussion of Wertheimer's Tefen Model and its implications for peace, see "Trialogue of Cultures in the Age of Globalization" at the Sinclair House Debates, Herbert-Quandt Stiftung Foundation at http://www.h-quandt-stiftung.de/root/index.php?lang=en&page_id=333 , and Ari Goldberg's "Israeli tycoon urges help for Palestinians," BBC News on-line at http://news.bbc.co.uk/1/hi/business/1944846.stm.

Using the Tefen Model within Israel, Wertheimer has already built a series of industrial parks that bring together Arab, Druze, and Jewish Israelis.[50] Are they successful? Yes, already by 2002 the four Israeli industrial parks had launched 150 new firms and had created 5000 new jobs.[51] By 2004 the same four industrial parks accounted for more than $2 billion in annual revenue, representing 10 percent of Israel's total industrial exports.[52]

Will Wertheimer's network of industrial parks ultimately become a major factor in bringing peace to the Middle East? It is too early to tell, but there are already 10 industrial parks either built or planned throughout the eastern Mediterranean, including sites in Israel, Jordan, Lebanon, Turkey and Gaza. Many people are optimistic about their current and future success. Wertheimer believes that "industry is the engine of economic stability"; and that without economic stability, there can be no peace.[53]

As Wertheimer graphically stated to the United States Congress, "The Middle East has a way of besmirching the entire world with its conflicts. It is of global interest to quiet this area."[54] An industrial development plan for this region, based on the Tefen Model, would produce a variety of benefits, perhaps the most important of which would be "a reduction of terrorism worldwide. The majority of the world's terrorists hail from [the Middle East]. ... Terrorism thrives in areas of poverty. Narrowing the gap between the financial status of neighboring countries and enhancing a population's standard of living automatically changes attitudes. Job opportunities and a higher standard of living for people in this area will reduce the power that terrorist groups offer to the deprived masses."[55]

---

[50] Fast 50 — 2003 Winners: Meet the Winners (2003) appearing on the *Fast Company* website, in a complement to the March 2003 print edition. It is part of the section, Link: http://www.fastcompany.com/fast50_04/2003winners.html.

[51] Op cit., Wertheimer (2002).

[52] Op cit., Fast 50 — 2003 Winners: Meet the Winners (2003).

[53] Op cit., Wertheimer (2002).

[54] Ibid.

[55] Ibid.

American Evan Kaizer's appreciation of Wertheimer's contribution is perhaps the best summary of the potential benefits this business model could contribute to the world:

> *Few individuals have achieved the business success of Stef Wertheimer ... and then have decided to dwarf the importance of their own contributions to the business marketplace with their commitment to promoting a peaceful coexistence of warring parties based upon respect and economic vitality. We can all learn from his model.*[56]

Natural capitalism: Sustainability at a profit

In addition to implementing poverty-reduction and Middle-East peacemaking strategies, businesses are also involved in highly innovative environment-enhancing strategies. According to *Harvard Business Review*, "Business strategies built around the radically more productive use of natural resources can solve many environmental problems at a profit."[57] Using the label "natural capitalism", Amory and Hunter Lovins along with their colleague Paul Hawken introduced a process by which business can gain a competitive edge and earn substantial profits by systemically focusing on the health of the natural environment:[58]

> *"The first stage [of natural capitalism] involves dramatically increasing the productivity of natural resources, stretching them as much as*

---

[56] Op cit., Fast 50 — 2003 Winners: Meet the Winners (2003).

[57] Lovins *et al.* (1999).

[58] In addition to their excellent *Harvard Business Review* article, for an in depth discussion of natural capitalism, see Hawken *et al.*'s (1999) *Natural Capitalism: Creating the Next Industrial Revolution*. For further discussion on the role of business in protecting the environment, see the journals *Green@work* and *Reflections*, 1(4), 2000 — special issue on sustainability. In addition see Lovins and Altomare (2000) *Harvard Business Review on Business and the Environment;* Nattrass and Altomare's (1999) *The Natural Step for Business;* McDonough & Braungart's (2002) *Cradle to Cradle;* and Laszlo's (2003) *The Sustainable Company: How to Create Lasting Value Through Social and Environmental Performance.*

100 times further than they do today. In the second stage companies adopt closed-loop production systems that yield no waste or toxicity. The third stage requires a fundamental change of business model — from one of selling products to one of delivering services. For example, a manufacturer would sell lighting services rather than light bulbs, thus benefiting the seller and customer for developing extremely efficient, durable light bulbs. The last stage involves reinvesting in natural capital to restore, sustain, and expand the planet's' ecosystem.[59]

Why haven't most businesses considered such profit-making, environment-enhancing strategies before? Because the benefits often don't show up on the balance sheet. Most businesses treat the natural environment as a free resource. Yet "recent calculations... conservatively estimate the value of all the earth's ecosystem services to be at least \$33 trillion a year. That's close to the gross world product, and it implies a capitalized book value on the order of half a quadrillion dollars. What's more, for most of these services, there is no known substitute at any price, and we can't live without them."[60]

If there are such cost savings to be found in natural capitalism, why didn't business embrace it years ago? The answer is not that business values are somehow skewed or abhorrent, but rather that "...scores of common practices in both the private and public sectors systematically reward companies for wasting natural resources and penalize them for boosting resource productivity. For example, most companies expense their consumption of raw materials through the income statement but pass resource-saving investment through the balance sheet. That distortion makes it more tax efficient to waste fuel than to invest in improving fuel efficiency. ... [T]he compass that companies use to direct ...[themselves] is broken."[61]

Amory and Hunter Lovins and Paul Hawken offer examples of many companies that are already benefiting from natural capitalism.

---

[59] Lovins *et al.* (1999, p. 145).
[60] Ibid.
[61] Ibid.

Perhaps only one example, that of Interface Corporation, a leading maker of materials for commercial interiors, is needed to tell the much larger and highly optimistic story of what business could be contributing to societal well-being. In Interface's

> *"...new Shanghai carpet factory, a liquid had to be circulated through a standard pumping loop similar to those used in nearly all industries. A top European company designed the system to use pumps requiring a total of 95 horsepower. But before construction began, Interface's engineer, Jan Schilham, realized that two embarrassingly simple design changes would cut that power requirement to only 7 horsepower-a 92% reduction. His redesigned system cost less to build, involved no new technology, and worked better in all respects.*

How did Interface succeed in such a significant energy-consumption reduction? They used two small but highly leveraged innovations.

> *First, Schilham chose fatter-than-usual pipes, which create much less friction than thin pipes do and therefore need far less pumping energy. The original designer had chosen thin pipes because, according to the textbook method, the extra cost of fatter ones wouldn't be justified by the pumping energy that they would save. This standard design trade-off optimizes the pipes by themselves but "pessimizes" the larger system. Schilham optimized the whole system by counting not only the higher capital cost of the fatter pipes but also the lower capital cost of the smaller pumping equipment that would be needed. The pumps, motors, motor controls, and electrical components could all be much smaller because there'd be less friction to overcome. Capital cost would fall far more for the smaller equipment than it would rise for the fatter pipe. Choosing big pipes and small pumps-rather than small pipes and big pumps-would therefore make the whole system cost less to build, even before counting its future energy savings.*[62]

---

[62] Ibid.

The second innovation was to make the pipes straight and short rather than crooked and long, which further reduced the friction. Interface accomplished this:

> ... *by laying out the pipes first, then positioning the various tanks, boilers, and other equipment that they connected. Designers normally locate the production equipment in arbitrary positions and then have a pipe fitter connect everything. Awkward placement forces the pipes to make numerous bends that greatly increase friction. The pipe fitters don't mind: they're paid by the hour, they profit from the extra pipes and fittings, and they don't pay for the oversized pumps or inflated electric bills. ... Schilham's short, straight pipes were easier to insulate, saving an extra 70 kilowatts of heat loss and repaying the insulation's cost in three months.*[63]

The Interface example has implications far beyond both Interface and China for two reasons:

> *"First, pumping is the largest application of motors, and motors use three-quarters of all industrial electricity. Second, the lessons are very widely relevant. Interface's pumping loop shows how simple changes in design mentality can yield huge resource savings and returns on investment.*[64]

Inventing small changes, such as those at Interface, "that are cheap, free or even better than free" (because they generate big savings) rely on whole-systems thinking.[65] With whole-systems thinking, "the right investment in one part of the system can produce multiple benefits throughout the system.[66]

The logic of natural capitalism is compelling. In the 21st century, unlike during the industrial revolution, natural resources, not people,

---

[63] Ibid.
[64] Ibid.
[65] Ibid.
[66] Ibid.

are scarce. Ultimately, the companies that most effectively manage their scarcest resources will win, as will society. Those that don't will cease to exist. Where natural capitalism can eclipse Wangari Maathai's tree-planting efforts is not in its commitment or values, but rather in the private sector's much higher leverage to make substantial and lasting worldwide changes. As more businesses embrace natural capitalism, however, they would be wise to carefully observe the efforts of such leaders as Shirin Ebadi, Wangari Maathai, and Gro Harlem Brundtland when searching for approaches that are most likely to succeed.

From Despair to Optimism: An Ecology of Hope

In his 2004 presidential campaign, United States Congressman Dennis Kucinich described his desire to create a Department of Peace as the first step in "making nonviolence an organizing principle in society."[67] According to Kucinich, "Creating a structure of peace ensures that economic structures can be sound, affirmative of human needs, and restorative of human values."[68] There is no question that the world needs peace to prosper, and prosperity to have peace. The world, however, cannot attain peace without all of society's primary actors actively working to create the conditions for peace. For too long, business has been left out of that equation. Now, as we enter the 21st century, forward-thinking leaders from all sectors are searching for new partnership options that include business as a co-creator of a society we can be proud of.[69] Increasingly, business is taking the lead in some of the most innovative and exciting initiatives that offer hope for the planet.

---

[67] "Iraq and the Economy" by United States Representative Dennis J. Kucinich at his Swearing-In Ceremony on Sunday, January 5, 2003, in Cleveland, Ohio; as reported at Common Dreams News Center website: http://www.commondreams.org/views03/0113-05.htm.

[68] Ibid.

[69] For a particularly important and innovative approach, see the Ethical Globalization Initiative (http://www.eginitiative.org/), founded and led by Mary Robinson, the former President of Ireland and former executive director of the United Nation's Human Rights Commission.

Arnold Toynbee, in observing societal dynamics, clearly believed society could do better:

"The [21ˢᵗ]...century will be chiefly remembered by future generations not as an era of political conflicts or technical inventions, but as an age in which human society dared to think of the welfare of the whole human race as a practical objective."[70]

Nobel Peace Prize Laureate Joseph Rotblat, after all his warnings about the dire consequences of war, also offers reasons to be hopeful:

"I do not believe that there is scientific evidence that biology condemns humanity to war."[71]

Former Prime Minister Golda Meir's insights likewise offer hope for society to change its thinking and behavior, and to achieve heretofore unimaginable aspirations:

"War is an immense stupidity. I'm sure that someday all wars will end. I'm sure that someday children in school will study the history of the men who made war as you study an absurdity. They'll be astonished; they'll be shocked, just as today we're shocked by cannibalism. Even cannibalism was accepted for a long time as normal. And yet today, at least physically, it's not practised any more."[72]

References

Adler, NJ (1998). Societal Leadership: the Wisdom of Peace. In *Executive Wisdom and Organizational Change*, Suresh Srivastva and DL Cooperrider (Eds.), pp. 205–221, San Francisco: Jossey-Bass.

---

[70] Arnold J. Toynbee as quoted in the opening of the introduction to Bruce Mau *et al.*'s *Massive Change* (2004, p. 15).

[71] Franck *et al.* (2000) as published in the original edition: Nyack, NY: Circumstantial Productions Publishing, 1998, p. 71.

[72] Former Israeli Prime Minister Golda Meir, as cited in Fallaci (1976).

Adler, N (1994). Globalization, government, and competitiveness. *Optimum*, 25(1), 27–34.

Adler, NJ and F Ghadar (1990). Strategic human resource management: a global perspective. In *Human Resource Management in International Comparison*, Rudiger Pieper (Ed.), pp. 235–260, Berlin: deGruyter.

Adler, NJ and F Ghadar (1993). A strategic phase approach to international human resource management. In *International Management Research: Looking to the Future*, Durhane Wong-Rieger and Fritz Rieger (Eds.), pp. 55–77, Berlin: deGruyter.

Caputo, P (2005). *Acts of Faith*. New York: Alfred A. Knopf.

Creswell, J (2005a). Citigroup agrees to pay $2 billion in Enron Scandal. *New York Times*, June 11.

Creswell, J (2005b). J.P. Morgan chase to pay investors $2.2 billion. *New York Times*, June 15.

Diamond, J (2005). *Collapse: How Societies Choose to Fail or Succeed*. New York: Viking.

Fallaci, O (1976). *Interviews with History*. Boston: Houghton Mifflin.

Franck, F, J Roze, R Connolly (Eds.) (2000). *What Does It Mean to be Human?* New York: St. Martin's Press (Originally published 1998: Nyack, NY: Circumstantial Productions Publishing).

Friedman, M (1970). The social responsibility of business is to increase its profits. *New York Times Magazine*, September 13, pp. 32–33, 122–126.

Friedman, TL (2005a). C.E.O.s, M.I.A. *New York Times*, op-ed, May 25.

Friedman, TL (2005b). It's a flat world, after all. *New York Times*, op-ed, April 3.

Friedman, TL (2005c). *The World is Flat: A Brief History of the Twenty-First Century*. New York: Farrar, Straus & Giroux.

Fast 50 — 2003 Winners: Meet the Winners (2003). Complement to the March 2003 *Fast Company* print edition appearing on the *Fast Company* website at: http://www.fastcompany.com/fast50_04/2003winners.html.

Hart, SL (2005). *Capitalism at the Crossroads*. Upper Saddle River, New Jersey: Wharton School Publishing (Pearson Education).

Hart, S and CM Christensen (2002). The great leap: driving innovation from the base of the pyramid. *Sloan Management Review*, 44(1), 51–56.

Hawken, P, A Lovins and LH Lovins (1999). *Natural Capitalism: Creating the Next Industrial Revolution*. Boston: Little Brown & Company.

Kakutani, M (2005). For Americans in Sudan, good deeds turn sour. *New York Times*, May 3.

Laszlo, C (2003). *The Sustainable Company: How to Create Lasting Value Through Social and Environmental Performance*. Washington DC: Island Press.

Lovins, AB, H Lovins and P Hawken (1999). A road map for natural capitalism. *Harvard Business Review*, 77(3), 145–158.

Lovins, AB, H Lovins, P Hawken, F Reinhardt, R Shapiro and J Magretta (2000). *Harvard Business Review on Business and the Environment.* Boston, MA: Harvard Business School Publishing.

Mau, B and The Institute without Boundaries (2004). *Massive Change.* London: Phaidon Press.

McDonough, W and M Braungart (2002). *Cradle to Cradle.* New York: North Point Press.

McLean, B and P Elkind (2003). *The Smartest Guys in the Room: The Amazing Rise and Scandalous Fall of Enron.* New York City, NY: Portfolio (Penguin Group).

Mjøs, OD (2003). The Nobel Peace Prize for 2003, announcing Shirin Ebadi on December 10 in Oslo, Norway: Norwegian Nobel Committee (as cited at http://www.nobel.no/eng_lect_2003a.html).

Mjøs, OD (2004). The Nobel Peace Prize for 2004, announcing Wangari Maathai on December 10 in Oslo, Norway: Norwegian Nobel Committee (as cited at http://nobelprize.org/peace/laureates/2004/presentation-speech.html).

Nattrass, B and M Altomare (1999). *The Natural Step for Business.* Gabriola Island, British Columbia, Canada: New Society.

Prahalad, CK (2005). *The Fortune at the Bottom of the Pyramid: Eradicating Poverty Through Profits.* Upper Saddle River, NJ: Wharton School Publishing (Pearson Education).

Prahalad, CK and A Hammond (2002). Serving the World's poor, profitably. *Harvard Business Review*, 80(9), 48–57.

Prahalad, CK and SL Hart (2002). The fortune at the bottom of the pyramid. *Strategy + Business*, 26(1), 2–14.

Roblatt, J (2005). The 50-year shadow. *New York Times*, May 17.

Scott, AO (2005). Those you love to hate: a look at the mighty laid low. *New York Times*, April 22.

Sorkin, R (2005). Ex-chief and aide guilty of looting millions at tyco. *New York Times*, June 18.

Schwab, K (2003). Capitalism must develop more of a conscience. *Newsweek*, February 24, 41–42.

Wertheimer, S (2002). Statement by Stef Wertheimer. Washington, DC: June 24, 2002 Hearing of the United States House Committee on International Relations (as sited at http://www.israelnewsagency.com/stefwertheimer.html).

The Worldwatch Institute (2005). *State of the World 2005: Redefining Global Security.* Washington DC: Worldwatch Institute.

Section Three

THE VIRTUOUS ORGANIZATION AND EXEMPLARY TIMES

Section Editor: Karen P. Manz

How do we imagine "exemplary times" for our work life? Is it evidenced by windfall profits and a bulging portfolio? Does it appear as a time when everyone is enthused, creative and empowered to do their very best work? Is it when a leader of extraordinary demeanor and skill inspires others to stretch a little farther or to trust a little more? Or rather, is it a rare occasion occurring every other decade when all the stars are aligned and we feel "just right"?

We may recognize some truth in all of the above scenarios. However, in considering the chapters of this section, there appears the possibility that *exemplary times may simply occur when we experience the abundant capacity and positive benefit of having developed a connection with virtue either as an ideal or actual behavior.* As this process is developmental, it can be viewed as how one might acquire wisdom over time. The following chapters are ordered to represent means of recognizing, developing, and realizing virtue in individuals and organizations — in obvious and not-so-obvious ways — and which can facilitate greater opportunity for exemplary times in work and life.

The authors of this section take a focused look at aspects of the relationship between virtues and the exemplary nature of people, places and work by drawing upon theory, research, philosophy, case studies, practices or personal reflection. We begin with Pearce, Waldman and Csikszentmihalyi who propose a model of virtuous leadership which identifies individual characteristics and cues in the environment which may contribute to enhanced moral decision making and positive organizational learning.

Next, Mitroff and Mitroff present a unique case study and reflective analysis of noted children's television creator Fred Rogers. They take a lifespan perspective of moral development as they point to the many places, time periods and ways in which Rogers' exemplary life philosophy has touched the lives of children. Yesterday's TV-viewing children are today's leaders and Rogers' legacy for adult managers is discussed.

Meyerson and Quinn look at those individuals — tempered radicals — who seek to bring positive change to an organization for the benefit of others who may be marginalized due to their values or personal attributes. The authors compare the sometimes subtle, incremental, long-term and honorable efforts of tempered radicals with the positive deviance concept of POS.

In the next chapter, *Fortune* magazine senior writer, Marc Gunther, is in conversation with Judi Neal about CEO's and enlightened organizations. An exemplary CEO is highlighted as a case study of one who has exhibited virtuous behaviors which link to exemplary results in his work and life. Neal continues the conversation as she explores the capacity of organizations to exercise virtuous behavior.

Rosabeth Moss Kanter closes this section by calling for greater attention to and engagement with higher order values in the economic life of communities, regional areas and national society. In particular, the "Corporate Conduct Continuun" is introduced as a means for enhancing a broader view of corporate responsibility. Numerous company cases are noted and extolled whereby exemplary corporate citizenship has been developed. Kanter reiterates the view of the authors in this volume that we should seek "the best in us all in all places".

Chapter Ten

VIRTUOUS LEADERSHIP: A THEORETICAL MODEL AND RESEARCH AGENDA

Craig L. Pearce

Claremont Graduate University

David A. Waldman

Arizona State University

Mihaly Csikszentmihalyi

Claremont Graduate University

A discussion of a model for virtuous leadership is presented by Pearce, Waldman and Csikszentmihalyi. The import and interplay of work relationships and task accomplishment are considered along vertical and shared leadership connections. These authors contend that individual characteristics and cues in the environment may point to greater ethical and moral decision making as well as enhanced positive organizational learning. The idea of a continuum ranging from absence to full presence of virtuous leadership has implications for exemplary work.

In this manuscript we attempt to shed light on the concept of virtuous leadership. We first attempt to identify the nature of virtuous leadership. Next, we specify two potential antecedents of virtuous vertical leadership. Specifically, we identify the personal characteristic of responsibility disposition, as well as environmental cues, as potential predictors of subsequent virtuous leadership. Moreover, we articulate how virtuous vertical leadership might result in virtuous shared leadership. We also demonstrate how both vertical and shared virtuous leadership can act as key factors in the creation of organizational learning. Importantly, we specify several important research implications of our theoretical model. Finally, we illustrate several practical considerations when it comes to developing and enhancing virtuous leadership.

Virtuous Leadership: A Theoretical Model and Research Agenda

The purpose of this manuscript is to provide definition to the concept of virtuous leadership, to identify potential antecedents of virtuous leadership and to articulate its potential relationship to organizational learning. The issue of virtue in organizations has taken on more prominence in recent years. Reflecting general thinking on positive psychology (e.g., Csikszentmihalyi, 1990, 1993), scholars have begun to take a keen interest in positive organizational psychology (e.g., Csikszentmihalyi, 2003; Cameron *et al.*, 2003). Numerous, recent high-profile corporate scandals, such as those at Enron, Worldcom, and Aldelphia, among others, have no doubt also heightened interest in the virtues, or lack thereof, demonstrated by the leaders of our organizations. Accordingly, we begin by briefly reviewing leadership theory and scholarship on organizational learning. We subsequently specify what we believe to comprise the nature of virtuous leadership in organizations. We then develop a theoretical model of virtuous leadership, including potential antecedents and outcomes. Finally, we discuss the research and practical implications of our model.

Numerous definitions of leadership have been put forth in the literature, with many focusing on influence processes used in pursuing a goal or set of goals (Sashkin, 1988; Yukl, 2002). For example, Rauch and Behling (1984, p. 46) defined leadership as a "process of influencing the activities of an organized group toward goal achievement." In a similar manner, House *et al.* (1999) posed the definition, "the ability of an individual to influence, motivate, and enable others to contribute toward the effectiveness and success of the organization ..."

Some recent definitions of leadership, however, have begun to stress how the influence process involves a relationship component (e.g., Lord and Brown, 2001, 2004; Waldman *et al.*, 2001). Leadership, according to these recent definitions, entails a relationship between a leader and followers, although the relationship can be hierarchically or geographically distant and not require face-to-face interaction (Waldman and Yammarino, 1999). Pearce and colleagues (e.g., Pearce and Conger, 2003; Pearce *et al.*, 2008; Pearce and Manz, 2005) have built on the idea of leadership as embedded in relationships in their articulation of shared leadership theory. According to shared leadership theory, leadership can flow in multiple directions in organizations, including both up and down the vertical hierarchy as well as horizontally among peers. More specifically, shared leadership can be defined as the serial emergence of multiple leaders based on the task demands and the knowledge, skills and abilities of those involved in the task. Recent research has documented the importance of shared leadership in a wide variety of contexts including top management teams (Ensley *et al.*, 2006), change management (Pearce and Sims, 2002), research and development (Hooker and Csikszentmihalyi, 2003), the military (Shamir and Lapidot, 2003) and social work (Pearce *et al.*, 2004). In sum, virtuous leadership can be displayed by formally designated, vertical leaders, as well as through shared leadership.

The concept of organizational learning has also taken on increased prominence in recent years, as scholars have attempted to link it to firm strategy and effectiveness (Bligh *et al.*, 2006; Senge, 1990). Crossan *et al.* (1999), for instance, view organizational learning as a dynamic process of change in both thought and action, characterized by the challenge between acquiring new learning, while utilizing what has already been learned. Vera and Crossan (2004) point toward linkages between leadership behavior at strategic levels, and organizational learning — especially with regard to feed-forward processes that allow a firm to innovate and renew itself. As such, organizational learning can provide a means of long-term competitive advantage.

We, in the text that follows, argue that virtuous leadership is an important facilitator of learning within organizations. Virtuous leadership can establish the conditions of trust and openness that are critical to the creation and transformation of knowledge within organizations. Accordingly, in the next section we illuminate the nature of virtuous leadership by specifically considering the role of the vertical leader. Later we articulate how shared leadership might likewise be virtuous in nature.

The Nature of Virtuous Leadership

While various definitions of leadership are clearly sensible, we believe that they have not adequately specified how leadership can be virtuous in nature. The dictionary equates virtuous to righteousness and morality. As such, any definition of virtuous leadership should specifically include the pursuit of righteous and moral goals for both individuals and the organizations in which they work. Accordingly, we define virtuous leadership as distinguishing right from wrong in one's leadership role, taking steps to ensure justice and honesty, influencing and enabling others to pursue righteous and moral goals for themselves and their organizations and helping others to connect to a higher purpose.

Burns (1978) originally advanced the argument that transforming leadership is tantamount to virtuous leadership, and that both followers and leaders progress to the highest levels of moral development (Kohlberg, 1976) as a result of such leadership. That is, transformational leaders are able to progress to Kohlberg's post-conventional stage, in which they act in an independent and ethical manner, regardless of the expectations of other individuals. Along similar lines, Kuhnert and Lewis (1987) and Kuhnert (1994) outlined a constructive/developmental personality theory of understanding the world and resulting behavior on the part of leaders. This theory would suggest that transformational leaders are likely to progress to a superior stage of development, involving deeply-held personal values and standards (e.g., integrity, justice, and maintaining the societal good). Bass and Steidlmeier (1999) also addressed moral values, suggesting that *authentic* transformational leaders attain advanced levels of moral development. Additionally, Further, Turner *et al.* (2002) present evidence of an empirical relationship between leadership and moral development, according to the Kohlberg (1976) typology.

Along similar lines, Kanungo (2001) and Mendonca (2001) argued that charismatic leadership, a concept similar to transformational leadership, can be rooted in strong ethical values. The essence of this argument is that such leaders are likely to be guided by morally altruistic principles that "reflect a helping concern for others even at considerable personal sacrifice or inconvenience" (Mendonca, 2001, p. 268). As such, their visions are just and in sync with the demands of various stakeholders, not just shareholders — a notion to which we will return below. Further, their fortitude gives these types of leaders the courage to face risks and work at overcoming obstacles in the pursuit of goals (Mendonca, 2001). We should caution, however, that as noted by previous authors (e.g., Bass and Steidlmeier, 1999; Howell and Avolio, 1992), not all leaders with charismatic appeal will have strong moral values, and indeed some may have motives leaning more toward personal power and self-aggrandizement, which we address in the following section.

Most interacting groups with time develop a hierarchy that includes various levels of power and responsibility (Leavitt, 2004). Even though hierarchies vary considerably in terms of how centralized vs. diffuse the authority relations within the group are, leadership — either formal or informal — is likely to emerge. The ideal type of virtuous leadership would have the following characteristics: (1) the leader is successful in fulfilling the goals of the group — which usually involves external criteria such as profitability, market share, and so on; (2) the leader invests time and energy in trying to optimize the individual goals of the group members; (3) the leader is able to align the goals of the group with the goals of a larger ideal or community; and (4) the leader believes in his or her mission, and enjoys its performance. In reality, such an ideal may rarely be attained in its entirety. While some leaders fall short on each of these four counts, others are able to manage one or more of them creditably. Thus virtuous leadership may be seen as a continuum ranging from absence to full presence.

A Model of Virtuous Leadership and Organizational Learning

In Fig. 1, we present a model of virtuous leadership. The model has three primary features. First, we link the enactment of virtuous *vertical* leadership to two likely antecedents. Second, we conceptualize how virtuous vertical leadership can affect the display of virtuous

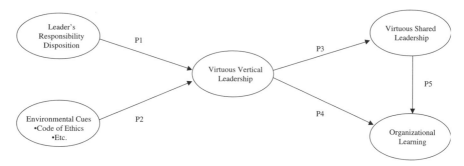

Fig. 1:   A model of virtuous leadership antecedents and outcomes.

shared leadership. Finally, we articulate the importance of virtuous leadership, both vertical and shared, to organizational learning.

Antecedents of virtuous vertical leadership

We expect two broad types of antecedents of virtuous vertical leadership. On the one hand, personal characteristics should play a major role in the virtuousness of one's leadership. Accordingly, we examine the leader's responsibility disposition. On the other hand, we expect the environment to play an important role as well. Accordingly, we examine the role of environmental cues (e.g., ethics codes, reward systems, etc.). Below we further explicate the potential nature of these relationships.

Responsibility disposition: leaders can be classified according to two types of need for power: (1) socialized, and (2) personalized. The key distinction between these types of need for power lies in the leader's underlying responsibility disposition. Socialized leaders tend to have a high responsibility disposition, whereas personalized leaders have a low responsibility disposition. Winter (1991) proposed that individuals with a strong sense of responsibility have beliefs and values reflecting high moral standards, a feeling of obligation to do the right thing, concern about others, and a high degree of self-judgment or critical evaluation of one's own character. These types of leaders apply restraint in their use of power, and they use their influence to achieve goals and objectives for the betterment of the collective entity, rather than for personal gain (House and Howell, 1992; Pearce *et al.*, 2008). Similarly, Avolio *et al.* (2004) suggested that authentic leaders set a personal example of moral standards and integrity, thus building a high level of identification with the leader.

In contrast, leaders high in a need for personalized power desire positions of power for their personal benefit, rather than the benefit of the larger group or organization (Conger, 1990; Hogan *et al.*, 1994). Indeed, these types of leaders are often described as narcissistic. They can become extremely self-absorbed, have an exaggerated sense of self-importance, have a strong desire to be admired by others, and view the manipulation of others as a sport (Hogan, 1994; Hogan *et al.*, 1994; Kets de Vries, 1993; Maccoby, 2004). Such individuals raise impression management to the level of an art (Gardner and Avolio, 1998; Giacalone *et al.*, 1998). Accordingly, such leaders are adept at scheming ways to enhance their own image (Gardner and Avolio, 1998; Giacalone *et al.*, 1998), and persuasively emphasize the importance of personal allegiance to them as the leader, rather than the greater organization (Hogan *et al.*, 1994). Indeed, these types of narcissistic leaders often have great difficulty in building a team because of their counter-productive need for personal power over others (Hogan *et al.*, 1994). As such, we believe the leader's responsibility disposition plays a key role in how virtuous one behaves as a leader. The following proposition more formally articulates this viewpoint.

P1: The leader's responsibility disposition will be related to how virtuously the leader behaves.

Environmental cues: Mischel (1977) articulated the concept of situational strength. Strong situations are characterized as providing very clear cues as to appropriate behavior, while weak situations are characterized as being ambiguous with regard to what constitutes appropriate behavior. While situational strength may provide cues to expected behavior, there is nothing that guarantees those cues will indicate virtuous behavior. Take Enron for example. At Enron there were numerous cues that continuous improvement in short-term financial numbers was paramount: Those who found ways to increase the numbers, no matter the means, were those most highly rewarded and recognized. The environmental cues at Enron were quite strong.

Nevertheless, it is possible to manage environmental cues such that they are in support of virtuous leadership. Consider, for example, the work of Manz and Sims and colleagues (e.g., Manz and Sims, 1990, 2001). These authors have specifically articulated the importance of managing one's environment in support of effective leadership. At the organizational level, cues can take on many forms, from ethics codes (e.g., Weaver *et al.*, 1999), to leadership selection and development systems, to the manner in which rewards are distributed. Accordingly, we believe that environmental cues will be predictive of virtuous leadership. This position is stated more formally in the following proposition.

P2: Environmental cues will be related to how virtuous the leader behaves.

Likely outcomes of virtuous leadership

While there are likely to be many potential outcomes of virtuous leadership, we focus on two specific outcomes in our model. First, we articulate the potential relationship between virtuous vertical leadership on the development of virtuous shared leadership. Second, we link virtuous leadership, both vertical and shared, to organizational learning.

Virtuous vertical leadership and shared leadership: we expect virtuous vertical leadership to result in virtuous shared leadership. As defined above, the virtuous vertical leader has deep concern for equity and justice, as well as helping others to achieve moral and righteous goals. These types of vertical leaders have been labeled alternatively as either "empowering" leaders (e.g., Pearce and Sims, 2002; Pearce *et al.*, 2004) or as "SuperLeaders" (Manz and Sims, 1990, 1991, 2001). Houghton *et al.* (2003, p. 133) specifically linked virtuous vertical leadership to the development and display of shared leadership in teams: "SuperLeadership may be viewed as the art of creating and facilitating...shared leadership."

Bass *et al.* (1987) found that subordinates tended to emulate the transformational leadership they experienced from above, and labeled the phenomena the "falling dominoes effect". More recently, Pearce and Sims (2002) identified that this domino effect applies across a wide range of leader behavior, ranging from aversive leadership — the use of threats and intimidation, and the like — to virtuous forms of leadership, such as empowering leadership. Accordingly, virtuous, vertical leadership seems likely to result in virtuous shared leadership. The following proposition more formally articulates this position.

P3: Virtuous vertical leadership is positively related to the development and display of virtuous shared leadership.

Virtuous vertical leadership and organizational learning: to better understand how virtuous vertical leadership might affect organizational learning we turn to stakeholder theory. Stakeholder theory specifies that a firm has a variety of different constituencies, such as employees, suppliers, customers, shareholders, and the broader community (Donaldson and Preston, 1995; Freeman, 1984). All of these constituencies have a strategic and/or moral stake in the firm, and they are each guided by their own interests and values. The key issue addressed by virtuous leaders is how to enhance the welfare of the firm, while simultaneously balancing the needs of the various stakeholders. Many scholars claim that by far the most important stakeholder to which top leaders must attend are the shareholders since they are the owners of the company. However, because of their broad-ranging moral and justice values, virtuous vertical leaders will attempt to balance the interests of all stakeholders (Bass and Steidlmeier, 1999; Waldman *et al.*, 2005), providing a more robust framework from which to leverage the learning potential of the firm.

As an example of the effect of virtuous vertical leadership on organizational learning, Waldman *et al.* (2005) described the case of a CEO of a Fortune 500 company that had been trying to energize his executive leadership team and other senior managers to focus on a totally new conceptualization of the firm's strategy. Yet because of the uniqueness and change involved in the strategy, it was facing skepticism and neglect from the executive team. The CEO had organized a three-day retreat with his top 200 executives to discuss the new strategy and build commitment to its implementation. During the first day, the CEO and other speakers provided details on the new strategy and engaged in a variety of discussions. By mid-afternoon, it was clear that the CEO was not fully connecting to the group. He changed gears and started talking about how the new strategy would help the company contribute to the global fight against AIDS, specifically how the war against AIDS could benefit from the new strategy even though the company is not in the medical field.

The impact of the five-minute talk about AIDS was apparent. The mood of the group showed a discernable change. Managers started showing a stronger interest in the topic. During all formal and informal discussions that evening and the next two days, many references were made to the battle against AIDS. Upon completion of the retreat, the participants rated the discussion about AIDS as one of the highlights of the retreat. The gathering started with a large group of skeptical executives and seemed to have ended with a large group of energized and mobilized executives. The upshot is that followers may be more motivated and energized to contribute to the learning capacity of the firm, when the leadership is clearly virtuous in nature.

P4: Virtuous vertical leadership is positively related to organizational learning.

Virtuous shared leadership and organizational learning: we also expect virtuous shared leadership to result in enhanced organizational learning, which is consistent with extant theory. Burke *et al.* (2003), as well as Conger and Pearce (2003), specifically link shared leadership with team-level cognition, while Vera and Crossan (2004, p. 227) purported that "the ideal leader might recognize his or her limitations and share the leadership of organizational learning."

The empirical evidence on shared leadership also suggests that it should be positively related to organizational learning. To date, studies of shared leadership have consistently linked it with positive organizational outcomes (Avolio *et al.*, 1996; Ensley *et al.*, 2006; Hooker and Csikszentmihalyi, 2003; Pearce, 1997; Pearce and Sims, 2002; Pearce *et al.*, 2004; Shamir and Lapidot, 2003). Most of the studies have examined some dimensions of performance, however, several have examined other constructs, such as team dynamics. Shamir and Lapidot (2003), for example, found shared leadership to be inextricably linked to moral and ethical decision making in the military. Moreover, Pearce *et al.*, (2004) found shared leadership to be an important predictor of problem solving quality in virtual teams of social workers. Perhaps most relevant in terms of the current model, Hooker and Csikszentmihalyi (2003) found shared leadership to be an important ingredient in creativity in research and development labs. Their case study reveals that shared leadership, under certain conditions, can enhance the conditions for flow (Csikszentmihalyi, 1988, 1990), which in turn bolsters the creative process. Accordingly, we expect shared leadership to result in enhanced organizational learning. The following proposition more formally captures the essence of our logic on the linkage between virtuous shared leadership and organizational learning.

P5: Virtuous shared leadership is positively related to organizational learning.

Implications

There are multiple implications of the theoretical model we presented. Below we first identify the key research implications before proceeding to its practical implications.

Research implications

There are several important research implications that are relevant to the current model. First, there is a notable dearth of research dealing with how virtuous leadership might ultimately result in organizational outcomes. Indeed, it is a challenging area in which to conduct research. Although many different survey measures of leadership exist (e.g., Bass, 1985; Conger and Kanungo, 1998), comparatively little has been done to measure virtuous leadership. Nonetheless, the work of Manz and Sims (1990, 1991, 2001) on SuperLeadership, alternatively labeled as empowering leadership (e.g., Pearce and Sims, 2002), provides a very useful starting point for launching work in the area of virtuous leadership and its impact in organizations.

Second, the temporal nature of the model presented here would suggest the need for longitudinal research. Issues such as organizational learning indeed take time to develop. Accordingly one might assess the antecedents at an early stage of research, virtuous vertical leadership at an intermediate stage, shared virtuous leadership at a later stage and organizational learning at a final stage. Clearly, experimental work might also be useful in regard to identifying the causal nature of these relationships.

Third, levels of analysis issues are relevant to the current model. The model includes individual-level, group-level and organizational-level phenomena. The work of Kozlowski and Klein (2000) is relevant to research of this nature. They proposed that "bottom up processes" portray how lower-level properties emerge to form collective phenomena (Kozlowski and Klein, 2000, p. 15). Relevant to the concept of organizational learning, it is possible for emergence to occur through *compilation*, whereby there is theoretical reason to believe that lower-level properties may sometimes emerge in a discontinuous manner. The result is a collective-level phenomenon with *configural* properties. Kozlowski and Klein (2000) describe how unit properties conceptualized in configural terms are relatively rare in the organizational literature, although they are not rare in actual organizations. More specifically, they note that according to dispersion theory, non-uniform phenomena characterized by potential disagreement, competition, coalition formation, and so forth, may indeed be quite common.

In the present model, if vertical and shared leadership emerge in a configural manner, this would be a sign of the type of personalized leadership discussed earlier. That is, in the case of the vertical leader, while some followers might be enamored by the leader and attribute virtuous qualities, others might pick up on fraudulent or self-serving tendencies. As such, we would expect that compilation or configural properties of leader emergence to not be in line with the model shown in Fig. 1. Instead, compositional or isomorphic models would be more in line with our model (Kozlowski and Klein, 2000). Such a model would entail the emergence of relatively uniform perceptions of virtuous leadership among followers.

Practical implications

There are several important practical implications that can be derived from the model that we have presented. Our model specifies that personal characteristics and environmental cues may play parts in the enactment of virtuous leadership. While codes of ethics seem a useful starting point, we believe a far more comprehensive approach is warranted. For instance, given that potential leaders can vary in their responsibility disposition, leader selection systems would appear to be a particularly important component of the organization's environment that not only signals what is valued but also helps to reinforce those values.

While we articulated a distinction between those who have a personalized versus a socialized need for power, identifying and clearly separating these two drives can be challenging. This is particularly true because those who are high in the need for personalized power are also generally quite skilled at impression management (Giacalone *et al.*, 1998). Couple this with the fact that the way leaders are selected is often a less-than-rigorous process, and this is true even at the top of organizations (Charan, 2005). As such, leader selection requires serious attention. Accordingly, one potential strategy would be the employment of sophisticated psychological testing as an important component of the leader selection process, at all levels of the organization. For example, Hogan and Hogan (2001) offer an approach that has promise for uncovering the hidden motives of would-be narcissistic leaders. Nonetheless, this is an area that would benefit from increased attention.

Leadership development is another important environmental cue that can both signal the importance of virtuous behavior and educate would-be leaders in virtuous approaches to leadership (Pearce, 2007; Quatro *et al.*, 2007). Unfortunately, evidence suggests that organizations rarely provide sufficient training and development (Pearce, 2004). Moreover, the vast majority of leadership development is focused on those individuals who are currently in formal leadership positions or have been identified as leadership candidates, as opposed to providing leadership skills, learning opportunities to the wider work force which typically represents an important source of leadership for the future (Cox *et al.*, 2003).

Perhaps this lack of attention to leadership development is what accounts for the general level of dissatisfaction with leaders that is so prevalent in organizations (Cranny *et al.*, 1992; Fisher and Locke, 1992). After satisfaction with pay, satisfaction with leadership is generally the second most dissatisfying aspect of most employees' organizational lives (Hackman and Oldham, 1980), and this is quite consistent across a broad assortment of contexts, ranging from service workers, to employees in the machine trades, to professional and technical employees, and even to the ranks of management. Accordingly, the development of virtuous leadership, both vertical and shared, is an area that would benefit from emphasis in organizations.

Reward systems appear to be another important environmental cue when it comes to encouraging virtuous leadership. People search for cues about what is and what is not rewarded in their organizations. They subsequently engage in (or at least create the appearance that they engage in) those behaviors that they believe are rewarded. Unfortunately, organizational reward systems are often out of synch with the desires of those who create the reward systems (Kerr, 1975). It is naïve, however, to suggest that simply paying people to be virtuous will miraculously result in virtuous leadership across the board. Realistically, we can expect that some people may not be motivated to behave in a virtuous manner. Again, this is where leader selection and development systems may prove important.

While we have highlighted several important environmental cues that can aid in the development of virtuous leadership, we do not believe this to be a comprehensive list of all that can be done to encourage virtuous leadership. Rather we illustrated these cues because they seem to be representative of what can be managed and seem to apply across organizational contexts. We believe that when it comes to managing environmental cues in support of virtuous leadership, a holistic, systems approach is warranted. The key, it would appear, is to have integrated and aligned systems that collectively support the development of virtuous leadership in organizations.

Conclusion

We have attempted to shed light on the concept of virtuous leadership. We specified two potential antecedents of virtuous vertical leadership. Specifically, we identified the personal characteristic of responsibility disposition and environmental cues as potential predictors of subsequent virtuous leadership. Moreover, we articulated how virtuous vertical leadership might result in virtuous shared leadership. We also indicated how both vertical and shared virtuous leadership might act as key factors in the creation of organizational learning. Importantly, we identified several important research implications of our theoretical model. Finally, we illustrated several practical considerations when it comes to developing and enhancing virtuous leadership. Clearly, virtuous leadership deserves more theoretical and empirical attention.

References

Avolio, BJ, D Jung, W Murray and N Sivasubramaniam (1996). Building highly developed teams: Focusing on shared leadership process, efficacy, trust and performance. In *Advances in Interdisciplinary Studies of Work Teams*, MM Beyerlein, DA Johnson and ST Beyerlein (Eds.), pp. 173–209, Greenwish: JAI Press.

Avolio, BJ, WL Gardner, FO Walumbwa, F Luthans and DR May (2004). Unlocking the mask: a look at the process by which authentic leaders impact follower attitudes and behaviors. *The Leadership Quarterly*, 15, 801–823.

Bass, BM (1985). *Leadership and Performance Beyond Expectations.* New York: Free Press.

Bass, BM, DA Waldman, BJ Avolio and M Bebb (1987). Transformational leadership and the falling dominoes effect. *Group and Organizational Studies,* 12, 73–87.

Bass, BM and P Steidlmeier (1999). Ethics, character, and authentic transformational leadership behavior. *The Leadership Quarterly,* 10, 181–217.

Bligh, M, CL Pearce and J Kohles (2006). The importance of self and shared leadership in team based knowledge work: toward a meso-level model of leadership dynamics. *Journal of Managerial Psychology,* 21(4), 296–318.

Burke, CS, SM Fiore and E Salas (2003). The role of shared cognition in enabling shared leadership and team adaptability. In *Shared Leadership: Reframing the Hows and Whys of Leadership,* CL Pearce and JA Conger (Eds.), pp. 103–122, Thousand Oaks, CA: Sage.

Burns, JM (1978). *Leadership.* New York: Harper Row.

Cameron, KS, JE Dutton and RE Quinn (eds.) (2003). *Positive Organizational Scholarship.* San Francisco: Berrett-Koehler.

Charan, R (2005). Ending the CEO succession crisis. *Harvard Business Review,* February, 28–37.

Conger, JA (1990). The dark side of leadership. *Organizational Dynamics,* 19, 2, 44–55.

Conger, JA and RN Kanungo (1998). *Charismatic Leadership in Organizations.* Thousand Oaks, CA: Sage Publications.

Conger, JA and CL Pearce (2003). A landscape of opportunities: Future research on shared leadership. In *Shared Leadership: Reframing the Hows and Whys of Leadership,* CL Pearce and JA Conger (eds.), pp. 285–303. Thousand Oaks, CA: Sage.

Cox, JF, CL Pearce and HP Sims (2003). Toward a broader agenda for leadership development: Extending the traditional transactional-transformational duality by developing directive, empowering and shared leadership skills. In *The Future of Leadership Development,* SE Murphy and RE Riggio (Eds.), pp. 161–180, Mahwah, NJ: Lawrence Earlbaum.

Cranny, CJ, PC Smith and EF Stone (Eds.) (1992). *Job Satisfaction: How People Feel About Their Jobs and How it Affects Their Performance.* New York: Lexington Books.

Crossan, M, H Lane and R White (1999). An organizational learning framework: From intuition to institution. *Academy of Management Review,* 24, 522–538.

Csikszentmihalyi, I (1988). Flow in historical context: the case of the Jesuits. In *Optimal Experience: Psychological Studies of Flow in Consciousness,* M Csikszentmihalyi and I Csikszentmihalyi (eds.), Cambridge: Cambridge University Press.

Csikszentmihalyi, M (1990). *Flow: The Psychology of Optimal Experience.* New York: Harper Collins.

Csikszentmihalyi, M (1993). *The Evolving Self.* New York: Harper Collins.

Csikszentmihalyi, M (2003). *Good Business: Flow, Leadership, and the Making of Meaning.* New York: Viking.

Donaldson, T and L Preston (1995). The stakeholder theory of the firm: Concepts, evidence and implications. *Academy of Management Review*, 20, 1, 65–92.

Ensley, MD, KM Hmieleski and CL Pearce (2006). The importance of vertical and shared leadership within new venture top management teams: implications for the performance of startups. *Leadership Quarterly*, 17(3), 217–231.

Fisher, CD and EA Locke (1992). The new look in job satisfaction research and theory. In *Job Satisfcation: How People Feel About Their Jobs and How it Affects Their Performance*, CJ Cranny, PC Smith and EF Stone (Eds.), pp. 165–194, New York: Lexington Books.

Freeman, RE (1984). *Strategic Management: A Stakeholder Approach*, Boston: Pitman.

Gardner, WL and BJ Avolio (1998). The charismatic relationship: a dramaturgical perspective. *Academy of Management Review*, 23, 32–58.

Giacalone, RA, SB Knouse and CL Pearce (1998). The education of leaders: Impression management as a functional competence, *Journal of Management Systems*, 10, 2, 67–80.

Hackman, JR and GR Oldham (1980). *Work Redesign.* Reading, MA: Addison-Wesley.

Hogan, R (1994). Trouble at the top: Causes and consequences of managerial incompetence. *Consulting Psychologist Journal: Practice and Research*, 46, 9–150.

Hogan, R, GJ Curphy and J Hogan (1994). What we know about leadership effectiveness and personality. *American Psychologist*, 49, 493–504.

Hogan, R and J Hogan (2001). Assessing leadership: A view from the dark side, *International Journal of Selection & Assessment*, 9, 40–51.

Hooker, C and M Csikszentmihalyai (2003). Flow, shared leadership and creativity. In *Shared Leadership: Reframing the Hows and Whys of Leadership*, CL Pearce and JA Conger (eds.), Thousand Oaks, CA: Sage Publications.

Houghton, JD, CP Neck and CC Manz (2003). Self-leadership and superleadership: the heart and art of facilitating shared leadership. In *Shared Leadership: Reframing the How's and Why's of Leadership*, CL Pearce and JA Conger (eds.), pp. 123–140, Thousand Oaks, CA: Sage Publications.

House *et al.* (1999). Cultural influences on leadership and organizations: Project GLOBE. *Advances in Global Leadership*, 1, 171–233.

House, RJ, and JM Howell (1992). Personality and charismatic leadership. *The Leadership Quarterly*, 3, 81–108.

Howell, JM and BJ Avolio (1992). The ethics of charismatic leadership: submission or liberation? *Academy of Management Executive*, 6, 43–54.

Kanungo, RN (2001). Ethical values of transactional and transformational leaders. *Canadian Journal of Administrative Sciences*, 18, 257–265.

Kerr, S (1975). On the folly of rewarding A while hoping for B. *Academy of Management Journal*, 18, 769–783.

Kerr, S and JM Jermier (1978). Substitutes for leadership: Their meaning and measurement, *Organizational Behavior and Human Performance*, 22, 3, 11–14.

Kets de Vries, MFR (1993). *Leaders, Fools, and Imposters.* San Francisco: Jossey-Bass.

Kohlberg, L (1976). Moral stages and moralization: the cognitive-developmental approach. In *Moral Development and Behavior: Theory, Research, and Social Issues*, T. Likona (ed.), pp. 31–53, Austin, TX: Holt, Rinehart and Winston.

Kozlowski, SWJ and KJ Klein (2000). A multilevel approach to theory and research in organizations: Contextual, temporal and emergent processes. In *Multilevel Theory, Research and Methods in Organizations: Foundations, Extensions and New Directions*, KJ Klein and SWJ Kozlowski (Eds.), pp. 3–90. San Francisco: Jossey-Bass.

Kuhnert, KW (1994). Transforming leadership: developing people through delegation. In *Improving Organizational Effectiveness Through Transformational Leadership*, BM Bass and BJ Avolio (eds.), pp. 10–25, Thousand Oaks, CA: Sage.

Kuhnert, KW and P Lewis (1987). Transactional and transformational leadership: A constructive/developmental analysis. *Academy of Management Review*, 12, 648–657.

Leavitt, HL (2004). *Top Down: Why Hierarchies Are Here to Stay and How to Manage Them*, Boston: Harvard Business School Press.

Lord, RG and DJ Brown (2001). Leadership, values, and subordinates self-concepts. *The Leadership Quarterly*, 12, 133–152.

Lord, RG and DJ Brown (2004). *Leadership Processes and Follower Self-identity.* Mahwah, New Jersey: Lawrence Erlbaum Associates.

Maccoby, M (2004). Narcissistic leaders: the incredible pros, the inevitable cons. *Harvard Business Review*, 82(January), 92–101.

Manz, CC and HP Sims Jr. (1990). *SuperLeadership.* New York: Berkeley Books.

Manz, CC and HP Sims Jr. (1991). SuperLeadership: beyond the myth of heroic leadership. *Organizational Dynamics*, 19, 18–35.

Manz, CC and HP Sims Jr. (2001). *The New SuperLeadership: Leading Others to Lead Themselves*, San Francisco: Berrett-Koehler.

Mendonca, M (2001). Preparing for ethical leadership in organizations. *Canadian Journal of Administrative Sciences*, 18, 266–276.

Mischel, W (1977). The interaction of person and situation. In *Personality at the Crossroads: Current Issues in Interactional Psychology*, D Magnusson and NS Ender (Eds.), Hillsdale, NJ: Erlbaum.

Pearce, CL (1997). The determinants of change management team effectiveness: A longitudinal investigation. Unpublished doctoral dissertation. College Park, MD.

Pearce, CL (2007). The future of leadership development. *Human Resource Management Review*, 177(4), 355–359.

Pearce, CL (2004). The future of leadership: Combining vertical and shared leadership to transform knowledge work. *Academy of Management Executive*, 18(1), 47–57.

Pearce, CL, JA Conger and EA Locke (2007). Shared leadership theory. *Leadership Quarterly*. 18(3), 281–288.

Pearce CL and JA Conger (Eds.), (2003). *Shared Leadership: Reframing the Hows and Whys of Leadership*, Thousand Oaks, CA: Sage.

Pearce, CL and CC Manz (2005). The new silver bullets of leadership: the importance of self and shared leadership in knowledge work. *Organizational Dynamics*, 34(2), 130–140.

Pearce, CL, CC Manz and HP Sims Jr. (in press). The roles of vertical and shared leadership in enactment of executive corruption: implications for research and practice. *Leadership Quarterly*.

Pearce, CL and HP Sims Jr. (2002). Vertical versus shared leadership as predictors of the effectiveness of change management teams: an examination of aversive, directive, transactional, transformational, and empowering leader behaviors. *Group Dynamics: Theory, Research, and Practice*, 6(2), 172–197.

Pearce, CL, Y Yoo and M Alavi (2004). Leadership, social work and virtual teams: The relative influence of vertical vs. shared leadership in the nonprofit sector. In *Improving Leadership in Nonprofit Organizations*, RE Riggio and S Smith-Orr (eds.), pp. 180–203, San Francisco: Jossey Bass.

Quatro, SA, DA Waldman and BM Galvin (2007). Developing holistic leaders: Four domains for leadership development and practice. *Human Resource Management Review*, 17(4), 427–441.

Rauch, CF and O Behling (1984). Functionalism: Basis for an alternative approach to the study of leadership. In *Leaders and Managers: International Perspectives on Managerial Behavior and Leadership*, JG Hunt, DM Hosking, CA Schriesheim and R Stewart (eds.), pp. 45–62, Elmsford, NY: Pergamon Press.

Sashkin, M (1988). The visionary leader. In *Charismatic Leadership: The Elusive Factor in Organizational Effectiveness*, JA Conger and RN Kanungo (eds.), pp. 122–160, San Francisco: Jossey-Bass.

Senge, PM (1990). *The Fifth Discipline: The Art and Practice of the Learning Organization*. New York: Doubleday.

Shamir, B and Y Lapidot (2003). In *Shared Leadership: Reframing the Hows and Whys of Leadership*, CL Pearce and JA Conger (eds.), pp. 285–303, Thousand Oaks, CA: Sage.

Turner, N, J Barling, O Epitropaki, V Butcher and C Milner (2002). Transformational leadership and moral reasoning. *Journal of Applied Psychology*, 87, 304–311.

Vera, D and M Crossan (2004). Strategic leadership and organizational learning. *Academy of Management Review*, 29, 222–240.

Waldman, DA, GG Ramirez, RJ House and P Puranam (2001). Does leadership matter?: CEO leadership attributes under conditions of perceived environmental uncertainty. *Academy of Management Journal,* 44, 134–143.

Waldman, DA, D Siegel and M Javidan (2005). CEO transformational leadership and corporate social responsibility. Revision under review at the *Journal of Management Studies.*

Waldman, DA and FJ Yammarino (1999). CEO charismatic leadership: levels-of-management and levels-of-analysis effects. *Academy of Management Review,* 24, 266–285.

Weaver, GR, LK Trevino and PL Cochran (1999). Integrated and decoupled corporate social performance: management commitments, external pressures, and corporate ethics practices. *Academy of Management Journal,* 42, 539–552.

Winter, DG (1991). A motivational model of leadership: predicting long-term management success from TAT measures of power motivation and responsibility. *The Leadership Quarterly,* 2, 67–80.

Yukl, G (2002). *Leadership in Organizations* (5th ed.). Upper Saddle River, NJ: Prentice-Hall.

Chapter Eleven

SPIRITUALITY IN ACTION: THE FRED ROGERS' WAY OF MANAGING THROUGH LIFELONG MENTORING

Ian I. Mitroff

Alliant International University
University of Southern California

Donna Mitroff

Consultant, Children's Media

Mitroff and Mitroff present a reflective account of the exemplary work and life philosophy of Fred Rogers, originator of award-winning public television children's show, "Mr. Roger's Neighborhood". Although Fred Roger's is best known for his impact on children over the past 35 years, the Mitroffs examine his legacy on yesterday's children who are today's leaders. This "legacy look" at Rogers work is translated into seven key principles — "living virtues" — for adults which the Mitroffs frame within a lifespan perspective of learning and moral development.

"All life events are formative. All contribute to what we become, year by year as we go on growing. As my friend, the poet Kenneth Koch, once said, "You aren't just the age you are. You are all the ages you have ever been!"

> Fred Rogers (2003). *The World According to Mr. Rogers: Important Things to Remember*, p. 34. New York: Hyperion.

Introduction

On December 9, 2003, we were privileged to participate in a special memorial and "Tribute to Fred Rogers" at the Academy of Television Arts and Sciences in North Hollywood, California. Over the course of the evening, members of the Hollywood elite paid their regards to a kind and gentle man who was the antithesis of what the entertainment industry generally stands for. And yet, one after another, well-known personalities such as Lily Tomlin, David Hartman, Tyne Daly, Levar Burton, Scott Bakula, and others spoke, sang, danced, cried, and acknowledged his illustrious career, his enormous contributions to children's television, the overwhelming influence that Fred Rogers had on their lives, the lives of their children, and even their grandchildren. Everyone acknowledged Fred's genuineness, and especially, that he gave them hope that good television could be made.

Donna was one of the producers of the television academy's "Tribute to Fred Rogers." Donna met Fred in 1979 when she came to work at the Pittsburgh Public Television Station, WQED, as Director of Educational Services. Fred's production company, Family Communications, Inc., is still based at WQED. Donna worked with Fred and other members of his team over the next 20+ years and eventually came to know his wife, Joanne Byrd Rogers. While a member of the Board of Governors of the Academy of Television Arts and Sciences, Donna lobbied hard to get Fred elected to the Academy's Hall of Fame. Fred was inducted into the Academy in July of 2002.

During the months that it took to develop the "Tribute to Fred Rogers," Donna reviewed and reread most of Fred's writings. As she rediscovered the depth and breadth of Fred's ideas and shared these discoveries with Ian, a realization began to take shape — a realization that much of what Fred wrote and said about human development applied as much to adults as it did to children. That realization led to many hours of conversation and re-examinations of Fred's writings to see if the suspicion held up. It did! In fact, Ian pointed out that the process of translating the principles of Fred Rogers from helping children grow and develop to helping adults grow and develop resulted in more profound concepts than what is generally expounded in current management education.

The idea was crystallized when Ann Sweeney, then President of The Disney Channel, spoke at the Tribute about Fred's influence on her management style: "Fred not only influenced me as he did thousands of others when I was a kid, but he continues to influence me even more as an adult. The most important lesson I learned from Fred was the importance of listening with one's entire being. From him, I learned how to be fully and completely in the moment with whomever I was engaged. I learned how to listen to the inner person. That is the essence of being a true leader."

Through 35 continuous years on television and in the nation's consciousness, Fred Rogers has already had a powerful influence on today's leaders — an influence that many are not even aware of. Our goal with this chapter is to both expand upon that influence and to give Fred's legacy the recognition that it deserves.

The April, 2003 Issue of *Pittsburgh Magazine* was devoted entirely to Fred's legacy. The opening paragraph is a vivid testimony to Fred's long-lasting impact:

> During his lifetime, Fred Rogers did a remarkable thing: He created a brand-new language, comprising thousands of simple words and images that speak of truth, love, respect and caring. He hoped that adults and children would learn his language and apply it in their daily lives. Based on the more than 600 e-mail messages that flooded our website following his death on Feb. 27, many did indeed learn that language. In fact, one of the recurring themes in the e-mails is the value that adults continue to place on Fred Rogers' words. Unabashedly, they talk of tuning into "Mister Rogers' Neighborhood" after losing a job or when facing a personal crisis. They speak tenderly of the life lessons they learned during Fred's "television visits."[1]

---

[1] *Pittsburgh Magazine*, April, 2003, p. 6.

Rationale and Objectives

The entire rationale for this chapter can be summed up as follows: Fred played a crucial role in *starting* the process of helping young children to grow and to develop into healthy human beings. But the process needs to be *continued* throughout one's life.

While early growth and development are absolutely necessary, they are not sufficient. We believe that by extending Fred's ideas, he can continue to support the process of growth and development in managers so that they in turn can help those they supervise to grow and to develop as well. We also believe that further growth and development are absolutely essential if we are to produce healthy organizations that are capable of serving the greater, common good.

In short, Fred's ideas lead to a different set of principles for managing organizations. These "principles" are in effect "living virtues." To our knowledge no one has turned to Fred as a key source of wisdom and humanity for the next stage in the development of managers and the evolution of organizations.

Fred is perfect for the job. His background includes in-depth education and training in two fields that are rarely found in those who write about managers and organizations: spirituality and child psychology.

Before Fred was a household fixture, he was an ordained Presbyterian minister. His ministry was to work with children and families through the mass media. In 1968, his show, "Mister Rogers' Neighborhood" debuted nationally on PBS and has remained on the air since then.

Fred Rogers rejected the appalling state of television. He focused instead on "its great potential for good" as well as the promise of using it to really educate children. He prepared for his unique ministry by studying under some of the nation's leading child psychologists and child psychiatrists so that he could attain a deep understanding of the emotional needs of children, and thereby minister to those needs as effectively as possible. He used this knowledge to minister to the spiritual needs of children as well.

Fred Rogers' Legacy

There is no question whatsoever that Fred Rogers played an enormously important role in the development of children. He continues to do so through reruns of his popular series on PBS.

Fred helped children to deal with their deepest fears and emotions, for instance, the death of a close friend, relative, or parent; the growing sense of one's separate self, and hence, the fears around the separation from one's parents, issues of divorce, etc. Merely by naming them, he helped children to identify and thereby to manage their fears. Nonetheless, at precisely the time when children, and especially boys, need him the most, nature in the form of biology, and society in the form of one's parents and peers, conspire to play a cruel joke. It is a "joke" that often lasts an entire lifetime. It deeply cripples many men from developing their emotional, or feeling, sides.

Around the age of 5 or 6, most children, including both boys and girls, "develop out" of Fred Rogers. They find him babyish and corny. Action games, cartoons, and peers become the sources to which they turn for further development. But something even more insidious and devastating occurs in the development of boys. Harvard psychologist William Pollack refers to it as the Boy Code.

Around the age of 5 or 6, young boys learn to turn off and to bury their feelings. It is as though a giant emotional switch is permanently flipped to "Off." Furthermore, if boys do not learn how to switch off and to suppress their feelings, it can be devastating. They will be picked on and bullied relentlessly by other boys for being sissies.

To be sure, the feelings of young boys do not vanish altogether. This is impossible. They merely go underground where they remain primitive and undeveloped.

Where Fred openly acknowledged the fears and the emotions of very young children, and hence encouraged their expression so they can be dealt with in constructive ways, society sends a clear and a strong message that while it is acceptable for girls to express and to talk about their emotions, it is not for boys.

As young boys develop into adolescents, late teens, and early adulthood, they carry this numbing of their feelings with them, often for their entire lives. True, there is compelling evidence that nature finally comes to the rescue in the later years of men's lives where men actively seek to recapture and to redevelop their lost feelings. But, many men remain estranged and alienated from their feelings, throughout the vast body of their careers.

Many organizations have been designed, albeit unconsciously, to help men keep their feelings at bay. Instead of aiding emotional growth and development, many organizations conspire to keep them emotionally stunted. They do this by enacting strong and sharp barriers between different corporate functions, business units, products, services, etc. In short, they put people into different "silos." In this way, they effectively "wall off" people, and their messy emotions, from one another.

Likewise, as girls develop into women many of them develop feelings of low self-esteem and the fear of challenging men. But something just as ominous happens to them as well.

Too many young girls turn their greater sensitivities with regard to feelings and to human relationships into weapons for bullying and humiliating other girls. In turn, those who are bullied are often so desperate for relationships of any kind and extremely fearful of losing them that they will accept extremely harmful relationships over none at all. The phenomenon is akin to women who stay in abusive marriages. In short, those who are bullied often subordinate their needs for authentic relationships to those of any kind, however, harmful they are.

For these and many other reasons, Fred's principles cannot be simply applied to adults, let alone organizations, without substantial modification. For instance, one cannot confront directly the lack of emotional development of most men. To do so only drives them further into the Boy Code, i.e., the set of unwritten rules that governs the behavior of individual men and of largely male-dominated organizations. Instead, other strategies need to be employed to kick start, if not to re-start, the emotional development of men. Getting men to acknowledge and to develop their feeling sides is equivalent to getting them to commit to deep, long-lasting relationships, of which marriage is the supreme example.

Getting men to develop their feeling sides involves much more than merely getting them to enroll in short courses and programs for Emotional I.Q. It means dealing with the fact that the Boy Code underlies much of our current theories of business, economics, and organizations. It also means helping women to become more assertive and to overcome the hurtful relationships that they have had with other women in the past. Until these ideas are realized, and even more importantly, acted upon, then we will not be able to develop healthy managers and healthy organizations.

The Fred Rogers' Way of Managing Through Lifelong Mentoring

Fred Rogers understood what it took to be a good parent, and even more fundamentally, a great human being. He knew intuitively what it took to be a great manager and a great leader by being a great human being.

Seven principles, derived from Fred's writings and from analysis of his television programs, constitute the Fred Rogers' way of managing through lifelong mentoring.

Each principle is based upon Fred's enormous knowledge of and work with children, but *translated by the authors* into the realm of adults. That is, the principles for raising healthy children cannot be applied directly to adults without substantial modification. But the kernels, i.e., the grains of truth, are clearly there.

The seven principles are:

1. **Care**: "I like you just the way you are."
2. **Concern**: "Setting rules is one of the primary ways in which we show our love for children."
3. **Connect**: "Anything that is mentionable is manageable."
4. **Context**: "To know why a person is the way he or she is, one has to know his or her story."

5. **Creativity**: "The arts are the outer expression of our deepest, innermost feelings."
6. **Consciousness**: "At our core, all of us are spiritual beings; indeed, spirituality is our Essence," and;
7. **Community**: "We are part of everything that has come before us, that is now, and that will follow."

Principle 1 — Care: "I like you just the way you are."

One does not choose the family into which one is born. One *does choose* one's careers and the organizations in which one works.

A parent does not choose whether to love a child or not, or at least, he or she ought never to make such a choice. To produce healthy and productive adults, the basic job of every parent is to *accept* and to *love* each child totally and *unconditionally*. In contrast, the basic job of every organization is to *select* the right people for the right jobs within the right settings, i.e., work groups, teams, etc. In other words, if the acceptance of the parents is completely *un*conditional, the acceptance of organizations is highly *conditional*.

If the basic job of the parents is to produce healthy individuals, then the basic job of organizations is to *select* healthy employees and to help them *develop even further*, i.e., to reach their full potential as whole human beings. Ian's research shows that "realizing one's full potential as a whole human being" is the number one thing that people are seeking from their work (Mitroff and Denton, 2000). Those organizations that help people realize this goal are more profitable, more ethical, and happier places to work. Not only is this the right thing to do, but it is good for business as well.

In a word, organizations are not obligated to accept everyone that applies. In addition to appropriate technical skills, general and specific education, and demonstrated competency, a primary condition for employment is an acceptable level of emotional development and health.

The Container Store in Dallas is a premiere example of this principle (Berry, 1999). To select the right people, prospective employees spend an entire day in the organization to determine whether the organization is right for them, and in turn, whether they are right for it. They are interviewed extensively by those with whom they will work, their supervisors, and those they will supervise. They also witness dramatic sketches that have been written by the employees themselves. These illustrate vividly the kind of positive behaviors that are the core of the organization. In this way, the employees are an extension of the Human Resources department. In effect, those who are already members of The Container Store are a key mechanism in selecting future employees.

Notice carefully that this way of selecting employees also tears down the walls between different parts of the organization. It also helps everyone to become both more assertive and participative. By embedding principles of emotional health in their infrastructure, organizations such as The Container Store have discovered and put into place mechanisms for overcoming the inability and the general reluctance of many men to talk about their feelings, i.e. the Boy Code, without confronting it directly. Indeed, it has been found that confronting the Boy Code directly often intensifies it.

The very best organizations put an extremely high premium on selecting the right employees from the very beginning (Mitroff and Denton, 2000). It is in fact the "first principle" of healthy organizations. The best organizations often delay for months the opening of new stores, plants and facilities, and the start of key projects until they have found the right persons for the job.

Given the importance of emotional health and development, we are confident that knowledge of how humans develop over the course of their lives will become a key component in the education and the promotion of managers. We are so confident of it that we believe it will become the key for advancement in the organizations of the not-so-distant future.

Though small in number, there is an important sense in which leading companies embody Fred's principle, "You are special." They recognize and treat the uniqueness of everybody connected with the organization. This includes employees, customers, and suppliers.

The best companies embrace the philosophy of "small is beautiful." They deliberately break themselves down into the smallest units possible so that are able to focus on caring for one another and all of their stakeholders.

Principle 2 — Concern: "Setting rules is one of the primary ways in which we show our love for children."

One of the worst misperceptions of Fred Rogers was that because he was thoroughly genuine and loving, caring and accepting, he was totally permissive. The misperception was that he advocated no rules, discipline, or limits when it came to raising children. Nothing could be further from the truth. In fact, Fred describes discipline as "a loving gift" that parents give to their children when they need it.

Fred understood deeply that children desperately needed, and wanted, limits and rules. Furthermore, they needed and wanted discipline as well.

Fred knew that we showed our love for our children through demonstrating what was expected of them and what the consequences were if they did not meet those expectations. To think that healthy children and adults would result without sensible rules and appropriate discipline goes against every grain of research on children.

In The Container Store and other leading organizations the "rules" emerge from all of the stakeholders (Mitroff and Denton, 2000; Berry, 1999). For instance, the employees themselves with appropriate help from the outside, e.g., consultants who are experts in organizational behavior, formulate the rules for conducting meetings and for dealing with difficult people. In this way, the rules are anything but also abstract, academic, cold, and impersonal. The rules not only cover how to run meetings efficiently and effectively, but also how to encourage and to maintain civility. In formulating the rules, it is assumed that the feelings of everyone connected with the organizations are paramount. Above all, the rules are held to an absolute minimum.

It has been learned from the field of Crisis Management that the best organizations have clear-cut rules regarding employee misconduct, aggressiveness, and violence in the workplace (Mitroff and Anagous, 2001). From Day One, the best organizations make it perfectly clear that sexually offensive "jokes" or those featuring violence will not be tolerated for one instant. They make it perfectly clear that they have a "zero tolerance policy" with regard to sexual harassment and workplace violence. Anyone violating these rules is sent immediately to counseling in order to determine whether they are still fit to remain in the organization.

Principle 3 — Connect: "Anything that is mentionable is manageable"

Not only do humans have a deep need to connect with others, but also humans are hard-wired, i.e., "basically designed and built" so-to-speak, to connect with others. It is a fundamental part of our humanity. Without an ability to connect, we are not human.

The latest research in the neurosciences demonstrates that our brains — our whole systems — are hard-wired to experience the emotions that others are feeling. For instance, if another person experiences and noticeably exhibits anger, happiness, or sadness, then those parts of our brains that experience those same emotions will be triggered within us. We will feel the very same emotions that the other person is feeling and displaying, albeit to a lesser or a greater, degree than the person initially experiencing them.

Through deep connection with others, we find ultimate purpose and meaning within ourselves. One of the most interesting and important aspects of Fred Rogers' thinking is the way he treats "connectedness." For Fred, connectedness is embedded in his notion that "anything that is mentionable is manageable." For instance, in order to assuage the fears of children regarding, say, death and divorce, one needs to allow them to discuss these issues in ways that are acceptable, i.e., less threatening to them. Adults have the very same need. However, this only raises the thorny issue, "What are the limits, if any, of those issues that should, and should not, be discussed in the workplace?"

Once again, leading organizations approach these issues in innovative ways. For instance, The Container Store employees regularly get together to read and to share different texts on human development, and other important social issues. They regularly invite nationally recognized management experts such as Meg Wheatley and Peter Drucker to spend at least an entire day interacting with employees, customers, and other major stakeholders, in order to gain an outside perspective and a critique of the organization. Prior to their arrival, employees are encouraged to read and to discuss their works and ideas in small groups. In this way, the organizations are discouraged from turning into cults.

In reading these works, it is not assumed that the employees necessarily have advanced degrees. In fact, many of the employees have barely finished high school. The lack of formal education is not seen as a barrier, but as an opportunity.

Much of what occurs in these sessions is not only based on active listening, but also what we call "deep spiritual listening and learning" (Mitroff and Denton, 2000). An example from Donna's work experience is relevant. After the Columbine shootings, Donna invited leading experts on the development of boys, such as William Pollack, to conduct a one-day seminar at a network where she was then head of broadcast standards and practices. The purpose of the seminar was to expose the writers of children's television programs to the issues that young children, and especially boys, are struggling with, and to help explain why horrific events such as Columbine occur. Out of this unfortunate tragedy came a moment to reach the writers and the developers of children's programs so that they could be encouraged to produce programs that would first, do no harm and hopefully better serve the needs of children.

We contend that this principle needs to be continually broadened. The list of "mentors," "coaches," and "outside influences" that workers and managers need to be exposed to should be expanded to include experts on male and female psychology and emotional development so that everyone can continue to grow.

Principle 4 — Context: "To know why a person is the way he or she is, one has to know his or her story."

Fred Rogers was fond of saying that if we wanted to know why a certain person was mean, angry, or sad, then we had to know their "story," i.e., what made them, who they are, and what was going in their lives at the present. People don't act randomly. There are always reasons for their behavior, especially all the more when we don't like it.

The field of medicine has recently instituted a new specialty, "narrative medicine." Narrative medicine involves the training of future medical doctors to listen compassionately so that they can record more effectively the personal histories of their patients. The purpose is to understand the whole person for better treatment. To do this requires training doctors to understand the development of characters, stories, and plots both in world literature and in the stories of their patients. We believe that managers and leaders need to be similarly educated in order to learn how to listen to the stories of their employees, customers, communities, etc.

Stephen Denning (2004) has made a good start in his *Harvard Business Review* article, "Telling Tales." Denning identifies a number of archetypal stories told by managers. He also cautions how much to tell and when. In spite of this, Denning does not identify the full range of stories of which managers need to be aware. He neither identifies nor treats the "deep stories" that are fundamentally characteristic of human beings, for instance, the issues with which they struggled as children, teenagers, and adults. Telling and sharing stories is one of the central requirements for human growth and development.

Principle 5 — Creativity: "The arts are the outer expression of the deepest, innermost feelings."

To see the world again as a child is the fundamental basis of creativity. Creativity involves total immersion in one's work. Even more important, it involves feelings of joy, fun, and play. It is the very essence of spirituality.

One of Fred's most profound observations is that our play and creativity are two of the truest and most powerful windows into our innermost feelings. And, if anything is central to the Fred Rogers's way of managing and mentoring, it is the recognition of and the proper treatment of human emotions.

Principle 6 — Consciousness: "All of us are spiritual beings."

For Fred, the word "consciousness" was merely a small stepping stone to the deeper concept of "spirituality." If spirituality means anything, it is recognizing and treating the whole person (Mitroff and Denton, 2000). Spirituality teaches us that there are no artificial divisions between those parts of a person that "reason" and those parts that "feel" (Mitroff and Denton, 2000). To do so is to erect an artificial divide within the soul.

At the heart of The Container Store is a principle that is deeply spiritual: "Fill a person's whole basket." It means meeting the needs of the whole person who walks into the store. The Container Store often uses the metaphor of a person who is lost in the desert to convey this notion. The person's immediate need is water. However, the deeper need emanates from the reason why the person was in the desert in the first place, and the stress and the trauma that he or she has suffered as a result.

Once again, providing water services the person's immediate needs. But The Container Store wants to get to the deeper, underlying needs. They believe that if they meet these needs, then "the profits will follow." The first principle of The Container Store is meeting the true and the authentic needs of whole human beings.

Ian has found through his research that those organizations that practice spirituality believe in practicing it for its own sake (Mitroff and Denton, 2000). They believe firmly that one must not practice spirituality in order to make money, for personal gain, power, etc. They believe that if they practice spirituality other than for its own sake, then profits will not follow. Conversely, if one practices spirituality for its own sake, then profits will follow.

Spirituality also teaches us that it is not merely enough to recognize, let alone to treat, the "multiple intelligences" of human beings as separate aspects of their makeup. Cognitive, Emotional, and Spiritual I.Q. are not separable. What is needed is Integrative I.Q. We need to teach how to deploy all of the various known intelligences of the human spirit in an integrated manner.

In short, Fred Rogers is to human development what William James is to philosophy. Both developed and promulgated throughout their entire lives an integrative approach to the human condition. All of Fred's principles are part of one another. They form an inseparable whole. One cannot practice any of them without practicing all of them.

Principle 7 — Community: "We are part of everything that has come before us, that is now, and that will follow."

Community brings us back to connect. By community, Fred means that we are, and must be, connected to the broader world. It is not enough merely to be connected to our immediate friends, families, and our fellow employees. We must be connected to, and hence serve, the greatest, common good.

On more than one occasion when he was being honored and when it was Fred's turn to speak, he engaged his fellow honorees in the following exercise: "I want you to close your eyes and to think of that very special person in your life who 'loved you into being.' Take a minute to reflect on that person and how he or she continues to influence you today." The effect on the audience was both instantaneous and profound. It caused the rich, the powerful, and the famous to stop dead in their tracks and to connect with themselves and with all the others in the room.

The greatest organizations realize the value of community by very carefully selecting those few community groups and social causes with which to align themselves. They establish and demonstrate their commitment from Day One of their founding. They do not wait until they have made a certain amount of money, or reached a certain size, before their commitment to affecting the outside world kicks in. Instead, from Day One they give a certain predetermined amount to those organizations they support. In other words, they do not have an "ethical threshold," i.e., a certain boundary beyond which they will start being ethical or start caring about the larger outside world (Mitroff and Denton, 2000).

Concluding Remarks

Many of America's leading organizations, particularly those in the service area, already practice these principles, albeit by other names (Mitroff and Denton, 2002; Berry, 1999). But many more need to be aware of them and to internalize them deeply into their day-to-day operations and strategic vision.

While the number of organizations that actually practice these principles is very small, they are living proof that it is possible to follow them. Not only is it possible to build on these examples however limited they are, but also we desperately need to do so.

References

Berry, LL (1999). *Discovering the Soul of Service: The Nine Drivers of Sustainable Business Success*, New York: The Free Press.

Denning, S (May 2004). Telling tales. *Harvard Business Review.*

Mitroff, II and E Denton (2000). *A Spiritual Audit of Corporate America*, San Francisco: Jossey-Bass.

Mitroff, II and G Anagnos (2001). *Managing Crises Before They Happen: What Every Executive and Manager Needs to Know About Crisis Management*, New York: AMACOM.

Chapter Twelve

THE POSITIVE POTENTIAL OF TEMPERED RADICALS

Rand Quinn
Debra Meyerson

Stanford University

Meyerson and Quinn are interested in extending a scholarly look at the complementary aspects of *tempered radicals* and positive deviance behaviors defined within a Positive Organizational Scholarship perspective. Tempered Radicals, as defined in Meyerson's earlier works, are those who share an outsider/insider identity in groups or organizations and who seek to make things better for themselves and others. These authors focus on the tempered radical's "subtle, incremental and long-term strategies which slowly" make a significant difference. It is this source of positive change which is undertaken "with honor" that allows for a different notion of exemplary times to be viewed as long-term and enduring.

Over a career spanning several decades, an executive at a large financial firm implores employees he has hired to aggressively identify and hire other minority candidates (Meyerson, 2001). A closeted minister drawn to his faith but constrained by denominational unease to homosexuality decides to force open a discussion on the issue by coming out at an annual church conference (Creed, 2003). Two graduate students interested in studying feminist executives but counseled to pursue less "radical" research find ways to do both (Meyerson and Scully, 1995). An African-American woman successfully manages the opposing pulls of her career and her community (Bell, 1990). These individuals each see themselves as outsiders, not quite fitting in with the dominant culture and dynamics of their organization. But they are also insiders, working as change agents within the system, actively engaged in challenging the status quo. Through a variety of ways, these people seek to make things better, for themselves and for others. They are tempered radicals (Meyerson and Scully, 1995).

In this chapter, we argue that tempered radicals are a source for positive change and virtue in organizations. We do so by recognizing their potential to be sources of positive deviance. We begin by describing tempered radicals, who they are and what they do. We next address the positive potential for tempered radicals by bringing to bear emerging scholarship on positive deviance. We conclude by describing challenges faced by tempered radicals and offering lessons for leaders interested in cultivating and amplifying tempered radicalism.

Tempered radicals can be found everywhere, across all industries, in all positions, and in all manner of organizations, formal and informal, large and small. They make a difference by pursuing a variety of strategies, from quiet resistance to collective action. But their impact is often overlooked because as outsiders, they are compelled to pursue subtle, incremental, and long-term strategies. Rather than the heroic leaders we are too often captivated by, tempered radicals are the "cautious and committed catalysts who keep going and who slowly make a difference" (Meyerson, 2001, p. 5).

Who are Tempered Radicals?

Tempered radicals are people who "identify with and are committed to their organizations and are also committed to a cause, community, or ideology that is fundamentally different from, and possibly at odds with the dominant culture of their organization" (Meyerson and Scully, 1995, p. 586). Tempered radicals embody a tension between the existing institutional order and alternative orders. They are at once insiders and outsiders, negotiators of a middle path between conformity and rebellion (Meyerson, 2001). But they are not complacent. Tempered radicals question the prevailing logic. They are able to see ways in which normal patterns of behavior and sense-making do not meet the needs of groups of people, how the prevailing logic limits full participation, or how, in some cases, normal patterns constrain organizational effectiveness.

Tempered radicals are different from people who are in the majority in their organization in one of two ways. Either a social identity, such as race, gender, sexual orientation or religion marks them as different and positions them as outsiders within their organizations or their values or beliefs clash with those that are dominant in their organization (Meyerson, 2001). People in the first group — who work to succeed on insider terms, but are cast as outsiders — experience two types of tensions. For some people, the tension is experienced primarily as an identity-based struggle as they attempt to express a self that marks them as different and marginal. Others define the tension in terms of the challenges associated with change and resistance. These people attempt to change the organization to push outward the terms of membership and to adopt work practices that are mindful of differences so all members can thrive. Either way, whether people primarily experience the challenges of identity maintenance or the challenges associating with advancing change, when they express identities that deviate from the majority, they call into question taken-for-granted criteria of membership and norms of behavior. Thus, even those tempered radicals who experience their struggle in strictly personal terms must confront the unavoidable political implications of their enacted selves.

The men and women who fall into the second category — whose differences are rooted in value or ideological clashes — embrace change agendas rooted in those values and beliefs. The challenge facing most of these tempered radicals center around the struggle of finding ways to enact their deviant values and beliefs by effecting change while preserving the legitimacy within the very system they seek to change.

What is the Positive Potential of Tempered Radicals?

As outsiders within their organizations, tempered radicals often do not possess the authority and legitimacy needed to mandate systemic change. Any potentially "radical" action is "tempered" by their marginality and the organizational and environmental constraints these individuals face. As a result, the set of responses undertaken to push against opposing organizational norms tend to be subtle, incremental, and long range (Meyerson, 2001). It is important to note that tempered radicals are not *radicals* in the sense that they do not act in ways that represent a considerable departure from normal. Rather than working to dismantle systems, they work from within to strengthen them. Tempered radicals push against opposing organizational norms, but their actions are *tempered:* They recognize "modest and doable choices in between, such as choosing their battles, creating pockets of learning, and making way for small wins" (6).

For any set of strategies that tempered radicals employ, they face the challenge of expressing their identities or values or advancing a change agenda from within his/her organization. Different strategies meet these challenges to varying degrees. For example, tempered radicals can resist the dominant organizational culture by deliberately enacting their identities, cultures, or values through language, dress, and office decor. People employing these strategies are not necessarily seeking systemic change. They simply want to express their valued selves. Others who resist quietly may be more motivated to seek change. In our opening paragraph, we wrote about an executive at a large financial firm who worked for decades behind the scenes to improve the racial and ethnic diversity of the company. Other strategies aimed at advancing an explicit change agenda are more explicit and often collective. These include leveraging small wins and organizing collective action. As research has demonstrated, tempered radicals who engage in such activities over a period of time have the potential to affect widespread learning and change, although it is empirically challenging to isolate the causal contribution of an individual's actions to a given outcome that was conditioned by many factors (Meyerson and Tompkins, 2007; Sturm, 2006).

Research on tempered radicalism often highlights the tactic of small wins, a "limited doable project that results in something concrete and visible" (Weick, 1984). When framed in terms of their larger significance and used as a means of challenging the status quo, small wins can snowball into more significant changes. Returning to our example above, the executive's quiet recruitment initiative began as a circumscribed local effort early in his career. But by encouraging the minority employees he hired to actively recruit other minority candidates, the impact of his efforts was leveraged and led indirectly to the hiring of more than 3500 minority employees over several decades (Meyerson, 2001).

Despite the potential a small wins strategy holds, there are limits to what individuals can accomplish on their own. And while a "big win" strategy is possible, it is obviously more risky and more difficult to accomplish. When change efforts face significant institutional resistance or when immediate change is sought, tempered radicals often engage in a strategy of collective action. Compared to individuals, collectives possess greater legitimacy, power, and resources. "It stands to reason that people can drive large-scale immediate change more effectively by working in concert with others toward a common goal, particularly when they do not have formal authority to mandate desired changes" (Meyerson, 2001, p. 123).

Under some circumstances and for certain issues, quiet resistance may be more appropriate. And for other circumstances and other issues, tactics that place a change agenda front and center — whether small wins or collective action — are required. It is at this broader level, when tempered radicals choose to pursue strategies aimed at systemic or institutional change that we see the greatest opportunity for positive impact.

Tempered Radicals as Positive Deviants

Organizational virtuousness focuses on the "ennobling and uplifting aspects of the human conditions more than on achieving effectiveness, profitability, or notoriety" (Cameron, 2003, p. 63). The recent emergence of Positive Organizational Scholarship (POS) is based on the premise that the qualities associated with virtue, energy, and high quality connections have been under emphasized in organization studies (e.g., Cameron *et al.*, 2003; Dutton and Ragins, 2007). POS is a new domain of inquiry focusing on that which is invigorating, "life-giving," and positive in social life (Cameron and Caza, 2004; Cameron *et al.*, 2003). POS focuses on such things as "developing human strength, producing resilience and restoration, and fostering vitality," dynamics which are usually found in difficult and challenging situations (Cameron and Caza, 2004, p. 731).

A key construct within POS is positive deviance. Unlike the popular understanding of deviance, which connotes something negative or stigmatized (Goffman, 1963) and a threat to the welfare of an organization, positive deviance looks at *honorable* or *virtuous* action that departs from the norms of a particular referent group (Spreitzer and Sonenshein, 2003, 2004; Warren, 2003). Depending on the situation, the referent group might be a unit, an organization, an industry, or a profession. And while the definitional purview of positive deviance covers behavior, independent of outcomes, outcomes are clearly of underlying interest. For instance, Baker and Dutton (2007, p. 326) describe positive deviance as "extraordinary positive outcomes and the means that produce them".

Tempered radicals are often, but not always, sources of positive deviance. And the actors engaged in positive deviance are often, though not always, tempered radicals. In this section, we initiate a discussion of the complementary nature of the tempered radicalism and positive deviance constructs. We believe that tempered radicalism maps onto positive deviance to a fair degree and that they help fill silences for one another.

Intentional departure from normative behavior

To begin, the tempered radicalism and positive deviance constructs both examine intentional actions that depart from norms. While most of the early work on tempered radicalism focused on organizations and organizational norms, subsequent research has taken a wider view, acknowledging that organizational norms are often instantiations of professional or industry-wide norms. For example, Douglas Creed's (2003) study of voice and silence in organizations analyzes the professional constraints faced by lesbian and gay Protestant ministers. Denominations with restrictions against openly gay and lesbian ministers face many challenges, including when to remain silent and when to give voice to their identities, their relationships, and their experiences of homophobia in the church. Even in denominations that *allow* for the ordination of openly gay and lesbian people, ministers must contend with the vestiges of institutionalized homophobia. Despite a "don't ask, don't tell" standard for ministers, Creed describes several instances where tempered radicals within the church successfully forced discussions of the issue of homosexuality. Similarly, Spreitzer and Sonenshein (2004) describe departures from the norms of any of several referent groups — an individual's organizational unit, industry, or profession — as positive deviance. While both constructs focus on individual behavior, positive deviance covers organizational and extra-organizational levels of analysis as well (Spreitzer and Sonenshein, 2004).

Honor

Positive deviance describes action that is considered honorable or virtuous by some referent group (Spreitzer and Sonenshein, 2004). Spreitzer and Sonenshein offer, as an example, the honorable action of the pharmaceutical company Merck, which in 1978 decided to manufacture and distribute for free the drug that cures river blindness, even though doing so was likely not in the company's best interest. As a result, Merck helped eradicate river blindness in the developing world, costing the company millions of dollars (Spreitzer and Sonenshein, 2004).

Whether an action is meant or perceived to be honorable is not central to tempered radicalism. Rather, the point of focus is the source of action: whether an individual has a social identity that has resulted in exclusion or marginalization or whether an individual enacts values, beliefs, and agendas that are different from the majority. Yet, even though their actions are not explicitly tied to the notion of honor, tempered radicals are often motivated to express identities or values that result in marginalization because a given social identity group expects them to do so. For example, observant Muslims will be expected by other Muslims to adhere to the practices of Ramadan, though their refrain from eating during the day may be construed as deviant and mark them as different by their fellow workers.

Departure from norms

While theories of positive deviance and tempered radicalism imagine favorable outcomes such as improved effectiveness and more inclusive norms (Baker and Dutton, 2007; Meyerson, 2001; Meyerson and Scully, 1995), research on both constructs tends to center on actions leading up to those outcomes. Spreitzer and Sonenshein's (2004) paper emphasizes the *degree* of deviation from the norm. Significant departures from the norm constitute acts of positive deviance rather than departures in ways that are merely unexpected (p. 842). Such a focus may lead some to privilege "big wins" over "small wins." Conversely, tempered radicalism celebrates relatively small departures from organizational norms. For example, Meyerson (2001, p. 45) describes how an employee's quiet display of self-expression — displaying photographs of her same sex commitment ceremony on her desk — led to an improved workplace environment: "Over time her colleagues got used to the picture, and then some became more and more comfortable seeing Jennifer with her partner, not only in the picture but also in person".

What Challenges do Tempered Radicals Face?

The framework of tempered radicalism helps surface the range of strategies and tactics used by outsiders to change values and norms that are dominant within their organizations, often with the goal of making their organizations more inclusive and effective. But as one might expect, tempered radicals face risks. People manage to navigate between the opposing pulls of their workplace norms on one hand and their personal identities or values on the other to varying degrees of success. Some decide that the risks of pushing against organizational norms are too high and instead work to fit in. Others are marginalized further as a result of their strident actions that seem to disregard altogether existing rules of membership.

Ambivalence is a common psychological response to those who attempt to balance the competing pulls of being an outsider within (Meyerson and Scully, 1995). Ambivalence can induce assimilation. But ambivalence can also provide tempered radicals certain psychological advantages. To be ambivalent is to be both accepting *and* critical of the status quo. A tempered radical's insider status provides "access to opportunities for change," while outsider status provides sufficient detachment to recognize that the status quo needs to be challenged (Meyerson and Scully, 1995; Seo and Creed, 2002). In addition to ambivalence, several additional strains faced by individuals with "outsider" status have been identified: the lures of co-optation, reputational damage, and frustration leading to burnout (Meyerson, 2001).

Role of Leadership in Cultivating and Amplifying Tempered Radicals

An important yet under-theorized aspect of tempered radicalism is the role of organizational leaders in identifying, acknowledging, cultivating and amplifying the acts of tempered radicals. Meyerson's (2001) study found that tempered radicals placed high value in their relationships with their supervisors. As one might expect, given prior research on work teams, employees felt more willing to speak up and take risks when they shared a comfortable working relationship with their immediate supervisors. Leaders who proactively elicit input (as well as making explicit why input from everyone is essential) convey the importance of everyone's perspective, including those who might feel like outsiders, due to their social identity or cultural values, beliefs, and agendas. This kind of practice when enacted by leaders who are seen as sincere contributes to the psychological safety of a work environment (Edmondson, 1983).

In addition, leaders who sanction mistakes by revealing their own fallibility provide for their employees the freedom to experiment, express their values and beliefs, and push back on organizational norms and standards. Such leaders see failure as a natural part of work activity out of which learning and innovation flows (Edmondson, 2003). Without this safety and explicit or implicit permission to experiment, tempered radicals may determine that behavioral deviations, even relatively small ones, are too risky to initiate.

Conclusion: Advancing our Understanding of Positive Deviance and Tempered Radicalism

In this chapter, we take heed of Spreitzer and Sonenshein's (2003) call to focus on understanding how positive deviance relates to and differs from similar constructs. By undertaking this project, we believe that we have enriched both ideas. For tempered radicalism, positive deviance provides a framework for understanding and evaluating the action of tempered radicals. We know that tempered radicals push against the status quo, but the honor of those actions are not explicitly considered. Positive deviance opens the possibility for understanding how honor or virtue plays into the activities undertaken by tempered radicals.

In addition, efforts in POS to understand the determinants of positive deviance can help flesh out the psychological factors that are related to tempered radicalism, an area currently under theorized. For example, Spreitzer and Sonenshein (2003) identify five contributing psychological conditions for a mindset conducive to positive deviance: a sense of meaning, a focus on the other, self-determination, personal efficacy, and courage. How might a focus on these factors important for positive deviants (Spreitzer and Sonenshein, 2003) matter to tempered radicals?

For the positive deviance literature, its definitional emphasis on "significant departures" from organizational norms (Spreitzer and Sonenshein, 2004) tends to preclude consideration of relatively small acts, despite suggestions of their potential significance: a series of small wins can reveal "a pattern that may attract allies, deter opponents, and lower resistance to subsequent proposals" (Weick, 1984, p. 43). As prior work on tempered radicalism suggests, individuals with outsider identities, values, or beliefs face organizational constraints that often prevent them from taking radical actions. Focusing only on behavior that significantly departs from institutional norms may lead researchers of positive deviance to overlook the subtle, local acts of tempered radicals and disregard the positive — and significant — outcomes these individuals generate by bundling together multiple small wins over a period of time.

References

Baker, W and JE Dutton (2007). Enabling positive social capital in organizations. In *Exploring Positive Relationships at Work: Building a Theoretical and Research Foundation*, pp. 325–346. Mahwah, NJ: Lawrence Erlbaum Associates.

Bell, EL (1990). The bicultural life experience of career-oriented black women. *Journal of Organizational Behavior*, 11(6), 459–477.

Cameron, KS (2003). Organizational virtuousness and performance. In *Positive Organizational Scholarship. Foundations of a New Discipline*, KS Cameron, JE Dutton and RE Quinn (eds.), pp. 48–65. San Francisco: Berrett-Koehler Publishers, Inc.

Cameron, KS and A Caza (2004). Introduction: contributions to the discipline of positive organizational scholarship. *American Behavioral Scientist*, 47(6), 731.

Cameron, KS, JE Dutton and RE Quinn (2003). *Positive Organizational Scholarship: Foundations of a New Discipline*. Berrett-Koehler Publishers.

Creed, WED (2003). Voice lessons: tempered radicalism and the use of voice and silence. *Journal of Management Studies*, 40(6), 1503–1536.

Dutton, JE and BR Ragins (2007). *Exploring Positive Relationships at Work: Building a Theoretical and Research Foundation*. Lawrence Erlbaum Associates.

Edmondson, A (2003). Speaking up in the operating room: how team leaders promote learning in interdisciplinary action teams. *Journal of Management Studies* 40(6), 1419–1452.

Goffman, E (1963). *Stigma: Notes on the Management of Spoiled Identity*, New York: Simon and Schuster.

Meyerson, DE (2001). *Tempered Radicals: How People Use Difference to Inspire Change at Work*. Boston: Harvard Business School Press.

Meyerson, DE and MA Scully (1995). Tempered radicalism and the politics of ambivalence and change. *Organization Science*, 6(5), 585–600.

Meyerson, DE and M Tompkins (2007). Tempered radicals as institutional change agents: the case of advancing gender equity at the University of Michigan. *Harvard Journal of Law and Gender*, 30(2), 303.

Seo, MG and WED Creed (2002). Institutional contradictions, praxis, and institutional change: a dialectical perspective. *The Academy of Management Review,* 27(2), 222–247.

Spreitzer, GM and S Sonenshein (2003). Positive deviance and extraordinary organizing. In *Positive Organizational Scholarship. Foundations of a New Discipline,* KS Cameron, JE Dutton and RE Quinn (eds.), pp. 207–224. San Francisco: Berrett-Koehler Publishers, Inc.

Spreitzer, GM and S Sonenshein (2004). Toward the construct definition of positive deviance. *American Behavioral Scientist,* 47(6), 828.

Sturm, S (2006). The architecture of inclusion: advancing workplace equity in higher education. *Harvard Journal of Law and Gender,* 29(2), 247.

Warren, DE (2003). Constructive and destructive deviance in organizations. *The Academy of Management Review,* 28(4), 622–632.

Weick, KE (1984). Small wins: redefining the scale of social problems. *The American Psychologist,* 39(1), 40–49.

Chapter Thirteen

FORTUNE SR. WRITER MARC GUNTHER ON "THE ROLE OF VIRTUES IN SPIRITUAL LEADERSHIP"

Marc Gunther

Fortune Magazine

Judi Neal

International Center for Spirit at Work

A three-part movement begins with Neal, founder and CEO of the International Center for Spirit at Work, setting the stage for an interchange of ideas relating to virtues and leadership. Gunther, a senior writer for *Fortune Magazine,* is the dialogue partner. He draws upon his journalistic interviews with CEO's and especially upon the case of exemplary leader and CEO, Ricardo Levy, to examine the interaction between spirituality and business practice. The Levy case is followed up with a short interview whereby Neal asks pointed questions about the capacity of organizations to exhibit virtuousness and what may contribute to virtuous performance.

Judi Neal: The Role of Virtues in Spiritual Leadership

Marc Gunther is a senior writer at *Fortune Magazine.* He is highly respected for his articles on corporate social responsibility and faith at work. He is perhaps best known for a cover story he wrote called "God and Business: The Surprising Quest for Spiritual Renewal in the American Workplace." This article generated a tremendous amount of reader response, more than any other article that Marc had written for *Fortune*. And it was a hit on the newsstands as well.

Because of his own renewed faith in his Judaic tradition, and his strong belief that business is about more than the bottom line, Marc wrote a book titled *Faith and Fortune: The Quiet Revolution to Reform American Business* (Gunther, 2004). This book chronicles several enlightened organizations that believe that business can become a force for good in the world. The book profiles organizations such as Greyston Bakery, Tom's of Maine, Southwest Airlines, UPS, and Starbucks. It also explores the role religious leaders are playing in the marriage of faith and business, as well as the role of social investing and financial markets.

Marc contacted me because of my role as Executive Director of the Association for Spirit at Work, and asked me for suggestions on how he might get his book to reach a wider audience. In that conversation, we talked a lot about the importance of using the right language to reach the business community with the new ideas that are emerging in the spirituality in the workplace movement.

I told him about the book called *The Wisdom of Solomon at Work* (Manz *et al.*, 2001), that tells stories from the Old Testament that are relevant today. The book highlights the timeless virtues of faith, courage, compassion, integrity, and justice and makes the argument that these virtues provide wisdom and guidance for the difficult challenges faced by contemporary business leaders. Marc felt that a focus on virtues was most likely the best way to engage business leaders in a dialogue about spirituality and faith in the workplace.

As a result of that conversation with Marc, the editors of the *Journal of Management, Spirituality and Religion* special issue on values and virtues asked me to invite him to provide an excerpt from his book *Faith and Fortune*. The following excerpt profiles Ricardo Levy, a silicon valley CEO. It focuses on Levy's humility as a leader, and talks about why the virtue of humility is so needed in today's business world. I was fortunate enough to meet Mr. Levy at a conference in Montreal recently, and everything that Marc says about him is true. In spite of his amazing accomplishments, he was quiet and almost shy at the conference, and during his presentation, he constantly stressed the areas where he feels he needs to develop spiritually.

The next section is followed by a brief interview I conducted in May 2005 with Marc Gunther, about the importance of virtues in organizations.

Marc Gunther: What is a Spiritual Leader? Ricardo Levy[1]

Consider the celebrity CEO, that titan of American industry who graces the covers of business magazine and attracts a crowd to CNBC. He — and yes, the CEO is almost always a man — is often, although not always, a commanding presence, a charismatic figure who enjoys being the center of attention. His authority is unquestioned. His energy and ambition appear boundless. This man literally soars above the rest of us — did you know that corporate jets fly at higher altitudes than commercial planes? — and he is rarely plagued with self-doubt. You know the type. Jack Welch. Bill Gates and his successor, Steve Ballmer. In his heyday, Lee Iacocca. Ross Perot before he ran for president, and Michael Eisner before Disney stumbled — and, for that matter, after.

This isn't the only model of a chief executive, of course. Intel's Andrew Grove, a Hungarian refugee with a Ph.D. in engineering, comes across as a scholarly man of science, and Warren Buffett projects a folksy, midwestern charm along with his piercing intellect. But because the media relies on personalities to tell stories, television and the business press tend to portray business leaders as heroic, larger-than-life figures, giving them more credit than they deserve for a company's success — and more blame than they merit for its failure. One result is that we tend to be underwhelmed, at least initially, when we come across a CEO who does not fit the mold.

I felt that way when I met Ricardo Levy. His physical presence is unremarkable; he is balding, with brown curly hair, and he usually

---

[1] Excerpted from Chapter 12, "What is a Business Leader?" in *Faith and Fortune: The Quiet Revolution to Reform American Business*, New York: Crown Business, 2004/Used with permission.

dresses casually in clothes that seem like an afterthought. He speaks slowly and quietly, with a slight accent of his native Ecuador; my tape recorder barely captured his words when we first talked. Levy does not seek out the spotlight, and he is generous with his praise for others. Nor is he afraid to display uncertainty; indeed, he tries to be cognizant of his limits and seeks to practice humility, seeing that as a strength, not a weakness.

Yet there is no arguing with Levy's track record in business. In 1974, he and a partner started a tiny consulting firm that they called Catalytica in the basement of Levy's home in suburban New Providence, N.J. Twenty-five years later, Catalytica had grown into a publicly traded, high-tech research firm and manufacturer with headquarters in Silicon Valley, a factory in Greenville, N.C., that produced life-saving drugs, 1800 employees and a market capitalization that peaked at $1 billion. In August 2000, after considerable agonizing, Levy agreed to sell the bulk of the company to a Dutch pharmaceutical giant called DSM for about $800 million. Today, he remains Chairman of the board of Catalytica Energy, a small research-and-development firm that has developed a fuel-burning technology to reduce smog; essentially, it's what is left of the old Catalytica after the rest was sold. A wealthy man, he sits on the boards of several high-tech companies.

Levy would never describe himself as a model of a spiritual business leader — he's too self-effacing for that and, besides, no one person can embody that idea — but he is worth getting to know because, as much as any chief executive I've met, he has thought systematically about the interplay between spirituality and leadership. Fact is, he formally studied the topic. In 1997, Levy was one of a small group of CEOs and graduate students who took a course called *Spirituality for Business Leaders* that was taught by Professor Andre Delbecq at the business school of the University of Santa Clara, in the heart of Silicon Valley. I came across Delbecq on the Internet when I plugged the words "spirituality" and "business" into a search engine, and turned up the syllabus for his course. After we talked, he suggested that I get in touch with Levy, who was his star pupil and a friend. I visited Levy early in 2001, soon after the deal to sell Catalytica's pharmaceutical operations to DSM had closed. We've met several times since then, and stay in touch, occasionally, by e-mail.

We met that first time in a small conference room at Catalytica's headquarters, which occupy a nondescript, single-story building in Mountain View, California. Levy ordered in sandwiches, and began to tell me about himself.

Like many baby boomers, Levy has fashioned a personal brand of spirituality that draws from a number of religious traditions. He was born and raised Jewish, but he has not practiced conventional Judaism for many years. With his Asian-American wife, Noella, he enjoys practicing tai chi, a physical discipline rooted in Taoism. And while studying with Delbecq, he was exposed to such Christian thinkers as Thomas Merton and Thomas Keating, who made a strong impression on him.

"For me, spirituality is a very individual issue," Levy explained. "Although I consider myself fully Jewish, I'm not a member of a synagogue. Those of us who are less affiliated have to uncover our own path, and that's hard. Especially when, at the same time, we are CEOs of fast-growing companies. I didn't have a road map, although I felt I had the need."

Spirituality and business are intertwined in Levy's family history. His father, Leopold Levy, was an entrepreneur who fled Nazi Germany and settled in Ecuador in 1941; he started several businesses, including an insecticide company that Ricardo's older brother, Werner, still runs. Although Leopold Levy attended synagogue, and the family socialized with other German–Jewish immigrants, his mother was less observant and the Levys did not give their sons a rigorous Jewish education. "The best way to express it is to say that there was a spiritual undertone in the family," Ricardo said. Born just after the end of World War II, Ricardo spoke German at home, Spanish at school and enough Hebrew to become a bar mitzvah in 1958. He subsequently learned English well enough to attend college in the United States, where he earned advanced degrees from Princeton and Stanford. By then, he had drifted away from Judaism but not from spirituality. "My own mindset led me to be very interested in spiritual matters, so I would read a lot," he said. He and Noella were married by a Reform Rabbi; 25 years later, they invited him to preside over a ceremony where they renewed their vows, with their two grown children looking on.

After graduate school and a brief stint as a researcher at Exxon, Levy joined with two colleagues to start Catalytica. They didn't have a clear plan, other than to use their intellect and their ability to innovate to build a business; they began as consultants to the energy and petrochemical industry, focusing on technologies built around catalysts, or accelerators of chemical change. Many of their ideas failed, but they did come up with a couple of promising processes — a combustion system that reduces pollution by using catalysis to convert natural gas to energy, which is now at the heart of Catalytica Energy, and highly-efficient ways to manufacture complex molecules for the drug industry, which became their big business. They raised venture capital in the 1980s, took the company public in 1993 and then transformed Catalytica into a full-fledged operating company by buying a small California drug-manufacturing plant.

In 1997, Levy and his partners took a big gamble by acquiring a much larger, state-of-the-art factory in Greenville, N.C., from pharmaceutical giant Glaxo Wellcome for about $240 million. With that, Catalytica became one of the pharmaceutical industry's biggest contract manufacturers; its products included the cold-medicine Sudafed and the anti-AIDS drug AZT. Levy loved his work, and relished the idea that Catalytica's technologies were helping to make the world a better place. Speaking of AZT, he said, "These are life-saving drugs, and we produced the form that was then injected into a patient. Wonderful." But he also felt busier and more pressured than ever. "It meant moving into a completely different domain," he said. "We had been a notable company, in a small way, as a R&D company. Now we were running a company with well over 1000 employees."

Gradually, Levy's world became more hectic and complex. Instead of managing a small, private company, whose progress was measured by its technical accomplishments, he was leading a publicly traded company with significant capital requirements, sophisticated investors such as Morgan Stanley Capital Partners, coverage from stock-market research analysts and quarterly earnings targets. He faced a constant pull-and-tug between Wall Street's insistence that Catalytica make its numbers each quarter and the longer-term rewards that come from investing in research, plant and equipment, and people. "The pressures of quarterly earnings are very intense," Levy told me. "They are like a hungry monster. How to keep that balance between the long-term and the near-term is a fascinating and extremely difficult task for the CEO." The time pressures on Levy also intensified; his daily to-do list had never been longer. "One of the challenges," he said, "became how to make a transition like that and maintain your equilibrium and balance."

It was at this juncture, with his business expanding rapidly and the Silicon Valley economy exploding, that Levy took Andre Delbecq's course. The two men had known each other as members of the local chapter of a global business organization called *The Executive Committee*, where Delbecq, an expert on innovation, had talked about his burgeoning interest in spirituality. At age 60, Delbecq had taken a sabbatical from the Leavey School of Business at Santa Clara to explore the connections between spirituality and business leadership. He read widely outside of his own Catholic tradition, visited with such spiritual leaders as Rabbi Zalman Schachter Shalomi, the Jewish mystic, and Chung Liang Huang of the Living Dao Foundation and then spent a semester at the Graduate Theological Union at Berkeley developing his course.

Levy dove into the course with gusto. Catalytica's growth spurt had prompted him to ask himself some pointed questions about how to handle his expanding responsibilities as CEO. He wasn't even sure whether he still wanted the job. "Do I even belong here?" he asked. "Is this my calling? I was struggling with a lot of questions." The idea of being "called" by God to do a particular kind of work, which comes out of the Judeo-Christian tradition, was much discussed by Delbecq and the class. Everyone agreed that clergymen, teachers, social workers, medical professionals and the like could feel called to lives of service. But could business be a calling?

Delbecq was sure that it could be. Business plays such a central role in America, as the primary creator of jobs, wealth, goods and services, that without a robust economy fueled by business, there could be no helping professions or nonprofit institutions. What's more, because business has enormous potential to do both great good and great harm, Delbecq argued that business leadership can be seen as an invitation from God to service. Running a company, in this context, is not primarily a route to material well being or even self-fulfillment, but a way to serve the common good, provided the company operates with that purpose in mind. As the writer and theologian Michael Novak puts it in his book, *Business as a Calling*, which was part of the curriculum, business is "not only a morally serious vocation but a morally noble one." Levy had never thought about his work as a calling, although he had tried to behave ethically and he took pride in Catalytica's contributions to health care and pollution control. He found that the notion of business leadership as a calling helped him connect his work to a grander purpose.

For much of the course, Delbecq encouraged Levy and the other executives to read and think about spiritual leadership. This was worthwhile, but insufficient; he wanted to touch their hearts as well as their minds, and to persuade them to look inside themselves. So he urged them to try meditation, by exposing the class to several approaches: Buddhist and Hindu practices, the Christian centering prayer developed by Thomas Keating, and an ancient Benedictine contemplative practice known as Lectio Divina that includes reading, meditation, prayer and contemplative silence. Then Delbecq issued a challenge. He asked the executives to set aside 20 minutes a day to meditate for the next 30 days, and only then to decide whether to stay with it. He also organized a weekend retreat at a nunnery in the Santa Cruz foothills, where the business people tried meditation, story telling and prayer.

Finally, near the end of the term, Delbecq asked each of the CEOs and MBAs to take a field trip that would expose them to suffering in an unmediated way — that is, they were to spend time with poor people, AIDs patients, battered women or the elderly. They were to do so, not in their usual role as a volunteer or potential benefactor or a provider of business know-how, but simply as a fellow human being. "The focus is on being with, rather than doing for," Delbecq told the class. "This is an 'I-Thou' encounter with each person, not with a category of people. Listen to the individual voice, the life story, the sources of desolation and consolation." He urged the students to try to reach outside of their comfort zone, to travel to a place where they would rather not go. This, he hoped, would help the class to feel gratitude for their own good fortune, as well as connect them to the needy in a personal way.

Levy visited a homeless shelter in San Jose. He chose to spend time with homeless people because he realized that seeing them on the streets made him uncomfortable, and that bothered him. "I'd go to New York on a business trip, and I'd avoid these people," he said. "And then say to myself, 'Look, what are you doing? They're not animals. They're not going to attack you.' And yet I felt it." He visited the shelter twice, arriving in the late afternoon, helping to serve dinner, and then talking with people until they were ready to go to sleep. "It wasn't easy," he said. "I felt like that I didn't belong. It was a little strange because I had the luxury of being able to go home." But he was able to shed his prejudices and see the homeless as other people, not as a threat. "Some of them were a little bit gone in terms of their mental framework, and you have to be compassionate in that regard," he said. "Some of them were just plain stuck. They'd lost their jobs, and couldn't afford a place to live. They were no less worthy than I was." The experience was unsettling because it reminded him that he had not always been as compassionate as he would like to be. When he returned to work, Levy could not help but wonder about how receptive he was to the needs of his employees at Catalytica, and how clearly he was able to see them as who they are.

In the aftermath of the course, Levy's spiritual practice deepened — and it began to reshape him as CEO. In our interviews, he described three distinct but interconnected ways in which his spirituality had changed him as a leader. "One is the capability to center, the ability to quiet the mind through meditation. The second one is the ability to discern. The word discernment — I never really thought about it until I took the course — is a key to these issues. The third idea is recognizing the need to remind ourselves of our humility." Like Levy, I had tried meditation, so I had no trouble grasping the idea that a harried executive would benefit from a few minutes of quiet reflection, every day. But I knew nothing about discernment, which is an ancient Christian practice intended to divine the will of God. As for humility, well, that was a word I hadn't had much occasion to use in my years of writing about CEOs.

Humility was especially scarce in Silicon Valley during the 1990s tech boom that transformed legions of engineers, entrepreneurs and venture capitalists into swaggering millionaires. Levy, who had lived in the valley since 1974, had seen some of his neighbors change as they got rich. He'd felt the effects, too. "People lose perspective as they gain wealth and power," he said. "It is horribly seductive. Suddenly you feel, man, I made money, I must be good. You may not say it consciously, but the temptation is to suddenly feel a step above. As we went from 100 employees to 1000, I had to be careful not to get too giddy. I've felt the temptation, it's there, and it's treacherous." Treacherous, indeed — more than one promising career has been destroyed by the arrogance of a CEO.

But, if arrogance can derail a career, does it follow that humility can strengthen a business leader? Certainly the major religions speak of the importance of humility, often in similar terms. "Humility is the foundation of all the other virtues," wrote St. Augustine. Lao Tzu said: "Humility is the root from which greatness springs." In a business setting, as Levy explained it, humility is predominantly about knowing your limits, appreciating the contributions of others, learning to listen and striving to see things as they are, as opposed to seeing them through the distortions of ego. "It is not meekness. It is not passivity and neutrality," Levy said. "It is perspective. It is a recognition of what things are truly valuable. That means recognizing the fact that you have made a million dollars means squat."

More than a state of mind, humility should be reflected in the behavior of a spiritual leader. "It can be as little a thing as walking into an office and smiling at a receptionist, even if you are not having a good morning. Or how a CEO walks down the hall. He sets a tone," Levy said. "A CEO is really the ultimate source of comfort and concern in a company, but most people are afraid to talk to the CEO. How can you be effective leader if no one wants to talk to you? The effectiveness of an open-door policy is strictly a function of how open people feel you are, not how open you say you are. You can't just put up a sign." When coupled with a willingness to listen, humility opens up channels of communication between an executive and others in a company, as well as business colleagues, customers and suppliers. Its opposite, hubris, all but insures that an executive will operate in the dark.

Levy's argument — that humility translates into effectiveness for a business leader — appealed to my own softer side, but I wondered if it was a little naïve when I first heard him articulate it. Most of the media moguls I'd written about were anything but humble. Viacom's Sumner Redstone could be stunningly self-absorbed, Michael Eisner of Disney rarely owned up to his own shortcomings and blamed others for the company's troubles. Gerry Levin, the former CEO of AOL Time Warner, reacted to critics with a stubborn defensiveness. Nor are the business heroes celebrated by the press — Bill Gates, Jack Welch, Citicorp's Sandy Weill, Steve Jobs of Apple, Amazon's Jeff Bezos — reputed to be self-effacing. Occasionally, I had come across executives who seemed humble. Thomas Murphy and Dan Burke, the leaders of Capital Cities/ABC in the 1980s and early 1990s, were reluctant to claim credit for themselves when their company did well, and the late Frank Wells, Eisner's second-in-command at Disney during the company's glory years, was a modest man. But my experience as a reporter suggested that an outsized ego and success in corporate America often went hand in hand.

Then I read *Good to Great*, the best-selling book by Jim Collins published in 2001. Collins is a brilliant business researcher, consultant and writer who has spent years trying to understand corporate success; his first book, *Built to Last*, argued, among other things, that great companies are born out of a powerful vision that goes beyond making money. As an analyst, Collins has always been skeptical about the popular conceit that business success is all about leadership; the point of his extensive research projects, which take years to complete, is to dig deeper, analyze lots of data and uncover other forces at work. For *Good to Great*, he began by identifying 11 ordinary companies that made themselves great, using as his primary benchmark long-term stock-market return, relative to the firm's industry. All the companies, in other words, had been terrific investments. What else, he then asked, did they have in common? Collins discovered that one key to greatness is what he terms a Level 5 leader, which he defines as "an individual who blends extreme personal humility with intense professional will." There was that word again — humility.

When I went to see him in Boulder, Colorado, Collins told me that he was as surprised as anyone by the link between humility and leadership. "I have no religious background," he said, although several of his superstar CEOs turned out to be men of faith. "The research was purely secular, purely clinical, purely data-driven." And how humble were the CEOs he celebrates? Well, as a business writer, I'd never heard of any of them. (Their names and companies, if you're curious, are Fred Allen of Pitney Bowes, George Cain of Abbott Laboratories, Joe Cullman of Phillip Morris, Lyle Everingham and Jim Herring of Kroger, Ken Iverson of Nucor, David Maxwell of Fannie Mae, Colman Mockler of Gillette, Carl Reichardt of Wells Fargo, Darwin Smith of Kimberly-Clark, Cork Walgreen of Walgreen's and Alan Wurtzel of Circuit City.) All of these men, Collins found, were fiercely committed to building their companies, but they all shared a reluctance to claim credit for themselves and an eagerness to praise others. "It's not that Level 5 leaders have no ego or self-interest," Collins writes. "Indeed, they are incredibly ambitious — *but their ambition is first and foremost for their institution, not for themselves.*"

The more I thought about Collins' findings, the more they made sense: leaders who are humble are likely to be good listeners, they are likely to develop healthy and collegial relationships with others and they are likely to surround themselves with talented people. Most people would much rather work for a humble and big-hearted executive than they would for a boss who hogs credit. Out of curiosity, I went back and checked Capital Cities/ABC's stock-market performance; as I'd thought, the company had done far better when it was run by Murphy and Burke than it did after they sold it to Disney and Eisner took over.

"On one level, it's so simple," Collins said. "If we have any faith in what we know in our guts about the best in people, it's got to work." But, he found, the makeup of Level 5 leaders is actually quite complex. During his research, he asked the widow of one Level 5 CEO whether her husband had been a happy man; she seemed puzzled by the question, and said her husband didn't look at life that way. He could never be truly happy, she said, because he was almost "physically revolted by the idea of unrealized potential left on the table." That was why he was determined to bring out the best in others. Collins has come to think of Level 5 leaders as almost artistic in temperament. He said: "The drive is creative. The drive is compulsive. The canvas they were painting on was the company." Put another way, the spiritual leader has a burning desire to help others to flourish and build an enterprise with lasting value.

There's another bottom-line value to humility. It engenders curiosity, a healthy quality in any executive. After all, if you are aware of what you don't know, you are likely to seek out answers from others. This, at least, is one explanation that Sir John Templeton, the renowned money manager, gives for his success as an investor and, in particular, for his single greatest insight about investing — the idea that to diversify as well as to maximize returns, investors should seek opportunities outside of the United States. Nothing in Templeton's background led him to be a global investor — he grew up in a small town in Tennessee — but he came to believe that it was egotistical of other money managers to believe that all good companies and investment ideas were to be found in the United States. Even today, Templeton, a man of faith whose foundation awards a $1 million prize each year for innovation in religion, says that he continues to "work at being a humble person." (This can't be easy when you're known as Sir John.) Recently, he wrote: "Humility about how little I know has encouraged me to listen more carefully and more wisely." When I read this, I was struck by how few of the top executives I'd met had ever asked me a question and listened to the answer. They were accustomed to doing all the talking.

But can one, as Sir John Templeton says, "work at being a humble person"? Or is humility mostly a matter of character and upbringing? I put the question to Levy, who said that he believes that because pride and arrogance are learned traits, they can be un-learned as well. "Some people are hardened by life experiences," he said. "They become harsh." But they can then be softened by new experiences — by service to others, by reflection, by prayer, even by the inevitable daily setbacks of business life, so long as they are open to acknowledging them. I asked Delbecq the same question and got a blunter answer. "You learn humility by being humiliated," he said. "To be a leader is to be a magnet for criticism." The key, he said, is to listen to critics, and to learn from them.

Levy found that keeping his ego in check became easier after he began his daily meditation practice. This was the second way in which the course changed him. Before studying with Delbecq, he'd been intrigued by meditation but felt he couldn't take the time to sit every day; after Delbecq issued his 30-day challenge, Levy figured he would try it for a month. "Sure enough, it became habitual," he said. "Now, no matter what happens or where I am, early in the morning, the first thing I do is 20 minutes of quiet meditation." Even on busy days? "Especially on the busy days. It's on days when there's a lot of stress, a lot of tension that you really need it." Typically, Levy reads a short, inspiring passage from a spiritual book. Then he tries to let his mind settle into total quietness. When, inevitably, his thoughts intrude, and he's about to get caught up in whatever's on his mind that day, he tries, as he puts it, to "gently let the thought leave again, and invoke a spiritual word that reminds me of my intent to connect with the divine inside me."

On the simplest level, meditation and centering are about stopping and being quiet. "It has been very rare in my hustle and bustle of 25 years that I have paused," Levy said. "Until people attempt to do it, I don't think they realize how noisy our lives are. People kind of know, I'm getting too many phone calls or too many people want to see me or my schedule is too crowded. Those are the surface manifestations. Beneath that, our mind is just trained to spin its wheels, to create little scenarios, to look at alternatives. Even if we don't do it consciously, it's happening all the time." One goal of meditation is to stop, or at least slow down, all these mental gymnastics, which some Buddhists call the monkey mind. Levy said: "If I had not started to develop the ability — or let's say, the intent, or at least the habit of taking time to quiet myself and reach in — I would have been a much less capable executive," particularly during the months leading up to the Catalytica sale. "So if we talk about what does spirituality do, a very real part is how it helps to quiet the innumerable noises that an executive hears. It's a very salutary thing just to get into that mode." Once in a rare while, he told me, he'll figure out the answer to a thorny business problem during or after a meditation session, although that is not the purpose of the practice. More often, he finds that the quieting of the mind is a "rejuvenating tonic" that helps him be more present and more open during the rest of his day. These qualities — being present, open, calm and receptive to others — are all elements of spiritual leadership.

In August 2000, Catalytica agreed to sell its drug business to DSM; its combustion division now operates as Catalytica Energy Systems, a stand-alone public company that Levy serves as a part-time, unpaid chairman of the board. "I go to the office when I think I can be of help, but my schedule is my own, and I'm enjoying that," he told me recently. He serves on the boards of several other high-tech companies, including one called Stem Cells Inc., so he is trying to learn more about molecular biology. And he continues to read widely about spirituality and business leadership so that he can "discern" his next steps. "One day a week, I spend several hours really studying," he says.

Religious traditionalists probably won't be much impressed by Levy's personalized brand of spirituality. He is, after all, a Jew who doesn't go to synagogue, who meditates like a Buddhist and who relies on an ancient Christian practice to make up his mind. The whole deal, admittedly, sounds mushy. Why, then, should we pay attention to him at all? One reason is that he's more typical than you might think. Millions of Americans, like Levy, proudly exercise their right to pick and choose the values and rituals that suit them from the extravagant buffet of American religious practices. A recent survey of business executives found that more than 60% had positive feelings about spirituality and a negative view of religion. Their religious practices, it's safe to assume, are neither conventional nor orthodox.

The bigger reason to listen to Levy is that he's enjoyed a great deal of success in business, building a company that he sold for

$800 million and spun off another enterprise with great promise. He's done a lot of good, too, by helping companies make drugs more efficiently and developing emission-control processes for utilities. He's also one of the most thoughtful executives I know. Sometimes when he talks about humility and centering and discernment, I have to remind myself that the words are coming from a Stanford-educated scientist and a battle-tested CEO, who's at home both in the laboratory and the boardroom. By their nature, scientists don't just accept a theory when it comes along; they test it to see if it works. Levy's done just that with his spiritual practices. His approach, at heart, is a disciplined way of trying to stay close to the values that matter to him and to the people who are crucial to the success of any business enterprise. "People are the most intangible, the most complex element of any business equation," Levy said. "The only way to reach people is to start by reaching into yourself — by understanding yourself." He does not claim his approach will work for everyone, or that there is any road map to becoming a spiritual leader. "This subject matter, by definition, is not a matter of 10 steps," he says. "It's a matter of awakening to what's inside."

Judi Neal Interview With Marc Gunther

JN: In your book, *Faith and Fortune*, you write a lot about spirituality in the workplace. How have you found people responding to words like "spirituality," "faith," and "virtues"? In our recent conversation, you stated that you thought there would be less resistance to a word like "virtues" than to the other words. Why is that?

MG: These questions of language are difficult and very important. I don't think that most of corporate America — of course, there are exceptions — is ready to talk about "spirituality" or "faith" at work. Spirituality is a vague term. To many people, it has New Age connotations. There's nervousness about faith as well because of the political debate over "faith-based" initiatives of the Bush White House. My friend David Miller, who runs the Center for Faith and Culture at

Yale, has talked about developing "faith-friendly"companies, as in "family-friendly" companies. I like that phrase.

JN: Is anyone in the corporate world using words like "spirituality," "faith" and virtues"?

MG: "Virtues" was a word used by Jeff Immelt, the CEO of General Electric, when I interviewed him last year. That surprised me. GE's a big, tough company. But Immelt said he wants it to be known as a virtuous company, in order to attract and motivate the best people.

Despite that, I think corporate America remains most comfortable with the secular language of corporate citizenship or corporate social responsibility. Still, I'm often struck by how much overlap there is between the language of religion and the language of business. Think about it — we talk about service in business, we talk about being good stewards of corporate assets.

JN: You describe Ricardo Levy as a man who exemplifies the virtue of humility. What other virtues does he seem to embody?

MG: He is thoughtful, considerate and purposeful. He is also a good listener. And he's curious. Most CEOs I interview don't ever ask me a question and when they do, they don't listen to the answer.

JN: Ricardo's companies in Silicon Valley are probably not as traditional or conservative as many mainstream companies in other parts of the U.S. Can traditional business values and virtues work together in the average workplace?

MG: They can and do work well together. I'd describe all the companies I write about in *Faith and Fortune* — even the biggest ones like UPS, Southwest Airlines and Starbucks — as virtuous. They set out to truly serve their own people and their customers. As a result, they are fabulously successful and they do well for their shareholders. I assume that's what you mean by a "traditional business values."

JN: Yes, I meant the bottom line when I was asking about "traditional business values." What would you say is the relationship between virtues and various kinds of individual and organizational performance?

MG: It's complicated. There are plenty of virtuous people and companies who fail in business, for a lot of reasons. And there are corrupt people and companies who succeed — although not indefinitely, as the scandals have taught us. I do believe that in the long run, all other things being equal, there is alignment between virtue and commercial success. It's logical — people want to work for people and companies they believe in, companies with a purpose that goes beyond the bottom line. Maybe I'm naïve, but I think the good people win in the end.

JN: If that's true, then what role do virtues play in organizational leadership?

MG: They are crucial. Look at the obvious and very important issue of executive pay. A greedy CEO who takes home $10 or $20 million a year sets a terrible example. He is poor steward of shareholder money. He has an inflated sense of his own self-importance. By contrast, a more modest pay package indicates than a CEO is working for the good of the enterprise, not to enrich himself, and that he or she understands that success belongs to everyone, and that the fruits of success should be distributed fairly. Which CEO would you want to follow?

JN: It's pretty obvious, isn't it. I had the opportunity to interview Bob Catell, CEO of Keyspan Energy, and co-author with Kenny Moore of the book *The CEO and The Monk*. Bob told me in very clear terms that he could easily earn more money somewhere else, but that he was committed to this organization and to the communities it serves, and that it wasn't about the money. It's inspiring to know that there are virtuous CEOs out there like Ricardo Levy and Bob Catell. So that brings me to another question: Can virtues be taught? If so, how?

MG: I do believe they can be taught, but it's not easy. Andre Delbecq, a very wise man who teaches at University of Santa Clara, runs a class in spirituality and leadership that I'm told is superb. He sends executives and MBA students out to work with the poor, among other things. UPS and Xerox run programs where they pay people to spend extended periods of time working in the inner city. These are ways to learn virtues.

JN: Can an organization be virtuous, or are virtues only a characteristic of individuals?

MG: Yes, I think an organization can become virtuous. Great schools or volunteer organizations are virtuous. So are some public interest groups. And, yes, so are the best companies. They develop people's capabilities, help their customers solve important problems, create the wealth that allows the educational and nonprofit sectors to flourish. I'd call those virtues.

JN: If organizational virtuosity is a good thing, how would a leader or a change agent help that organization to become more virtuous?

MG: By focusing on service. The late Robert Greenleaf, a Quaker and former AT&T executive, wrote a book about servant leadership. He suggested that the role of a leader is to serve others — his workers, customers, partners, shareholders. Trying to imbue an organization with an ethic of service would be one way to promote virtuous behavior.

JN: It's important to look at the shadow side of promoting virtuous behavior. What potential problems, if any, arise from focusing on virtues in organizations?

MG: Any organization's strength, taken to an extreme, can become a weakness. Herman Miller, a truly wonderful company, became so focused on its virtues in the early 1990s that its business performance fell off. Hewlett Packard had the same problem, I'm told. People came to work there because it was family-friendly, or to play in the company orchestra — not because they cared about making great technology. Running a business requires leaders to balance a variety of demands. You can overemphasize goodness. Of course, it would be nice if that were the problem with more companies.

References

Gunther, M (2004). *Faith and Fortune: The Quiet Revolution to Reform American Business*. New York: Crown Business.

Manz, C, K Manz, R Marx and C Neck (2001). *The Wisdom of Solomon at Work: Ancient Virtues for Living and Leading Today*. San Francisco: Berrett-Koehler.

Chapter Fourteen

THE CORPORATE CONDUCT CONTINUUM: FROM "DO NO HARM" TO "DO LOTS OF GOOD"[1]

Rosabeth Moss Kanter

Harvard Business School

Kanter introduces the idea of a values and economic based continuum, "The Corporate Conduct Continuum," as a means to assess corporate integrity and degree of positive engagement with communities, regions and global networks. She points to rising expectations by the general public for good to better corporate citizenship. Cases and role model companies who take innovative and highly successful steps to meet triple bottom line accountability are highlighted. Kanter contends that these kinds of exemplary efforts and effects are imperative for moving local and national interests to higher ground in the 21st century marketplace and world.

The land of opportunity depends on private enterprise to produce opportunity by innovating and creating jobs, and Americans increasingly expect that companies not only behave ethically but that they go beyond the letter of the law to help society as

---

[1] This chapter is excerpted and adapted from Kanter, *America the Principled: 6 Opportunities for Becoming a Can-Do Nation Once Again* (New York: Crown Publishers, 2007). Copyright 2007 by Rosabeth Moss Kanter/Used by permission. See the book for additional notes and background text that provides context for this excerpted material.

Bell Atlantic (today's Verizon) did in its' Union City, NJ science and technology school reform program or IBM does through its dynamic virtual and flexible workplace program. The corporate good conduct continuum ranges from avoiding illegal, unethical, or harmful acts at the minimum to doing as much good as possible at the voluntary high end. The low standard is the domain of laws and regulation; the other end signifies higher ideals. It is guided by publicity, reputation, and enlightened self-interest; the best companies are already well along toward being guided by values that encourage them to make a positive difference in the world.

"Value-based capitalism" is my catchall phrase for the wide swath from ethical behavior to above-and-beyond social contributions. It means being guided by standards and principals that are not reducible to economics. It implies responsibilities toward employees, customers, consumers, suppliers, communities, and the public that are shaped by social norms about appropriate, or better, treatment, even when there are no specific laws governing the relationships. Role model companies such as Procter and Gamble (P&G) and IBM have already made values, principles, and standards the core of their management controls. They are regularly taught in training programs, posted everywhere on the Web and in facilities, and used by people to guide decisions — as I saw when P&G managers in India echoed those in Cincinnati by reciting exactly which principles they used to guide the acquisition and integration of Gillette.

Excellent leaders in businesses with a tradition of meeting high standards steer their companies to contribute to society, above and beyond what is legally required — such as Procter & Gamble's A. G. Lafley or IBM's Sam Palmisano. But with prosecutors and the press focused on bad guys, segments of the public find it hard to imagine that there are any corporate good guys. Many still equate big business with bad business. On a 2005 national survey of confidence in leaders, business scored near the bottom (beating only government officials) in lack of public confidence. Back-dating of stock option awards to make sure that option holders earn lots of money is just the latest in a series of unfolding corporate financial scandals. By late 2006, about 200 companies were either under investigation by federal authorities or conducting their own probes of this practice, and some executives faced criminal charges.

A Few Good Companies? Rising to Rising Expectations

Americans need many more examples of how business can make a positive difference — and even more businesses doing it. One source of role models is the Ron Brown Award for Corporate Leadership, given by the White House after a review of scope, impact, and sustainability (I was a judge for the first seven years). Some of the winners include:

- IBM, one of the largest corporate elephants, was a two-time winner, first for workplace diversity and later for its "Reinventing Education" initiative, started in 1994 and reaching about a third of the United States and a dozen other counties, including Brazil, China, India, and Vietnam. Reinventing Education involves partnerships with public school systems to use technology to help solve such pressing problems as parent involvement in North Carolina, teacher support in West Virginia, or massive information needs in Broward County, Florida. IBM is also a perennial number one, or close, on *Business Ethics* magazine's list of the best companies in terms of ethics and integrity.
- Cisco Systems won for its Networking Academies, which teach information technology-related skills that prepare students in economically disadvantaged areas for jobs or higher education in engineering and computer science. About 10,000 Academies in 150 countries involve more than 400,000 students, who are taught in nine languages.
- BankBoston, now part of Bank of America, brought banking services back to inner cities, financing opportunities for poor people and new immigrants while educating them about money. Its network of community banks helps revitalize distressed neighborhoods, providing employment and hope along with reasonably priced loans.

- Timberland mobilizes employees, suppliers, and retailers for community projects in 25 countries, including global events on Earth Day. Saying that its shoes and boots help people "hike the path to service," the company gives employees 40 hours a year of paid company time for projects of their choice and "service sabbaticals" for temporary assignments with nonprofit organizations.

Skeptics claim that such activities are self-interested. Of course they are. And they should be. Enlightened self-interest makes efforts sustainable because employees, customers, and share-holders reward good conduct with their loyalty. Over 90 percent of 25,000 citizens of 23 countries reported on a global Millennium Survey that they want companies to focus on more than profitability. In another survey, two-thirds of American consumers said they feel more trust in products aligned with social values.

Numerous investors also support social responsibility. Over the decade between 1995 and 2005, socially screened assets under management increased slightly faster than the broader universe of managed assets. Total social investment rose more than 258 percent, going from $639 billion in 1995 to $2.29 trillion in 2005. The universe of professionally managed portfolios during this same period increased less than 249 percent, from $7 trillion to $24.4 trillion. (During the 2001–2003 recession, social investment funds grew 6.5 percent, while professionally managed portfolios as a group declined by 4 percent.) Criteria for social investments included screens for alcohol, tobacco, gambling, defense/weapons, animal testing, environment, human rights, labor relations, employment equality, community investment, and/or community relations. Internationally, the Japanese Federation of Economic Organizations (Keidandren) features a Charter for Good Corporate Behavior. The Association of British Insurers, whose members control a quarter of Britain's stock market, asks companies to report on social, environmental, and ethical factors that might pose significant risks to short- and long-term value. The *Financial Times* called this a significant shift for investors who had traditionally seen social responsibility as an extraneous distraction. In South Africa, the Johannesburg Stock Exchange has called for "triple bottom line" reporting — financial, social, and environmental performance.

The standard for corporate conduct can be raised from "do no harm" to "do lots of good." Organizations associated with values increasingly gain goodwill benefits that contribute to financial performance, from brand enhancement to employee recruitment and retention. That's why Michael Ward marked his appointment as CEO of railroad giant CSX with a community-based strategy to improve the wrong side of the tracks. That's why "cause-related marketing" is a growing phenomenon, as companies parade their philanthropy and compete to ally with the best nonprofit organizations. But please note that some of the worst corporate crimes have been committed by companies with good track records of philanthropy. Neither corporate contributions nor individual donations should give executives a "Get Out of Jail Free" card.

As parents know, you can't change behavior through punishment alone; you must also praise good deeds. The American public should want the good company models to spread — here and around the world. Awards and recognition can honor the exemplars, but such praise must be accompanied by disclosure to shame and shun the offenders.

Making Values-Based Capitalism the American Way

Pushed by federal Sarbannes–Oxley regulations and nudged by negative publicity, corporate boards of directors are finally doing the right thing. More disclosure, firmer audits, and independent directors are required by law. Boards are also issuing tighter codes of conduct and holding CEOs accountable for performance, including firing them for lapses in ethics or judgment.

During one week of business infamy in March 2005, Maurice (Hank) Greenberg was ousted from AIG, the company he founded, by his board, and former WorldCom head Bernard Ebbers was convicted of an $11 billion accounting fraud. Fox News anchor Neal Cavuto asked me on national television whether boards are now too quick to terminate CEOs who crossed ethical lines but had done nothing illegal, such as Harry Stonecipher, whose romantic e-mails led to his ouster at Boeing. I replied that the CEO job is not a reward for staying out of trouble; directors, shareholders, and the public need confidence in a leader's judgement going forward. And those who get the biggest financial rewards should be held to the highest standards.

It is difficult and contentious to strike an appropriate balance between overly stringent regulation and overly zealous prosecution. We must proceed cautiously in loosening controls so that markets rather than politicians guide corporate conduct. We must debate what can and should be demanded of American companies — what is appropriate, and what violates our sensibilities and standards.

What those standards are derives from a public consensus about values and principles. Economic logic plays a role, of course, but quality of life is not reducible purely to equations, as the *Economist* said when it found the cost-benefit analyses of various actions to reduce global warming too equivocal to guide policy. The concept of sustainability has become a convenient way to talk about business actions today that do not destroy the basis for doing business in the future.

It takes leaders of good character who exhibit humility rather than imperial arrogance to guide good companies. But relying on individual attributes alone is insufficient. Good leadership is made possible not just because people have the right values, but because institutions have the right checks and balances, including abundant opportunities for dialogue and dissent. We can do the following:

- *Continue to demand transparency*: disclosure and discussion are among the best ways to steer business behavior toward high standards — and high standards include high performance. Hiding bad news undermines business success and hurts the economy. Good companies can provide plausible answers to the tough questions the press and the public **ask**. Give airtime to the NGOs that investigate; give equal time to companies to respond.
- *Keep score*: triple bottom-line reporting (financial, social, and environmental performance) is common in Europe but at its infancy in the United States. Companies such as General Electric and IBM are issuing "corporate citizenship" reports and seeking standards

for evaluating their performance against citizenship goals. Consumers can ask about every aspect of performance; investors can demand it. People should applaud the good companies, and vote with their wallets.

- *Use bully pulpits to push the highest standards*: the United Kingdom has a minister for corporate social responsibility; in the United States, we prefer convening committees and councils with a private-sector chair, such as President Bush's corporate responsibility committee. In either case, public officials can make noise and broadcast a big message about what is expected. The stick of regulation can be waved in front of companies even when not being used to strike. The carrot of praise and publicity for voluntary compliance and above-and-beyond contributions can be held out frequently, and not just at annual award dinners. Political leaders can use their convening power to bring companies to the table to sign on to sets of principles in relevant areas, akin to the Equator Principles, which puts their commitments on record. And business schools represent another set of pulpits for educating future business leaders and rising executives about values.

- *Encourage local action*: when the Chicago city council passed its own minimum-wage law for large retailers, such as Wal-Mart, above the national minimum wage, the mayor (appropriately) vetoed it; but the action brought attention to public concerns about the discounter's employment practices. Communities can set standards and work with businesses to meet them. If communities are sufficiently strong in the assets world-class companies seek, such as human talent, communities can make their other values clear. BankBoston's inner-city banking initiatives were triggered by a Massachusetts report on racism and the failures of banks to provide services in poor neighborhoods; that one bank's response established financial services for neglected areas, which became a profitable business for the bank. And sometimes communities can act on issues without waiting for the government. California and Maryland did this with stem cell initiatives. Or consider the coalition of U.S. cities committed to implement the Kyoto Protocol for environmental standards that the Bush administration refused to sign.

- *Expect politicians to raise standards to what the public wants*: politicians should not be creating standards to save money for an industry (a perennial consideration invoked around minimum wage, health benefits, or energy consumption). Higher standards can stimulate innovation because creative companies identify efficient new ways to meet them. And innovation, is the best way to secure the future.

CLOSING COMMENTS: REFLECTIONS ON WHAT MATTERS MOST

David A. Whetten

Brigham Young University

In 2000, David Whetten delivered his Presidential Address "What Matters Most" in his role as president of the Academy of Management. In the way of concluding comments for the book, this final chapter shares David's memorable speech. It is prefaced by new comments from him providing a preamble that represents some of his current thinking related to his timeless original remarks. We believe this is a particularly fitting way to end a book titled "*The Virtuous Organization*" and David agrees. In fact, he views the title of this volume as capturing the essence of his original vision of how a large association such as the Academy of Management might effectively support its membership with a foundation of manifest virtues such as trust, respect, civility and nurturance. We are reminded that organizations, after all, consist of people and virtue originates in the way we interact and treat one another. Ultimately, his comments leave us with a call to action. Specifically, we are exhorted to help bring to realization the spirit of virtuous organizations wherever we work and reside through the decisions we make, the actions we take, and the relationships we build throughout our lives and careers.

In preparation for writing a chapter on the history of organizational behavior for a volume commemorating the 50th anniversary of the ILR School at Cornell, I asked a fellow ILR graduate, Walter Nord, to describe the field during an early period — the decade of the 1960s. He reported, "To the extent that intellectuals in the U.S. have ever been radicals, those were the people who were doing OD at that time. The desire to humanize our organizations attracted many students to OD-type classes. They were looking for solutions to social problems that they believed were the effluent from poorly managed organizations. Many scholars of my age were attracted to OD during this era because it provided a legitimate means for protesting inequity in organizations and for doing something about it. The prevalence of this orientation is evident in the extensive research on alienation during this decade" (Goodman and Whetten, 1998, p. 38). Walter's description of the "intellectual radicals" who were attracted to this field during that era reminds me of a recently retired BYU colleague, Bonner Ritchie. The first time I met him was at a professional conference. His presentation, entitled something like "Making Organizations Safe for Humans," was the talk of the conference.

Nearly a half century later, the concept of "virtuous organizations" conveys a similar sentiment: organizations often are, *but need not be,* contributors to personal alienation and associated social problems. The chapters in this volume give us glimpses of organizations that actively promote high ideals — that build rather than destroy character. It is hard to say if there are more of these organizations now than earlier, or if those of us who study organizations are more inclined or better equipped to see the virtuous "side of organizational life. Either way, I'm confident that Walter and Bonner would count this as progress.

The premise of this chapter is that professional associations, like the Academy of Management, provide those who "profess" these ideals for all organizations an opportunity to implement them within a single organization. Surely, if we aspire to be catalysts for virtuous behavior in "those" organizations, we should first model that role within "our" organization — where we serve as both members and leaders.

In retrospect, this was the objective of my 2000 presidential address. At an individual level, I wanted to offer encouragement to members of our field, especially graduate students and newly minted, assistant professors, who wondered if they were made of the "right stuff" — who questioned their ability to succeed as an academic. At an organizational level, I wanted to encourage members to collectively work against the sense of alienation expressed by some, especially new, members who questioned the value of actively participating in an organization that they experienced as overgrown and elitist.

The notion of a virtuous organization is consistent with my vision for the Academy of Management. My dream is that this organization will serve as a mental referent among its members for how organizations, generally, can actively promote nurturance, civility, tolerance, respect, trust, and responsibility. Nearly a decade later, in my mind, that's still "*What Matters Most*."

The 2000 Presidential Address: What Matters Most[1,2]

In the process of preparing this talk, I gained a new appreciation for Samuel Johnson's observation "There is nothing that focuses the mind like being hanged in a fortnight." I want to express appreciation to my dear friends and colleagues Kim Cameron and Bob Quinn for helping me understand yesterday at breakfast why this podium has appeared so gallows-like in my mind for much longer than a fortnight.

---

[1] David A. Whetten (2001). 2001 Presidential address: What matters most. *Academy of Management Review*, 26(2), 175–178. Reprinted with permission.

[2] Members who attended the 1998 Academy of Management meeting in San Diego may recognize this as the theme I selected as program chair. In my introduction of the theme in the conference program notes, I referred to a conversation I had with Lou Pondy, my mentor at the University of Illinois. After reflecting on my complaint that no matter what teaching method I used I was not succeeding as a teacher, he said, "You will warrant the title 'professor' when you discover what you are willing to profess." Building on the notion that this provocative advice to a young professor seems equally appropriate for a young profession, I continued, "What matters most is that we come together to discover what we are willing to profess." I view my presidential remarks as a personal response to the charge I issued to the Academy as program chair, as well as a tribute to my deceased mentor, Lou, who gently prodded me to speak from my heart.

With their wise, gentle, but persistent probing, they pulled from me an admission of fear. The prospect of speaking to my colleagues was not intimidating, but the unresolved tension within me between what I wanted to say and what I was terrified of expressing had a death grip on my thinking and my feelings. Although I had already prepared several different presidential messages, Kim and Bob helped me understand that I was using the pretense of crafting a better expression from my head as an excuse for ignoring what I wanted to say from my heart.

My association with Kim and Bob has spanned three decades. As master's students in the sociology department at Brigham Young University, we shared a common teaching assistantship. Our supervising professor had an owl-like visage that seemed highly appropriate for a man of profound wisdom. At the beginning of the semester, it was our lot as TAs to handle the myriad complaints from students about the professor's teaching objectives. You see, as we had learned from others in the department, there was a high negative correlation between the age of this particular professor and the amount of canonized sociological content he taught in his courses. By the time we came on the scene, he was near retirement and much more interested in sharing with his students sound, enduring principles for creating effective relationships within families, formal organizations, and even communities — than in teaching them the reigning sociological pronouncements on these matters.

My response to the disgruntled students was something like this: "You must decide how important it is to you to learn the content of this course as it was described in the catalogue. If you need this information so you can be prepared for upper division classes or graduate school, then I suggest you switch to another section of the course. However, if you are willing to release your professor from his obligation to teach you the discipline of sociology and, instead, allow him to teach you what he believes matters most, this class could change your life."

Today I would like to make a similar request: that you release me from the obligation of speaking to you as your president so that I can share with you some of the things that have changed my life.

To begin, I wish to acknowledge that Kim and Bob have been a large part of not only what I have to say today but also what I have said in academic settings for the past 30 years. But more important, they account for an even larger part of who I am today as a person. Indeed, I wish to use our 30-year relationship as a model for the kind of associations among professionals that I hope become more common within this professional association.

The modern terminology for describing social intercourse among academics includes words like colleague and college, which are formed from the Latin root col, meaning "together," as reflected in the Latin word *collegium,* meaning "a fellowship." These terms suggest that the business of academe is best accomplished when it is encompassed within a social fabric characterized by open, honest, and trusting relationships. Although some might argue that "compassionate intellectual" is an oxymoron, it has been my experience that rigorous reasoning is best accomplished among academics-as colleagues, whose interest in one another extends beyond "picking brains" and testing wits.

My understanding of this subject was enriched by a novel experience Saturday night, when Anne Huff; my wife, Zina; and I had dinner with members of the "Ph.D. Project." As many of you probably know, this is a group of about 100 students and supporting faculty who are predominantly African-American. This support group is the result of the vision and commitment of a senior KPMG partner, Bernie Milano.

After being extended the traditional gracious academic greeting normally offered to senior members of the profession — something like "I read your article on such and such" — Zina and I found ourselves quickly drawn into conversations about children, extended families, summer vacations, hobbies, and former jobs.

Following dinner, the group "hooded" 22 members who had received their doctorates this year. Many said this was a more meaningful graduation ceremony than the one they had just completed at their respective universities, because it included their academic support group. After this activity, the student introducing the guest speaker fainted. She was attended to by EMT personnel and taken from the room; the elected president of the group, Jeff, then came back and gave the following report: "Pat is fine. She is speaking, she is coherent, and she doesn't want us to worry. They've taken her to a hospital nearby, but I'm not going to tell you which one, because I know you'll all want to go there as soon as the dinner is over, and they can't accommodate a group this size. I will call the hospital regularly, and you can call my room for updates. Either myself, or my room-mate, Greg, will be there to take your calls." (Incidentally, Pat is fine, and yesterday she chaired a conference session.)

Later that evening, as I reflected on this experience, I thought how ironic it was that this group of academics, who feel marginalized and who are striving so hard to become integrated into the main-stream of their profession, has actually created a model professional association. I saw in that setting the kind of relationships longed for by many established members of this profession.

The holistic form of social intercourse I observed Saturday night brings to mind something I learned from my wife many years ago. While living in Urbana, Illinois, Zina taught disability awareness in the local schools. Her teaching objective is captured nicely in the notion "If you know one blind person, you know one blind person," meaning the experience of every blind person is different, because each is a different person.

As part of a program called "Kids on the Block," Zina used life-size puppets to help elementary school children view their disabled schoolmates as whole persons. One of her favorite puppet characters, Mark, had cerebral palsy and was in a wheelchair. He introduced him-self by saying, "Hi, I'm Mark, and I have a birth defect that makes it difficult for me to do some things. But there is more for you to know about me than the fact that I can't walk." He then proceeded to describe his interests, his hobbies, his dreams, and his worries. Before long, the audience was laughing *with* Mark and not *at* Mark. The timeless message those elementary school kids learned from Mark is that we dehumanize our relationships when we restrict our awareness of others to a single characteristic, attribute, or role.

Admittedly, our primary purpose for traveling to Toronto was not to attend a convention for parents or gardeners or mountain climbers, or to participate in a support group for grandparents of newborns with birth defects, or of sons and daughters who have recently buried their parents, or of individuals whose spouses or significant others are dying of cancer. Yet, these are but a few of the facets of the human condition present in this room today.

I remember hearing a colleague describe his highly enjoyable and productive professional relationship with a colleague as "nonredundant." By this he meant that what they did together and what they shared with each other went beyond the typical, common forms of professional discourse and association. These two colleagues had chosen to move beyond a one-dimensional view of each other — to not be satisfied with a superficial professional relationship, circumscribed by the typical identifiers of name, rank, and university affiliation. In brief, it's as if they were saying to each another, "Hi, my name is Mark, and I'm an academic, but don't hold that against me. There's more to my life that I think you'll find interesting and important."

All the examples of professional relationships I've highlighted today share at least two things. First, the participants released one another from the obligation of acting within a particular role or acting out a single characteristic that constrained them from sharing their struggles and their successes — the messy stuff that characterizes holistic associations, the kind that are wonderfully nonredundant. Second, these relationships were characterized by mutual trust, including appropriate expressions of support and intimacy.

Intuitively, we understand that the gift of trust involves the choice of forbearance. We trust others because we believe they won't take advantage of us. They won't use their understanding of our vulnerabilities to embarrass or to denigrate or subordinate. The reciprocal of the gift of trust is the gift of disclosure. By exposing more of ourselves to others, we give them the opportunity to become trustworthy. Unfortunately, most professional relationships are so burdened by the complications of presumed competence and confidence — and the accompanying implications for power and status — that the level of disclosure required to establish norms of trust is seldom reached. Studies of organizational transformation show that in order for norms to change, they must be broken by those who have the most to lose from the resulting social instability. Paradoxically, these individuals are often those in positions of power and high status.

This brings us to the admission of fear that Kim and Bob had to pull out of me. I was not afraid of speaking to a large group; I do that for a living. The reason I kept writing new drafts of my presidential address, each of which looked remarkably like the others, was that I was terrified of breaking our professional norms governing scholarly discourse. I wanted to speak from my heart to address the experience of Academy members who consider themselves to be marginal members because they feel so removed from the experience of the successful but I was concerned that this might appear self- serving or disingenuous and feared that some would be disturbed by such an uncharacteristic presidential address. So, you can either thank or blame Kim and Bob for what is to follow, because without the encouragement of these trusted colleagues, I would not have had the courage to be so personal in this setting.

Let me begin here by telling you a story. Soon after I was elected an Academy officer, I was visiting with a master's student at Brigham Young University who was leaving to enter a doctoral program at a leading university. He had taken a class from me and had served as my research assistant for a year, so we had developed a close professional relationship. Toward the end of our conversation, as he rose to leave, he turned and made the following astonishing observation: "I wish there were some basis for hoping that in 30 years I would be as successful as you. All I see behind you is success, and all I see in front of me is struggle." In response, I invited him to sit down and listen to "the rest of the story." I felt it was important to share with him the personal and professional struggles that were at least as typical of my life as the successes he presently admired. Absent a more complete understanding of the relationship between struggle and success, I feared he might become discouraged and give up when he encountered a rough patch in his life's journey, thinking that because he was struggling, he would never be successful.

Following are some of the highlights of that conversation. At the conclusion of my first year as a doctoral student at Cornell, I did poorly on a comprehensive exam. I'm grateful to my advisor, Howard Aldrich, for giving me a second chance, although he had no empirical support for such an action. During my last semester at Cornell, my wife died unexpectedly. As a single parent, with no extended family in the area and in the process of interviewing for jobs, I decided to send my two children to live with my parents, not knowing when or how my family unit would be restored.

A few months later I felt extremely fortunate to be hired by the University of Illinois. Unfortunately, I made the mistake of telling my professional associates that I had been hired to replace Jeff Pfeffer. I soon realized how inappropriate it was to compare myself with a highly productive scholar. While the two other new hires in organizational behavior churned out article after article from their lab studies, I was lost in an impenetrable forest of my own making; although I had succeeded in collecting the largest data set on interorganizational relationships for my dissertation, I had failed to figure out how to combine my theoretical questions with my empirical findings in an article-length format. It was three agonizingly long years before I received my first acceptance from a major journal. As an aside, based on the empirical data I collected during three cycles of reporting "0" publications on my annual productivity report, I am convinced that, despite what the mathematicians might claim, the distance between "0" and "1" is greater than between any other two numbers.

I remember how difficult it was to attend professional conferences during that time, feeling as though others viewed me as a fizzled rising star. And although I'd like to report that while I was off to a slow start as a researcher the students loved me in the classroom, I was equally clueless about how to teach organizational sociology to undergraduate business students.

But things turned around. I finally arrived at a much longed for, long-overdue deflection point in my downward trend. I learned how to consistently publish in our top journals, and my teaching ratings steadily improved. Along the way I was supported by many wonderful colleagues and friends. My struggles allowed them the opportunity to show their humanity, and this cemented our professional associations on the foundation of truly human relationships.

Please don't misunderstand the intent of my personal disclosure today. My point is not to make my professional accomplishments appear heroic, nor do I assume that my challenges and struggles are comparable to others. But I do hope that those of you who are feeling discouraged because you weren't drafted by your favorite university, or because you have just struck out in a particular inning of your career, will not take yourself out of the game of scholarship because of the misconception that those you consider successful are strangers to profound struggle.

I am, by nature, what my wife would graciously refer to as a "tender-hearted" person. So, I tend to be rather emotional. But I have even surprised myself at how often my voice has quivered the past few days as I have welcomed new Academy members, given Anne Huff her plaque as the former president, and conducted my last Board of Governors meeting. This morning, as I reflected on this pattern, I realized it stems from a profound disbelief during the first decade of my career that I would ever amount to anything professionally. I truly hope that my presence here today will serve as a lasting source of inspiration to those who feel discouraged, who wonder if hard times will be tempered, and, most of all, who might believe that success comes without struggle.

In conclusion, I'd like to return to the title of my talk. What I believe matters most to the future of this organization is predicated on our willingness as individual members to share with one another what truly matters most to us as complicated, complex, sometimes internally inconsistent, but always aspiring to be better, human beings. Specifically, I believe that one measure of our success as an organization is our ability to continually spawn collegial relations like the one I've shared with Kim and Bob and expressions of support like those I observed among members of the PhD Project this weekend.

This is not an easy path. I expect that the Academy of Management will continue to grow and that our large size will continue to prompt complaints about the impersonal nature of the sociality among members, especially during our annual conference. If we let nature take its course, so to speak, I am troubled by the prospect that those who are new to our field, or who bring different academic interests or training, or who are venturing out on the professional stage for the first time, might leave their encounters with us feeling socially unconnected and professionally unfulfilled. Fortunately, members of our profession have identified numerous remedies for the harmful consequences of large organizational size on social relations. Hence, I invite all those who have influence over organizing decisions within the Academy to act in accordance with our best understanding of how to build social processes that foster interpersonal intimacy as an anecdote for organizational anomie.

But to only treat this as an intriguing, difficult organizational challenge would be inconsistent with the tone and intent of my remarks. Ultimately, the quality of our collective experience in this professional association is based on how fulfilled we feel in our individual associations among fellow professionals. To that end, I believe that along with expecting rigorous reasoning from one another, we should also offer one another unconditional, positive regard and acceptance, one conversation at a time, one encounter at a time, one relationship at a time. In this manner, each of us can contribute to building, from the bottom up, an academic professional association that reflects the truest expression of *collegium* — *a* fellowship among colleagues.

References

Goodman, PS and DA Whetten (1998). Fifty years of organizational behaviour from multiple perspectives. In *Industrial Relations at the Dawn of the New Millennium*, MF Neufeld and JT McKelvey (Eds.), pp. 33–54. New York: New York State School of Industrial and Labor Relations.

CONTRIBUTING AUTHORS

Nancy J. Adler is the S. Bronfman Chair in Management at McGill University. Dr. Adler conducts research and consults on global leadership, cross-cultural management, and women as global leaders. She has authored over 100 articles, produced a film, and published four books. She is a Fellow of the Academy of Management, the Academy of International Business, and the Royal Society of Canada. Nancy is also an artist working primarily in watercolor and ink.

Richard P. Bagozzi is a Professor of Marketing and Social and Administrative Science at the University of Michigan and Professor in the College of Pharmacy. He does basic research into human emotions, decision making, social identity, and action. He also publishes widely in multivariate statistics and its relationship to measurement, construct validity, theory, hypotheses testing, and the philosophy of science.

David S. Bright is an Assistant Professor in the Department of Management, Wright State University. He has also been a research fellow and visiting assistant professor at the Center for Business as an Agent of World Benefit, Department of Organizational Behavior, Case Western Reserve University. Bright's research interests focus on appreciative inquiry, organizational development, and forgiveness in organizations.

Kim S. Cameron is the William Russell Kelly Professor of Management and Organizations in the Ross School of Business and Professor of Higher Education in the School of Education at the University of Michigan. He is one of the co-founders of the Center for Positive Organizational Scholarship at the University of Michigan. His research on organizational virtuousness, effectiveness, quality culture, downsizing, and the development of leadership skills has been published in more than 100 scholarly articles and 11 books, including *Positive Organizational Scholarship* and *Positive Leadership*.

David L. Cooperrider is the Fairmount Minerals Professor of Social Entrepreneurship, Director of University Center for Business as an Agent of World Benefit, and Professor and Department Chair of Organizational Behavior at the Weatherhead School of Management at Case Western Reserve University. He is the co-creator of Appreciative Inquiry. His interests include the theory and practice of Appreciative Inquiry (AI) as applied to corporate strategy, change leadership, and positive organizational scholarship.

Mihaly Csikszentmihalyi is Professor of Psychology, the School of Behavioral and Organizational Sciences, at Claremont Graduate University and Director of the Quality of Life Research Center. He is also emeritus professor of human development at the University of Chicago. In addition to the influential *Flow: The Psychology of Optimal Experience* (1990), which was translated into 15 languages, he is the author of more than a dozen other books and more than 200 research articles.

Andre L. Delbecq is McCarthy University Professor at Santa Clara University. He served as Dean of the Leavey School of Business from 1979 to 1989. His scholarship has focused on executive decision-making, organization design, managing innovation, and leadership spirituality. He served as Eighth Dean of Fellows of the Academy of Management, President of the Western and Midwest Academies of Management, and Executive Director of the Organization Behavior Teaching Society.

Jane E. Dutton is the Robert L. Kahn Distinguished University Professor of Business Administration and Psychology at the University of Michigan. She is one of the co-founders of the Center for Positive Organizational Scholarship at the University of Michigan (http://www.bus.umich.edu/positive/). Her current research focuses on positive identity, compassion and work (compassionlab. com) and high quality connections.

Ronald E. Fry is Department Chair and Associate Professor at the Weatherhead School of Management at Case Western Reserve University. His research interests focus on the dynamics that foster system-wide, positive change. As a co-creator of the Appreciative Inquiry theory and method, he works with groups, organizations and institutions around the world to develop insights on large group dynamics, appreciative leadership, multi-stakeholder strategic planning, and business as an agent for world benefit.

Marc Gunther writes about the impact of business on society, with a focus on environmental issues. He is a senior writer at *Fortune* magazine, a columnist at CNNMoney.com and author of *Faith and Fortune: How Compassionate Capitalism is Transforming American Business* (Crown Business, 2004). He has written cover stories for Fortune about the greening of Wal-Mart and "God and Business." Gunther has contributed to *The New York Times* and *The Washington Post*, among other publications.

Geert Hofstede holds a Master's level degree in Mechanical Engineering from the Technical University of Delft (1953) and a cum laude doctorate in Social Psychology from the University of Groningen (1967). He had a varied and international career both in industry and in academia, retiring as a Professor of Organizational Anthropology and International Management from the University of Maastricht in 1993. Since the publication of his book *Culture's Consequences* (1980, 2001) he has been a pioneer of comparative intercultural research; his ideas are used worldwide.

Rosabeth Moss Kanter holds the Ernest L. Arbuckle Professorship at Harvard Business School, where she specializes in strategy, innovation, and leadership for change. Professor Kanter is the author or co-author of 17 books. Her latest book, *America the Principled: 6 Opportunities for Becoming a Can-Do Nation Once Again* (2007), offers a positive agenda for the nation, focused on innovation and education and a new workplace social contract. She chairs a Harvard University group which helps successful leaders at the top of their professions apply their skills not only to managing their own enterprises but also to addressing challenging national and global problems.

Fred Luthans is University and George Holmes Distinguished Professor of Management at the University of Nebraska . The former President of the Academy of Management and currently editor of *Journal of World Business, Organizational Dynamics, and Journal of Leadership and Organization Studies*, he is also the author of several well-known books and numerous research articles. His latest book, co-authored with Carolyn Youssef and Bruce Avolio, is *Psychological Capital* published by Oxford University Press. His research in recent years has been focused on the theory-building, measurement and performance impact of this positive approach.

Joseph A. Maciariello is Horton Professor of Management at the Peter F. Drucker and Masatoshi Ito Graduate School of Management and Academic Director of the Drucker Institute at Claremont Graduate University. He collaborated with Peter Drucker to publish *The Daily Drucker* (HarperCollins, 2004) and *The Effective Executive in Action* (HarperCollins, 2005). He has revised Peter Drucker's *Management: Tasks, Responsibilities, Practices* (HarperCollins, 1973) which is scheduled for publication on April 9, 2008 and Drucker's book *Management Cases* (HarperCollins, 1977) which is scheduled for publication in December 2008.

Charles C. Manz is a speaker, consultant, and author of over 200 articles and scholarly papers and 20 books including *Mastering*

Self-Leadership, 4th Ed., *The New SuperLeadership*, *The Power of Failure*, *Emotional Discipline*, and *SuperLeadership*. He is the Nirenberg Chaired Professor of Leadership in the Isenberg School of Management at the University of Massachusetts. Formerly a Marvin Bower Fellow at the Harvard Business School his clients have included 3M, Ford, Xerox, General Motors, P&G, and American Express.

Karen P. Manz is author and speaker in the area of values, spirituality and work life and co-author of numerous articles and the book, *The Wisdom of Solomon at Work: Ancient Values for Living and Leading Today*. She is adjunct Professor at Hartford Seminary, a Consulting Editor for the *Journal of Management, Spirituality and Religion*, and member of the American Academy of Management and the American Academy of Religion.

Robert D. Marx is Professor of Management at the Isenberg School of Management at the University of Massachusetts, Amherst. He is co-author of the *Wisdom of Solomon at Work: Ancient Virtues for Living and Leading Today* and co-author of *Management Live! The Video Book*. He recently serves as Board Chair of the Organizational Behavior Teaching Society and is the 2005 recipient of the Distinguished Teaching Award at the University of Massachusetts. He teaches regularly at several international graduate programs.

Debra Meyerson is an Associate Professor of Organizational Behavior at Stanford University's School of Education and (by courtesy) Graduate School of Business and co-director of Stanford's Center on Philanthropy and Civil Society. Meyerson's research focuses on conditions and change strategies that foster constructive and equitable gender and race relations in organizations, scaling social innovations, and the role of philanthropic institutions in shaping educational reform initiatives. She is the author of *Tempered Radicals: How People Use Differences to Inspire Change at Work*.

Donna Mitroff holds a Ph.D. in instructional design and is a specialist in media for families and children in television and other media forms. She has extensive background in program development and executive management and production. She has been a consultant to several of Hollywood's major children's programming organizations, has served on national advisory committees and international children's programming juries. She has been an elected member of the Board of Governors of the Academy of Television Arts and Sciences.

Ian I. Mitroff is currently a University Professor at Alliant International University in San Francisco. He is Professor Emeritus from the University of Southern California, where he was the Harold Quinton Distinguished Professor of Business Policy at the Marshall School of Business. He has authored 26 books, including *A Spiritual Audit of Corporate America, Smart Thinking for Crazy Times, The Essential Guide to Managing Corporate Crisis*, and *Managing Crises Before They Happen*. He is a Fellow of The American Psychological Association, The American Association for the Advancement of Science, and The American Academy of Management.

Judi Neal is a speaker, author and consultant, and received her Ph.D. from Yale in Organizational Behavior. Judi is founder and CEO of The International Center for Spirit at Work. She has published extensively on spirituality in the workplace and is the author of *Edgewalkers* (Praeger, 2006). She is Professor Emeritus at the University of New Haven and is the Academic Director of the Master of Arts in Organizational Leadership at the Graduate Institute.

Craig L. Pearce is an Associate Professor of Management at the Peter F. Drucker and Masatoshi Ito School of Management, The Claremont Graduate University. He received his Ph.D. from the University of Maryland. He is an active keynote speaker and consultant in the areas of leadership, team and organizational development. He has won several awards for his work on shared leadership including the 2000 Barclays American Award, the 2004 Ascendant Scholar Award and the 2008 Asia Pacific Leadership Award.

Edward H. Powley is Assistant Professor of Management at the Naval Postgraduate School. He teaches organizational behavior and studies organizational healing, positive change, and trust and mistrust in organizations. He has consulted and conducted research with Prudential Retirement, U.S. Environmental Protection Agency, U.S. Navy, Roadway Express, and the Society for Organizational Learning. He worked previously for The World Bank and the Corporate Executive Board. He received his doctorate from Case Western Reserve University and master's degree from The George Washington University.

Rand Quinn is a doctoral student at Stanford University's School of Education. He specializes in the politics of education and his general research interest is in the interplay of private and public institutions and action in education. Prior to graduate school, Rand was a community organizer and policy analyst working on welfare rights and other public benefits issues.

Seung-Yoon Rhee is Assistant Professor of Organizational Behavior at Korea Advanced Institute of Science and Technology. She received her Ph.D. in business administration from the University of Michigan, Ann Arbor. Her current research interests include shared emotions in groups, affect network, and social identity and identification.

David A. Waldman is Professor of Management and Director of the Center for Responsible Leadership (http://crl.asu.edu) at Arizona State University. He has authored approximately 100 scholarly and practitioner articles or chapters in many journals/series including *Journal of Applied Psychology,* and the *Academy of Management Journal,* and has published two books on 360-degree feedback, and leadership and open communication. Waldman is a Fellow of the American Psychological Association and the Society for Industrial and Organizational Psychology.

David A. Whetten is the Jack Wheatley Professor of Organizational Studies and Director of the Faculty Development Center at Brigham Young University. He has published numerous articles and books on a variety of subjects. He is co-author of *Developing Management Skills*, (with Kim Cameron). He has served as editor of the *Foundations for Organizational Science*, an academic book series, and the *Academy of Management Review*. Whetten is an Academy of Management Fellow, and in 2000, served as President of the Academy of Management.

Carolyn M. Youssef is Assistant Professor of Management at Bellevue University. She received her MBA from the American University in Cairo, Egypt, and Ph.D. from the University of Nebraska, Lincoln. She has published a number of articles and book chapters on positive organizational behavior and psychological capital. She is co-author (with F. Luthans and B. Avolio) of *Psychological Capital: Developing the Human Competitive Edge* (Oxford University Press, 2007).

ARTIST'S STATEMENT

Nancy Adler

"What we cannot comprehend by analysis, we become aware of in awe."[1]

In the midst of chaos, how do we see beauty? Surrounded by turbulence, how do we discover simplicity? Living together on one planet, how do we simultaneously celebrate our collective humanity and the unique resonance of our individual voices? Given the power of analytic understanding — driven as it is to claim life as *knowable* — how do we re-recognize the *unknown* and *unknowable*? How do we surrender to the humility it takes to stand in awe of life's mysteries? Where do we stand when we stand in awe?

Allowing a painting to be born is to stand in awe of one of life's most beautiful mysteries. Invited by the blank paper, the best of my intentions and experience enter into a dance with uncontrollable coincidence. Neither the process nor the resulting art are ever completely defined. Which way will the colors run? What surprises will the ink reveal as it, ever so gently, touches the paint? I purposely use water-based media that do not stay put where I place them on the paper. There's never any illusion that I control the process. I only enter the dance; paintings emerge out of the dance. For me, being an artist is about giving birth to the possibilities inherent

---

[1] Abraham Joshua Heschel (2001). In *I Asked for Wonder*, Samuel H. Dresner (ed.), New York: Crossroad.

in mystery. Creation — whether on a canvas of words, visual images, or life itself — is, in fact, about relearning to dance with God.

I have had the privilege of having many mentors: some known personally to me, many of whom I have studied with. They include visual artists (Barbara Bash, Jeanne Carbonetti, Elizabeth Galante, Frances Gafton, Gyokusen Meguro, John Leonard, Lew Yung-Chien, Tony Onley and Heather Yamada), poets (David Whyte), musicians (Tim Wheater and Ben Zander), and spiritual leaders (Andre Delbecq, Abraham Joshua Heschel, Zalman Schachter-Shalomi, and Lise Sparrow). I draw inspiration from such artists as Chagall, Jamali, and Kandinski. During his lifetime, many of Marc Chagall's contemporaries wrote him off for having refused the avante-garde's invitation to create art strictly for art's sake. They dismissed Chagall as a colorful, friendly painter whose art simply conveyed his *joie de vivre*. In this century, at a major retrospective of Chagall's work in Paris,[2] critics no longer write him off, but rather acclaim the striking humanity of his paintings, and offer him their highest praise, "Marc Chagall gave this nihilist century a worthy concept: hope."[3]

---

[2] "Chagall: Known and Unknown" an exhibition of 180 works of Marc Chagall at the Grand Palais in Paris through June 23, 2003.

[3] From Alan Riding (April 22, 2003). Anxiety and hope in a mystical fusion: Paris show offers Chagall's intense humanism beyond the *Joie de Vivre*. *New York Times*, p. B5.

SPECIAL PERMISSION

Permission from the Journal of Management, Spirituality & Religion (www.jmsr.org) has been granted to C. Manz, K. Cameron, K. Manz and Robert Marx (Eds.) to acknowledge and include with revision for publication in *The Virtuous Organization: Insights From Some of the World's Leading Management Thinkers* articles appearing in JMSR, Vol. 3, Issues 1 & 2, 2006.

These articles in their original printing are:

Values and Virtues in Organizations: An Introduction
Charles C. Manz, Kim S. Cameron, Karen P. Manz and Robert D. Marx

Organizational Healing: Lived Virtuousness Amidst Organizational Crisis
Edward H. Powley and Kim S. Cameron

Making Sense of Organizational Actions with Virtue Frames and its Links to Organizational Attachment
Seung-Yoon Rhee, Jane E. Dutton and Richard P. Bagozzi

Virtuous Leadership: A Theoretical Model and Research Agenda
Craig L. Pearce, David A. Waldman and Mihaly Csikszentmihalyi

Forgiveness From the Perspectives of Three Response Modes: Begrudgement, Pragmatism and Transcendence
David S. Bright, Ronald E. Fry and David L. Cooperrider

The Language of Virtues: Toward an Inclusive Approach for Integrating Spirituality in Management Education
Karen P. Manz, Robert D. Marx, Judith Neal and Charles C. Manz

Spirituality in Action: The Fred Rogers' Way of Managing Through Lifelong Mentoring
Ian I. Mitroff and Donna Mitroff

The Spiritual Challenges of Power, Humility, and Love as Offsets to Leadership Hubris
Andre L. Delbecq

Europe Versus Asia: Truth Versus Virtue
Geert Hofstede

Fortune Sr. Writer Marc Gunther on "The Role of Virtues in Spiritual Leadership"
Marc Gunther and Judi Neal

Peter F. Drucker on Mission-Driven Leadership and Management in the Social Sector: Interviews, and Postscript
Joseph A. Maciariello

INDEX